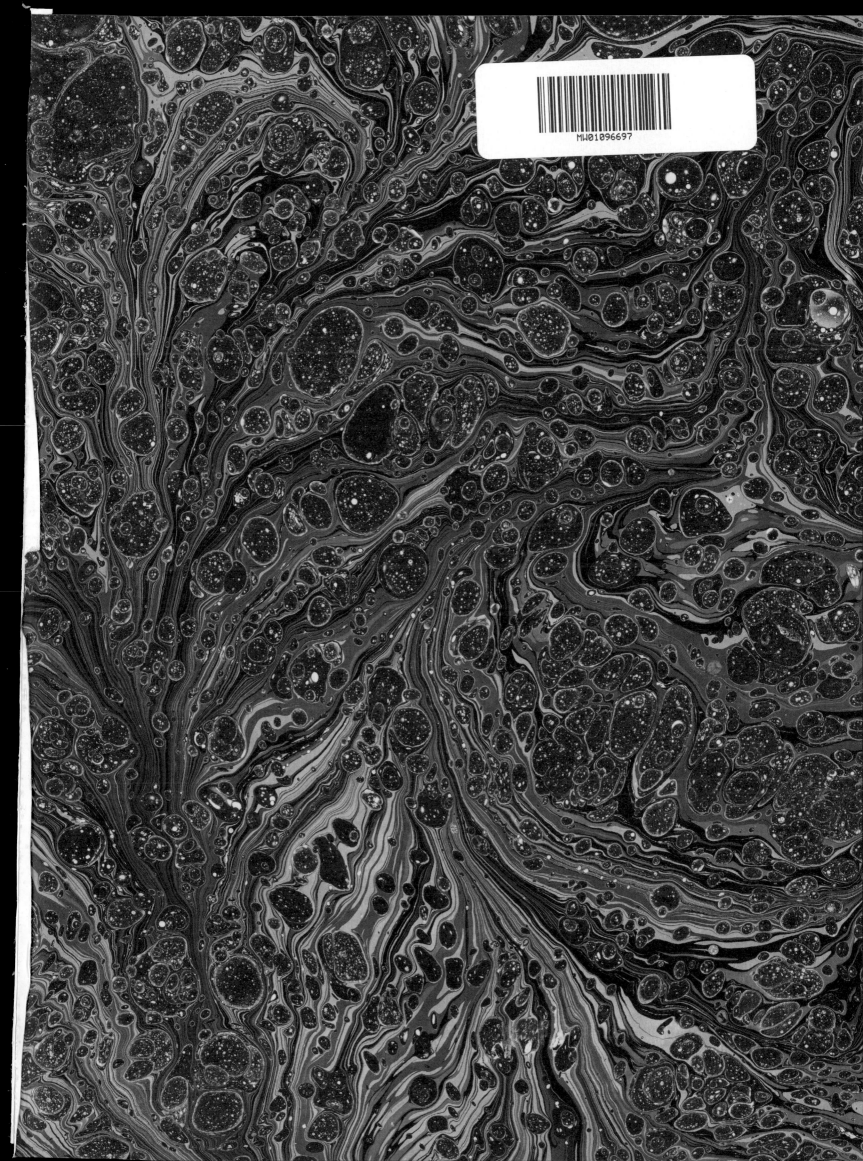

Battle Colors Volume III

BATTLE COLORS

Insignia And Aircraft Markings Of The Ninth Air Force In World War II

Volume III

Robert A. Watkins

**RESPECTFULLY DEDICATED TO ALL THOSE WHO SERVED
WITH THE NINTH U.S. ARMY AIR FORCE
DURING WORLD WAR II**

Book Design & Illustrations by Robert A. Watkins

Copyright © 2008 by Robert A. Watkins.
Library of Congress Control Number: 2007936610

Printed in China.
ISBN: 978-0-7643-2938-8

We are interested in hearing from authors with book ideas on related topics.

Published by Schiffer Publishing Ltd.
4880 Lower Valley Road
Atglen, PA 19310
Phone: (610) 593-1777
FAX: (610) 593-2002
E-mail: Info@schifferbooks.com.
Visit our web site at: www.schifferbooks.com
Please write for a free catalog.
This book may be purchased from the publisher.
Please include $3.95 postage.
Try your bookstore first.

In Europe, Schiffer books are distributed by:
Bushwood Books
6 Marksbury Avenue
Kew Gardens
Surrey TW9 4JF
England
Phone: 44 (0) 20 8392-8585
FAX: 44 (0) 20 8392-9876
E-mail: Info@bushwoodbooks.co.uk.
Free postage in the UK. Europe: air mail at cost.
Try your bookstore first.

Contents

INTRODUCTION

Owners Manual:

There is really nothing complicated about the use of this work, there are however a few items within that may perhaps warrant a wee bit of elaboration.

Dates: All dates contained herein have been expressed in a military format, i.e. day/month/year. As these relate to unit postings and command transitions, they indicate 'time-in' only, the duration of an assignment can be easily determined by addressing the next succeeding applicable date. When no additional data is available this simply indicates that the tenure of a given assignment carried through to the official end of hostilities in the European Theatre of Operations, this being V-E Day, 8-May-45.

Maps: Wherever possible station assignments have been depicted in chronological order. This order has been established by reading each station copy block counter-clockwise, beginning at the top left corner of any respective map. These copy blocks correspond to the accompanying text listings found on each page. My apologies in advance to readers in both Holland and Belgium for any awkwardness that may exist in listing the respective station province locations. Unfortunately, to date I have not had the opportunity to spend the time in either of these two countries that I would have liked. My knowledge of these lands has been confined primarily to written research, a situation that I hope to remedy in the near future.

Text: Some readers may wonder why the phrase 'No Known Insignia' is used repeatedly throughout this work instead of simply using the word 'None' in reference to missing insignia. Although many unauthorized insignia may not currently be known to me, this in no way negates their possible existence. The same is true of squadron colors, codes, etc. Use of the word 'None' implies that there is nothing more to be said on a given issue and this is simply not the case where this particular subject is concerned.

Ongoing Research:

Those readers familiar with the first two books in this series are aware of my acknowledgement that both of these works represent a work-in-progress, and the same is true in the case of this, my latest effort. In fact, due to the neglect with which the Ninth Army Air Force has been subjected since the conclusion of World War II, my efforts in cataloging both the combat insignia and tactical markings of this organization have been considerably more difficult than one might imagine, especially given the fact that the Ninth AAF was the largest tactical aerial armada ever assembled. It is a constant source of amazement that it is often easier to obtain certain types of documentation relating to much smaller USAAFs in more remote theatres of operation during the course of the war..

My primary concern is with the unofficial images that were so common during this period. Even with the advent of the Army's Heraldic Section, many units continued to display images and markings that had not gone through the official approval process. This was especially true once hostilities broke out and many of the AAF combat units were dispersed throughout the globe. Before this historical imagery is hopelessly scattered, I hope to collect and catalogue as much as possible concerning unit insignia and tactical markings of all combat units of the AAF. In this ongoing attempt to chronicle data as it relates to the original U.S. Army Air Service of 1918 through the transition to the current U.S. Air Force on September 18th, 1947, I continue to encourage those readers who have in their possession any data relating to this subject to contact me at the address below.

Robert A. Watkins
8462 Road 41
Mancos, Colorado
81328-8945
USA

NINTH U.S.A.A.F.
ORPHAN AIR FORCE OF THE E.T.O.

The Ninth Army Air Force has, for some reason, been sadly neglected in so many of the post war histories and documentaries in comparison to the exposure given the Eighth Air Force. This in spite of the fact that for much of World War II these two mighty air armadas fought side by side in the same skies over western Europe until final victory had been achieved.

This neglect may be in part due to the fact that the Ninth AF was not created among much pomp and circumstance, but rather evolved somewhat slowly over a period of time in a much more obscure theater than the one it ultimately ended up spending most of the war. Whereas the Mighty Eighth began its combat operations in the most highly publicized area of the conflict, the war in western Europe, the Ninth USAAF had its beginnings in the Middle East, and under an entirely different and obscure unit designation.

What would eventually become the largest tactical air force the world had ever seen actually came into existence under the code name HALPRO and the entire inventory of this new unit consisted of twenty-three B-24D Liberator heavy bombers recently transferred from the Tenth U.S. Army Air Force based in India.

The HALPRO mission of 12-Jun-42 was the first official USAAF combat operation within the Mediterranean area and the first in what would become many attacks on the stratigic oil fields at Ploesti, Rumania.

On 17-June-42, less than one week following this raid, the HALPRO contingent was combined with an initial detachment of B-17D's from the 7th Bomb Group (H) of Allahabad, India. This assortment of bombers would form the nucleus of the new U.S. Army Air Forces in the Middle East (USAMEAF) and designated the 1st Provisional Group / USAAF, which would continue operations from Cairo, Egypt.

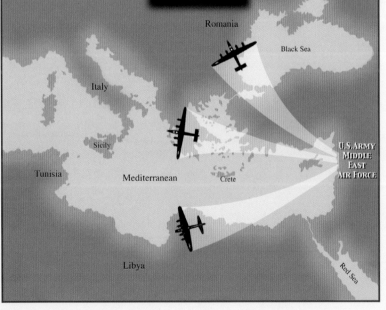

The 1st Provisional Group was shortly joined by the 57th FtrGrp, 12th Bomb Group (M) and the 98th Bomb Group (H). Also joining this assemblage were numerous C-47 Skytrain twin engine transports, all of which began combat operations against Rommels Afrika Korps. Sortieing from airfields located in both Palestine and Egypt, this unit assisted the British 8th Army in the Allied defeat of Axis forces at the Second Battle of El Alamein in November 1942.

It was during this period that USAMEAF was officially deactivated (12-Nov-42) and all of that organizations components transferred to the newly created Ninth U.S. Army Air Force. Many more additional units had been assigned to the newly formed Ninth and the overall command structure at that time was as follows: **IX Bomber Command** consisting of the 12th Bomb Group (M), 98th Bomb Group (H), 340th Bomb Group (M), along with the 376th Bomb Group (H), the latter having been created from the original 1st Provisional Group. **IX Fighter Command:** comprised of the 57th Ftr Group, 79th Ftr Grp, and the 324th Ftr Grp. Also assigned to the Ninth at this time was the 316th Troop Carrier Group. (Both the 12th Bombardment and the 57th Fighter Groups were on detached duty with the RAF during this time period.)

Beginning in August 1943 units within the Ninth AAF began to be transferred to the Twelfth AAF and with a stroke of the pen the Ninth officially ceased to exist within the Mediterranean Theater while magically being recreated thousands of miles away in southwestern England, and all on the same day, 16-Oct-43. For the Ninth AAF, heavy bombers were now a thing of the past as the new focus was to be on the tactical aspect of the war in western Europe.

THE GAUNTLET OF STEEL

Obtaining and maintaining control of the air over Western Europe did not come easily. Even with the decline of the Luftwaffe's ability to effectively counter the Allies aerial intrusions over German occupied territory, opposition from the ground was both intense and deadly. Field Marshall Erwin Rommel the 'Desert Fox' perhaps best summed up Germanys dilemma: "*Anyone who fights, even with the most modern weapons, against an enemy who dominates the air, is like a primitive warrior who stands against modern forces, with the same limitations and the same chance of success*". The Wermacht High Command knew this and in spite of seeing their Luftwaffe increasingly decimated, took the only remaining option open to them. As their own air force was being swept from the skies, a desperate effort was undertaken on the ground in an attempt to keep the massive Allied air armadas at bay.

By 1944 German anti-aircraft defences had reached an all time high and consisted of over 10,600 heavy AA guns as compared to 3,164 in 1940. During this same period production and deployment of light AA guns rose from 8,290 to 19,360 while the use of aerial searchlights went from 3,450 to 7,500. Additionally the Luftwaffe utilized radar directed fire control over their most sensitive target areas. Some of the more formidable of these were located in the feared Flak Towers built specifically to combat the Allied air incursions. These were massive bomb proof structures, some over six stories high, with weapons ranging from single, dual and quad mounted 20mm AA guns, the deadly effective 88mm cannon to the incredibly powerful 128mm Flak Guns. During the latter phase of the European air war, ground fire from German AA batteries accounted for the vast majority of allied aircraft and air crew losses.

All of this effort on the part of the Wermacht was never intended as a replacement for their own severely diminished loss of aerial defences. Time was what the German high command were hoping to gain through these efforts, time to rebuild the Luftwaffe with an inventory comprised of state-of-the-art aircraft like the jet powered Me 262, and equally important, time to train the pilots to fly these aircraft. It was an act of desperation that was to prove fruitless.

IN THE WAKE OF THE NINTH

From its humble beginnings at the eastern end of the Mediterranean Ocean the Ninth U.S. Army Air Force ultimately grew to become the greatest tactical air armada the world had ever seen.

From its inception the Ninth was charged with accomplishing three very basic combat principles:

1.) Gain air superiority.

2.) Deny the enemy the ability to replenish or resupply losses.

3.) Offer allied ground forces close support.

The Ninth was to become master of all three. Of all this units accomplishments throughout the conflict, the Normandy Invasion serves as a high-water mark achievement. Working closely with their British counterparts, the RAF's Second Tactical Air Force, the German war machine on the western front was successfully kept off balance during the D-Day landings thus ensuring a firm Allied foothold on the European Continent, but the cost was high. The Normandy Air Campaign officially lasted from June 6th thru August 28th 1944 and resulted in a total of 4,101 Allied aircraft lost, 1,637 of which were medium bombers and fighters. Over 389,400 sorties were flown during this campaign at a cost of 16,674 allied airmen. As horrific as these losses were however, they paled in comparison to the casualties inflicted upon the enemies forces, and the way had been paved for ultimate victory in the European Theater.

Neither the U.S. Ninth nor the British Second Tactical Air Forces would be afforded any respite at the conclusion of this campaign. In fact those engaged in the daily combat operations most likely wouldn't have been able to tell you the difference between August 28 and the 29th, it was all 'business as usual'. Operating from often hastily constructed Advanced Landing Grounds (ALG) the men of both the Ninth and Second Air Forces continued conducted daily flight operations against the enemy until wars end.

USAAF MARKINGS
THE EVOLUTION OF U.S. NATIONAL AIRCRAFT INSIGNIA

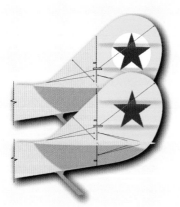

Circa 1916: The first national identification markings applied to U.S. aircraft appeared at the North Island Aviation School, California. Neither design was ever officially adopted by the Army Signal Corps. These applications appeared on the tail section only with no other images being applied to the surface area of the wings, top or bottom, nor the fuselage.

May 17, 1917: These two images represent the first authorized combination of national recognition insignia on U.S. military aircraft. During this period there were no standards in place regulating color uniformity, and as a result many applications varied from one aircraft to another and tended to be governed solely by those color shades currently on hand.

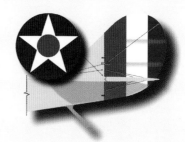

January 11, 1918: For reasons that may have been as much political as practical 'star-and-circle' insignia was replace with the cokade pattern depicted at left. This modification however affected only those AEF aircraft serving on the Western Front. The tail color configuration was itself modified from reading red-white-blue, right to left, to blue-white-red.

At the time of this writing no documentation has been located to explain the logic behind these changes, but the Army officially dropped this combination and reverted to the original 1917 configuration on all its aircraft in May of 1919.

Circa 1924-1927: The 'U.S. Army' designator was adopted for under-wing surface application on all Army Air Corps aircraft in 1924. The alternating pattern of horizontal red and white tail stripes came into existence three years later. Both of these adaptations were to disappear permanently from all Army Air Force warplanes in the wake of Pearl Harbor.

For a while it looked as if the Army had found a permanent solution regarding aircraft identification, Than reality came into play in the form of World War II and complicated the issue once more.

The first problem with the existing No.24102-K pattern came from the Pacific. Friendly fire incidences were far to frequent and one reason for this was allegedly due to the existing U.S. aircraft marking. It was reported that the first thing Allied anti-aircraft gunners reacted to when observing USAAF aircraft was the red circle in the center of the 24102-K insignia, with predictable and often disastrous results for U.S. pilots and flight crews. An attempt to remedy this problem resulted in the issuance of Amendment No.3 which ordered the immediate removal of the red circular device from all U.S. aircraft deployed outside the Continental United States. While this move solved one problem regarding recognition of American aircraft insignia, it was determined that additional research was needed. On June 18th 1943, a series of tests were held under authority of the Army / Navy Aeronautical Board to further study this problem.

A selection of both Allied and Axis national markings were applied to the U.S. aircraft, principally the P-47 Thunderbolt. A series of 'fly-by' runs were conducted at varying altitudes and distances to establish the optimum image for recognition of U.S. aircraft. The overall favorite was a new design recently added to the mix which included a set of horizontal white bars on each side of the circle and star configuration. The entire design was originally enclosed with a red outline but this was soon converted to the now familiar Insignia Blue contour line which, except for the addition of a red horizontal bar, remains in use by todays United States Air Force.

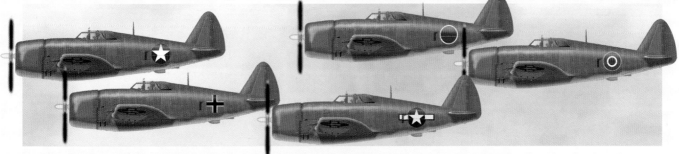

The images depicted below will serve to illustrate the modifications to U.S. military aircraft identification insignia between 20-Jul-41 and 14-Aug-43 with respective approval dates as indicated. The utilization of an Identification Yellow outer ring was ordered by Allied Force Headquarters. While used extensively during the North African campaign, it was employed only briefly in the UK.

JULY 20 1942	MAY 28 1942	OCTOBER 1 1942	JUNE 29 1943	AUGUST 14 1943

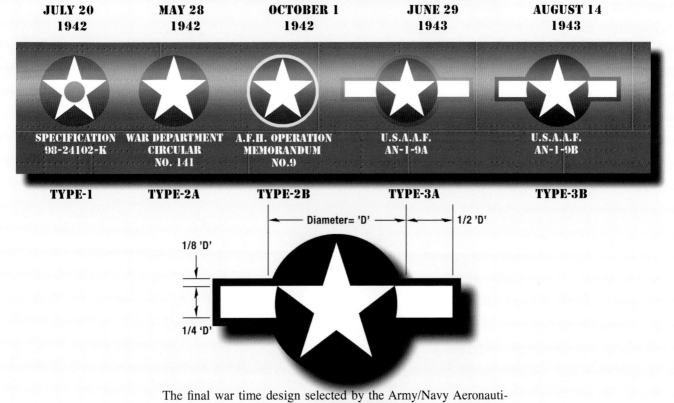

SPECIFICATION 98-24102-K	WAR DEPARTMENT CIRCULAR NO. 141	A.F.H. OPERATION MEMORANDUM NO.9	U.S.A.A.F. AN-1-9A	U.S.A.A.F. AN-1-9B
TYPE-1	TYPE-2A	TYPE-2B	TYPE-3A	TYPE-3B

The final war time design selected by the Army/Navy Aeronautical Board utilized only two colors; Insignia Blue and Insignia White. The specific ANA color codes changed constantly and are not addressed within the confines of this text. Readers wishing to pursue the subject of U.S. military insignia colors in finite detail are encouraged to consult the bibliography for additional subject sources.

COMBAT INSIGNIA AND TACTICAL MARKINGS

The question comes up from time to time as to why any real effort would go into such an obscure subject as unit insignia, and the answer is quite simple; It was a part of the everyday life of the vast majority of U.S. pilots, air and ground crew alike that the subject should be recorded and not forgotten by future generations. The generation that fought World War II didn't feel that they had to hide in a closet with the Sunday paper lest someone catch them reading, god forbid, the funnies. Those were simpler times and by today's standards much less sophisticated, which one might also successfully argue equates to less pretentious.

Social analysis aside, these images are important because they were important to the men that fought the war, period. If the generation that fought this war saw fit to invest a good part of their time and resources in displaying these images, the images are certainly worth preserving as part of their history.

RESEARCH PROBLEMS

Like so many other procedures required of military personnel, the process of preparing and submitting a group or squadron insignia design for official approval undoubtedly seemed like one more un-necessary task designed solely for the purpose of further tormenting the enlisted man. Actually the submission procedure was rather simple, it just took time to process the applications and this became especially true as the size of the Army Air Force increased as the war progressed. Aside from the original intent connected with the application procedure, mainly to review image content, un-official unit insignia lacks an empirical paper trail for the researcher to follow. The squadron insignia of the 455th Bomb Squadron / 323rd Bomb Group depicted at right is a perfect example of this problem. Depending upon the particular research source one consults at least three different images are presented as the image displayed by this squadron during WWII. Fortunately in this case there is photographic evidence to establish the correct image actually used by the 455thBS and with the help of grey scale analysis the colors originally used can be fairly well established. This may seem like a lot of trouble to go through for a single obscure insignia but without authoritative documentation it is the only way to insure as much historical accuracy as possible.

The vast majority of close-up aircraft photos taken during WWII were from a front angle, this perspective showing individual nose art to full advantage. Unfortunately for future historians however, the conclusive identifying tactical markings relating to unit assignment on most of these aircraft, and this is was especially true of the medium bombers, were located on the rear half of the aircraft

including the tail section. In many cases the only photos depicting this particular legible view of an aircraft were those taken immediately following an accident such as seen in the accompanying image depicting a runway mishap involving the 391stBG. While group designators were displayed on both upper wing surfaces as well as the tail section on the heavy bombers, the medium bombers of the Ninth AAF carried their Group designators *only* on their tail sections. This makes the positive identification of any given aircraft depicted in a war time photograph almost totally dependant upon a rear view angle of ship. It is sometimes possible to definitively identify an aircraft from it's nose art alone if adequate unit records were maintained. Even the configuration, or absence, of the Invasion Stripes and the particular design on the fuselage of the national insignia helps narrow the time frame of a given photo image.

If one can determine the aircraft serial number located on the vertical stabilizers of all U.S. war birds, the rest is fairly easy.

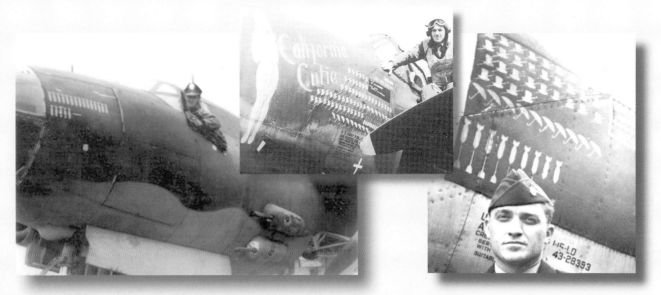

The images below represent *mission markings* and have no tactical significance whatsoever. However due to the presence of such markings on so many war time photographs, they are presented here for the benefit of those readers who may not have a working understanding as to their purpose or meaning. There were other symbols utilized but these represent the most commonly used. Additionally, there were no precise configurations adhered to when painting these markings to the fuselage of any given aircraft, therefore variations were common.

Yellow or white was the dominant choice of color for these symbols when applied to an olive drab surface. Red was sometimes also selected for use on both camouflaged and metal surfaces, however black paint was the dominant selection for most applications to a natural metal airframe.

The method of application varied greatly and ran the gambit of markings crudely slapped on freehand with a brush by a ground crew member lacking artistic skill, time or both, to still other examples painstakingly applied, sometimes using multiple colors.

PHOTO RECONNAISSANCE MISSION

ON A FIGHTER OR BOMBER, DENOTES A SUCCESSFUL ATTACK ON A RAILWAY AKA; 'CHATTANOOGA MISSION'

VISUAL RECONNAISSANCE MISSION

DEPICTS A COMBINED BOMBING AND STRAFING OPERATION

BOMBING MISSION

USED TO SYMBOLIZE A RESUPPLY DROP TO ALLIED GROUND FORCES

TOP COVER FOR ANY ALLIED AIRCRAFT

INDICATES DEPLOYMENT OF AIRBORNE TROOPS

FIGHTER ESCORT MISSION USUALLY FOR EITHER BOMBERS OR TRANSPORTS

TURNAROUND; A MISSION ABORTED DUE TO WEATHER CONDITIONS OR MECHANICAL PROBLEMS

COMBAT PATROL OR FIGHTER SWEEP OF ENEMY GROUND TARGETS

MEDICAL EVACUATION OF THE WOUNDED

DECOY MISSION TO DIVERT ENEMY FROM ACTUAL MISSION TARGET

COMBAT DEPLOYMENT OF GLIDER FORCE

AS APPLIED TO A TRANSPORT, DENOTES A FREIGHT HAULING MISSION

ALSO ON A TRANSPORT, EACH BOX CAR BEHIND A LOCOMOTIVE REPRESENTS AN ADDITIONAL FREIGHT MISSION

FIGHTER UNITS
OF THE
NINTH U.S.A.A.F.

14

A NEW HOME FOR THE NINTH

The transfer of the Ninth AA F from the Mediterranean to England entailed much more that adjusting to a change of climate, it included massive re-sizing and reorganization. As stated in the introduction the mission goals set for the Ninth were; 1.) Gain and maintain air superiority 2.) Disrupt enemy lines of transportation / communication and 3.) Attack enemy ground forces in cooperation with our own ground units.

At the height of its power during the war the Ninth AAF consisted of eleven bomb groups, eighteen fighter groups, fourteen transportation groups, two reconnaissance groups, five anti-aircraft battalions and four full battalions of combat engineers.

This does not factor in the multitude of additional special operations and support units necessary to

keeping the planes aloft. On any given day the Ninth would have an average of 2,000 combat aircraft sortied, and this is where the importance of tactical markings came into play. The two letter SD-110 code system for group recognition developed by the RAF had already been adopted by the Army Air Forces in the European as well as Mediterranean Theaters. Some commanding officers however felt the need to add the use of color recognition to the mix and five groups subsequently included the use of distinctive graphic patterns to their inventory of tactical markings.

Initially, most fighters of the Ninth displayed only the standard Allied Quick Identification Markings (QEM's), the exception to this were those groups equipped with the P-38 Lightning. Those units had previously adopted geometric symbols as a means of squadron identification and this practice was continued subsequent to their transfer to Great Britain.

There does not appear to have been any specific regulation in effect within the structure of the Ninth regarding the use of recognition patterns on combat aircraft, and this applies to the bombardment groups as well as the fighters.

Unlike their brothers in the Eighth AAF, which consistently utilized both color and patterns as a means of unit recognition, the same can not be said of the Ninth.

One reason, at least in part, for this low profile approach may be attributed, and rightfully so, to the close proximity of many combat units within the Ninth to enemy forces. This would also provide a plausible explanation as to the virtual absence of any squadron insignia on combat aircraft operating with the Ninth.

The use of such devices had of course long been discouraged in the European Theater, the theory being that such a display would give the enemy valuable intelligence, ie. unit assignment, place of origin, etc. It apparently never occurred to some of the great minds at S-2 that thanks to their agents within the British Isles, the Werhmacht probably had comprehensive lists of American squadron fuselage letter codes distributed throughout all of occupied Western Europe and the Fatherland before most of these units had completed their transitional training.

In all fairness to the boys of the Intelligence Branch, and perhaps more to the point, is the fact that unlike their strategic counterparts within the Eighth AAF, effective tactical operations such as those conducted by both the Ninth and British Second Tactical Air Force required engaging the enemy quickly and for as long a period as possible. Quite obviously, the closer you are to your opponent the easier it is to achieve these two goals, and thus we come to what the RAF referred to as Advanced Landing Grounds (ALG's) more commonly known within the USAAF as Forward Air Fields. Operating conditions at many of these facilities were basic at best, particularly during the first few months following the Normandy landings. The length of time a unit might spend at one of these ALG's could be little more than a matter of days. A lack of both time and materials may well have been the prevailing factors for the Ninth Army Air Forces comparatively austere aircraft tactical marking system.

The initial application of nose and tail unit marker patterns was obviously time consuming, especially with some of the more complex designs. Add to this equation the very basic, sometimes primitive working conditions, supply problems coupled with the ever present danger of enemy attacks, it is easy to speculate as to why more elaborate unit identification methods were not employed by forward units of the Ninth. To the pilots, air and ground crews alike, their new best friends became the anti-aircraft gunners assigned to defend their forward air fields. The Luftwaffe may have been down but they were most certainly not out and continued to attack Allied forward air fields at every possible opportunity.

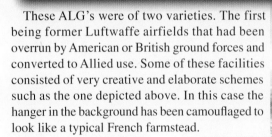

These ALG's were of two varieties. The first being former Luftwaffe airfields that had been overrun by American or British ground forces and converted to Allied use. Some of these facilities consisted of very creative and elaborate schemes such as the one depicted above. In this case the hanger in the background has been camouflaged to look like a typical French farmstead.

The second and more numerous type consisted of air strips created by combat engineers, specialists who's primary function was to constantly create operational air facilities in close proximity to enemy lines. So close in fact were these ALG's it those enemy lines that both RAF and AAF personnel were at times subjected to ground fire in addition to the aerial attack.

This situation brought back within some of these forward fighter units a brief re-introduction of camouflage paint to airframes. Some of these applications were to the upper surface areas only, leaving the under wing and fuselage surfaces in a natural metal finish. By this time it had become pretty much widely accepted that speed

and stealth, not camouflage, were the key factors to a fighter aircraft's chance of surviving an aerial attack on enemy held positions. Hit hard and fast, than get out of the area. All other methods of attack were an open invitation to disaster.

The Germans of course understood this tactic as well as the Allies and on January 1st, 1945 the Luftwaffe launched what was to be the last major air offensive on the Western front, and in fact the war. After action reports drafted by the Army Air Force estimated that between 700 and 800 German warplanes attacked American Ninth and British Second TAF bases near Brussels, Eindhoven and Metz destroying an estimated 127 Allied aircraft. The price of this raid was high however with GAF losses estimated at 460 combat aircraft.

Photos-top to bottom: No.1: AA Battery of the 51st Brigade / XIX TAC. No.2: 404thFG takes up residence at a former Luftwaffe hanger at St. Trond camouflaged to resemble French barn. No.3: Some of the results of the GAF Operation Bodenplatte, News Years Day, 1945. No.4: American aircrews set up shop among the wreckage at a captured Luftwaffe airbase.

The Allies could afford to sustain their losses, the Luftwaffe could not. The only real impact of this GAF effort were increased Allied air perimeter patrols and a quick coat of Olive Drab No.41 applied to upper airframe and wing surfaces.

3T-22ᴰFS • 7U-23ᴰFS • 6V-53ᴰFS } *36ᵀᴴFG: Pg.18*

F4-492ᴰFS • I7-493ᴰFS • 6M-494ᵀᴴFS } *48ᵀᴴFG: Pg.20*

T5-10ᵀᴴFS • 2N-81ˢᵀFS • W3-313ᵀᴴFS } *50ᵀᴴFG: Pg.22*

FT-353ᴰFS • GQ-355ᵀᴴFS • AJ-356ᵀᴴFS } *354ᵀᴴFG: Pg.24*

CH-365ᵀᴴFS • IA-366ᵀᴴFS • CP-367ᵀᴴFS } *358ᵀᴴFG: Pg.28*

E4-377ᵀᴴFS • G8-378ᵀᴴFS • B8-379ᵀᴴFS } *362ᴰFG: Pg.30*

A9-380ᵀᴴFS • B3-381ˢᵀFS • C3-382ᴰFS} *363ᴰFG: Pg.32*

D5-386ᵀᴴFS • B4-387ᵀᴴFS • C4-388ᵀᴴFS } *365ᵀᴴFG: Pg.34*

A6-389ᵀᴴFS • B2-390ᵀᴴFS • A8-391ˢᵀFS } *366ᵀᴴFG. Pg.36*

H5-392ᴰFS • 8L-393ᴰFS • 4N-394ᵀᴴFS } *367ᵀᴴFG: Pg.38*

A7-395ᵀᴴFS • C2-396ᵀᴴFS • D3-397ᵀᴴFS } *368ᵀᴴFG: Pg.40*

9D-401ˢᵀFS • E6-402ᴺᴰFS • 7F-485ᵀᴴFS } *370ᵀᴴFG: Pg.42*

9Q-404ᵀᴴFS • 8N-405ᵀᴴFS • 4W-406ᵀᴴFS } *371ˢᵀFG: Pg.44*

R3-410ᵀᴴFS • U9-411ᵀᴴFS • V5-412ᵀᴴFS } *373ᴰFG: Pg.46*

4K-506ᵀᴴFS • Y8-507ᵀᴴFS • 7J-508ᵀᴴFS } *404ᵀᴴFG: Pg.48*

G9-509ᵀᴴFS • 2Z-510ᵀᴴFS • K4-511ᵀᴴFS } *405ᵀᴴFG: Pg.50*

L3-512ᵀᴴFS • 4P-513ᵀᴴFS • O7-514ᵀᴴFS } *406ᵀᴴFG: Pg.52*

F5-428ᵀᴴFS • 7Y-429ᵀᴴFS • K6-430ᵀᴴFS *474ᵀᴴFG: Pg.54*

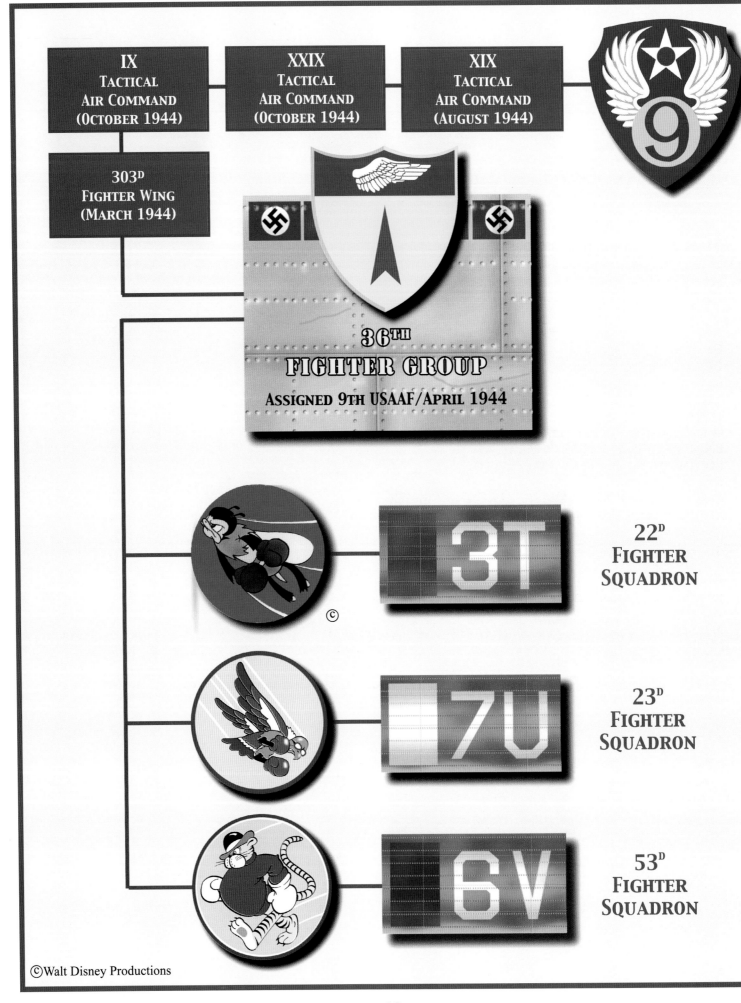

IX TACTICAL AIR COMMAND (OCTOBER 1944)

XXIX TACTICAL AIR COMMAND (OCTOBER 1944)

XIX TACTICAL AIR COMMAND (AUGUST 1944)

303D FIGHTER WING (MARCH 1944)

36TH FIGHTER GROUP
ASSIGNED 9TH USAAF/APRIL 1944

3T
22D FIGHTER SQUADRON

7U
23D FIGHTER SQUADRON

6V
53D FIGHTER SQUADRON

©Walt Disney Productions

18

P-47 'THUNDERBOLT'

36TH FIGHTER GROUP:

Motto: unknown
Sobriquet: unknown
Campaign Streamers:
Antisubmarine, American Theater; Air Offensive, Europe;
Normandy; Northern France; Rhineland; Ardennes-Alsace;
Central Europe.
Unit Decorations:
Distinguished Unit Citation - France, 1-Sep-44; Germany,
12-Apr-45; *Order of the Day* - Belgian Army, 1-Oct-44,
18-Dec-44 thru 15-Jan-45
Overseas Combat Commanders:
Lt.Col. Van H. Slayden; 12-Jan-44 thru Apr-45
Lt.Col. Paul P. Douglas ,JR.; Arp-45 thru V-E Day
Overseas Stations:
No.418 / Kingsnorth, Kent; Apr-44 thru Jul-44
A-16 / Brunchville, Basse-Normandie Jul-44 thru Aug-44
A-35 / Le Mans, Pays-de-la-Loire; Aug-44 thru Sep-44
A-76 / Athis, Champagne-Ardenne; Sep-44 thru Oct-44
A-68 / Juvincourt, Champagne-Ardenne; Oct-45
B-68 / Le Culot, Walls gewest; Oct-44 thru Mar-45
Y-46 / Aachen, Nordrhein-Westphalia; Mar-45 thru Apr-45
Y-62 / Niedermennig, Nordrhein-Westphalia; Apr-45
R-12 / Kassel/Rothwesten, Hessen; Apr-44

INSIGNIA / MARKINGS:

Group Insignia:
officially approved on 19-Jun-40
Squadron Insignia:
22d FS: officially approved 27-Jan-45
23d FS: officially approved 23-Sep-43
53d FS: officially approved 25-Oct-43

The image at right was
the original insignia when this
unit was still designated as the
22d Pursuit Squadron (Interceptor)

Squadron Codes:
22dFS - **3T** • *23dFS* - **7U** • *53dFS* - **6V**
A horizontal bar below these codes denoted
an individual aircrafts 'second-in squadron' status.
Squadron Colors:
22dFS - Red • *23dFS* - White • *53dFS* - Blue
Aircraft Markings:
Respective squadron colors applied to engine cowling and tail
rudder. Squadron codes and aircraft call-letter appeared black
on metal surfaces, white on Olive Drab painted finishes. Metal
finishes were dominate within the 36th Fighter Group.

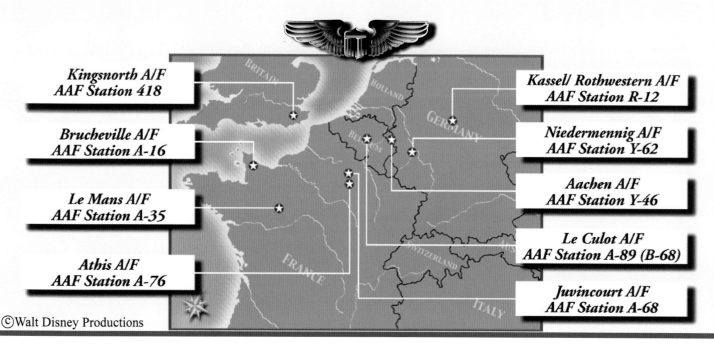

Kingsnorth A/F
AAF Station 418

Brucheville A/F
AAF Station A-16

Le Mans A/F
AAF Station A-35

Athis A/F
AAF Station A-76

Kassel/ Rothwestern A/F
AAF Station R-12

Niedermennig A/F
AAF Station Y-62

Aachen A/F
AAF Station Y-46

Le Culot A/F
AAF Station A-89 (B-68)

Juvincourt A/F
AAF Station A-68

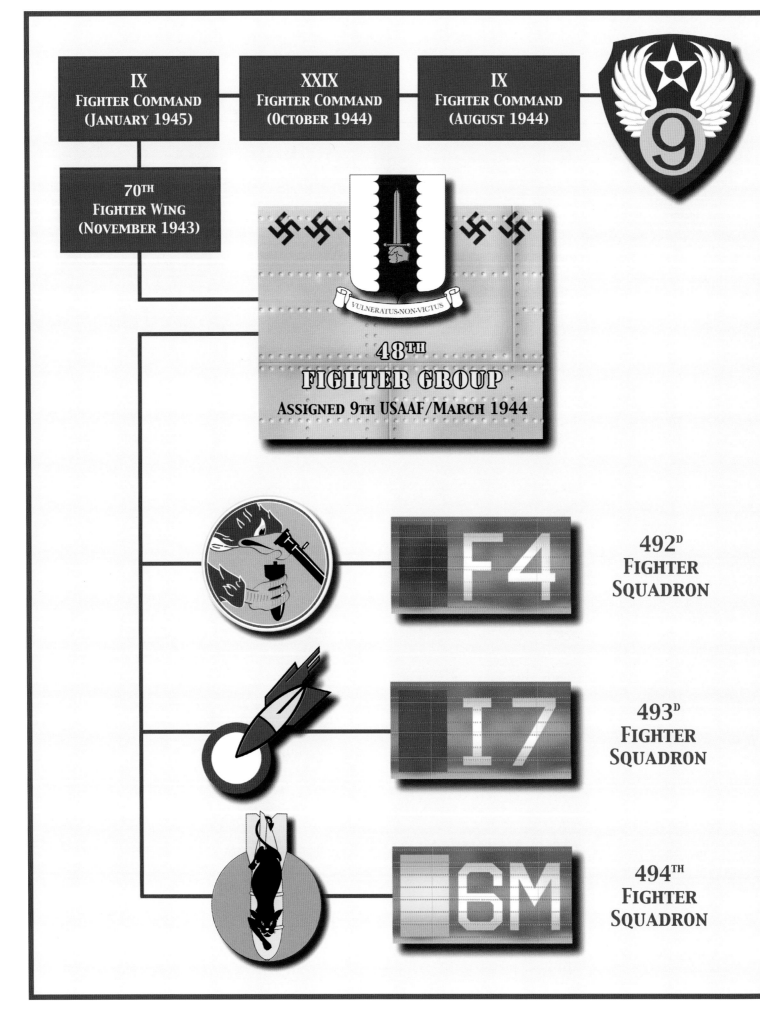

IX
FIGHTER COMMAND
(JANUARY 1945)

XXIX
FIGHTER COMMAND
(OCTOBER 1944)

IX
FIGHTER COMMAND
(AUGUST 1944)

70TH
FIGHTER WING
(NOVEMBER 1943)

VULNERATUS·NON·VICTUS

48TH
FIGHTER GROUP
ASSIGNED 9TH USAAF/MARCH 1944

F4

492D
FIGHTER
SQUADRON

I7

493D
FIGHTER
SQUADRON

6M

494TH
FIGHTER
SQUADRON

P-47 'THUNDERBOLT'

48th Fighter Group:

Motto: *Vulneratus Non Victus*
(*Unconquered Even Though Wounded*)
Sobriquet: unknown
Campaign Streamers:
Antisubmarine, American Theater; Air Offensive, Europe;
Normandy; Northern France; Rhineland; Ardennes-Alsace;
Central Europe.
Unit Decorations:
Distinguished Unit Citation - Germany, 6-Dec-44
Order of the Day, Belgium Army - 6-Jun - 30-Sep 1944,
1-Oct - 14-Dec 1944, 18-Dec44 - 15-Jan 1945.
Belgian Fourragere
Overseas Combat Commanders:
Col. George L. Wertenbaker, 23-Apr-44 thru Oct-44
Col. James K. Johnson, Oct-44 thru V-E Day
Overseas Stations:
No.347 Ibsley, Hampshire; 29-Mar-44
A-4 Deux Jumeaux, Basse-Normandie; 18-Jun-44.
A-42D Villacoublay, Ile-de-France; 29-Apr-44
A-74 Cambrai-Niergnies, Nord-Pas-De-Calais; 15-Sep-44
A-92 St. Trond, Province Limburg; 30-Sep-44
Y-54 Kelz, Nordrhein-Westphalia; 29-Mar-45
R-12 Kassel-Rothwestern, Hessen; 17-Apr-45
R-10 Illesheim, Bavaria Bayern; 29-Apr-45

Insignia / Markings:

Group Insignia:
officially approved on 12-Jan-42.
Squadron Insignia:
492d FS (formerly the 55thBS); fficially approved 25-Feb-43.
493d FS (formerly the56thBS); officially approved 24-Dec-41.
494th FS (formerly the 57thBS); officially approved 22-Aug-44.

493d FBS (alternate):
The insignia shown at right was an unofficial replacement for the approved
image depicted on the facing page. This
design was adopted by the squadron prior
to the overseas deployment of the 48thFG.

Squadron Codes:
492d FS - **F4** • *493d FS* - **I7** • *494th FS* - **6M**
Squadron Colors:
492d FS - Red • *493d FS* - Blue • *494th FS* - Yellow
Aircraft Markings:
Group marker; alternating red & white checker-board
pattern with squares measuring approximately six inches.
A red 'check' pattern was often the single color used when
applied to a natural metal finish. Respective squadron colors
were applied to both engine cowling and tail rudder. These
markings appear to have been introduced in late'44, early '45.

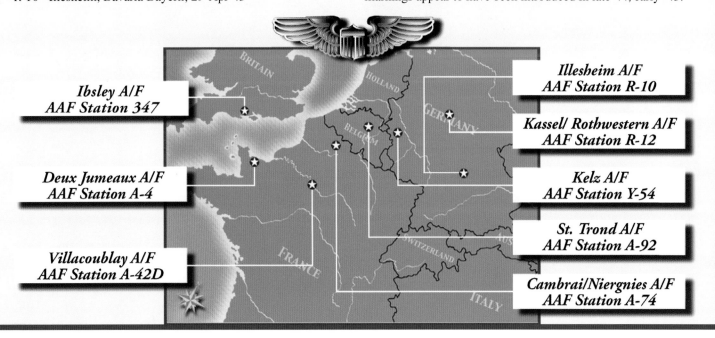

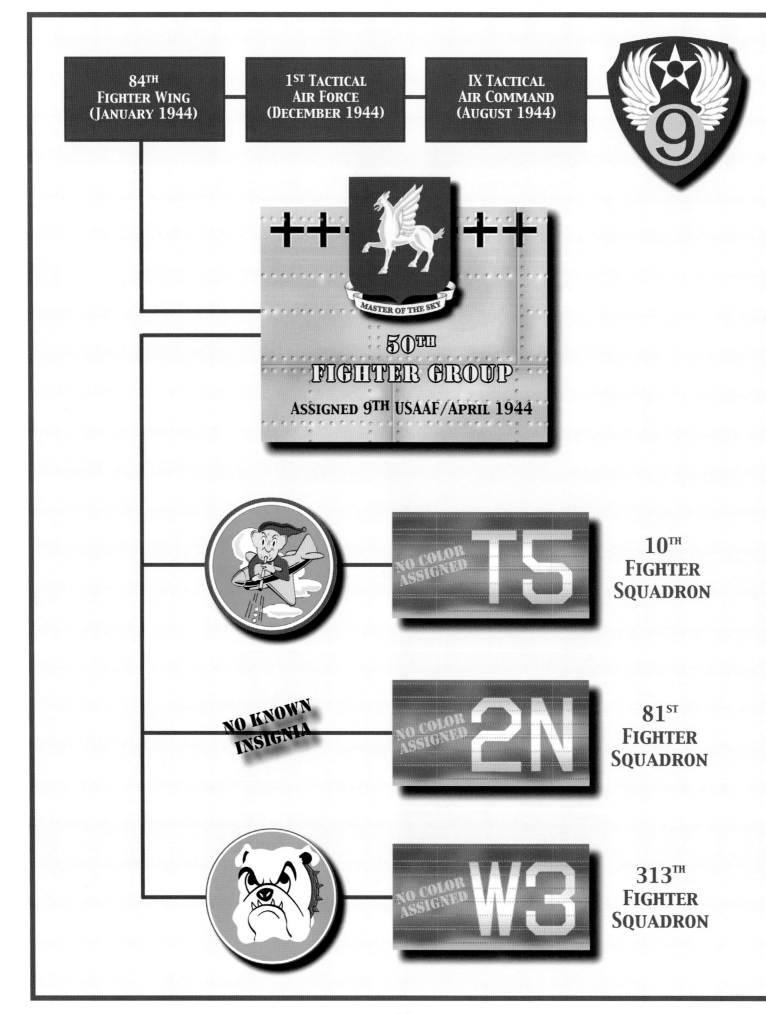

84TH FIGHTER WING (JANUARY 1944)

1ST TACTICAL AIR FORCE (DECEMBER 1944)

IX TACTICAL AIR COMMAND (AUGUST 1944)

MASTER OF THE SKY

50TH FIGHTER GROUP

ASSIGNED 9TH USAAF/APRIL 1944

NO COLOR ASSIGNED

T5

10TH FIGHTER SQUADRON

NO KNOWN INSIGNIA

NO COLOR ASSIGNED

2N

81ST FIGHTER SQUADRON

NO COLOR ASSIGNED

W3

313TH FIGHTER SQUADRON

P-47 'THUNDERBOLT'

227305

W3 ★ G

50th Fighter Group:

Motto: *Master Of The Sky*

Sobriquet: *Sky Masters*

Campaign Streamers:

Antisubmarine, American Theater; Air Offensive, Europe; Normandy; Northern France; Rhineland; Ardennes-Alsace; Central Europe.

Unit Decorations:

Distinguished Unit Citations - ETO, 13 - 20 March 1945; Germany, 25-Apr-45

Order of the Day, Belgium Army - 6-June thru 30 September 1944.

Overseas Combat Commanders:

Col. William D. Greenfield, 1-Dec-43 thru Nov-44.

Col. Harvey L. Case, Jr., Nov-44 thru V-E Day

Overseas Stations:

No.551 Lymington, Hampshire; 5-Apr-44

A-10 Carentan, Basse Normandie; 25-Jun-44

A-17 Meautis, Basse Normandie; 16-Aug-44

A-47 Orly, Ile-de-France; 4-Sep-44

A-69 Laon / Athies, Picardie; 28-Sep-44

Y-6 Lyon / Bron, Rhone-Alpes; 28-Sep-44

A-96 Toul / Ochey, Lorraine; 3-Nov-44

Y-90 Giebelstadt, Bavaria Bayern; 20-Apr-45

Insignia / Markings:

Group Insignia:

officially approved on 9-Jan-42.

Squadron Insignia:

10th FS; unofficial, details lacking

81st FS: unknown

313th FS; officially approved 16-Nov-42.

Squadron Codes:

10th FS - **T5** • *81st FS* - **2N** • *313th FS* - **W3**

Squadron Colors:

492d FS - (unkwn) • *493d FS* - (unkwn) • *494th FS* - (unkwn)

Aircraft Markings:

Other than the standard white or black United Kingdom Quick Identification Markings (QIM's) and the individual squadron codes, there does not appear to be any distinguishing tactcal markings associated with this unit during the war. There is some indication that the 50th did adopt some form of Group marking characteristics towards the end of hostilities. Definitive evidence regarding this issue is as yet forthcoming however, and thus the existing profile regarding this units markings remain as stated.

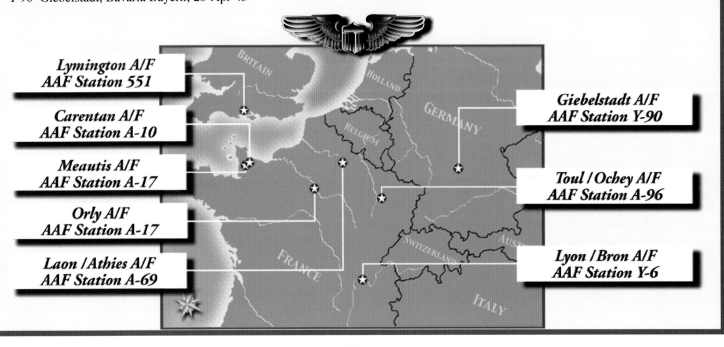

Lymington A/F
AAF Station 551

Carentan A/F
AAF Station A-10

Meautis A/F
AAF Station A-17

Orly A/F
AAF Station A-17

Laon / Athies A/F
AAF Station A-69

Giebelstadt A/F
AAF Station Y-90

Toul / Ochey A/F
AAF Station A-96

Lyon / Bron A/F
AAF Station Y-6

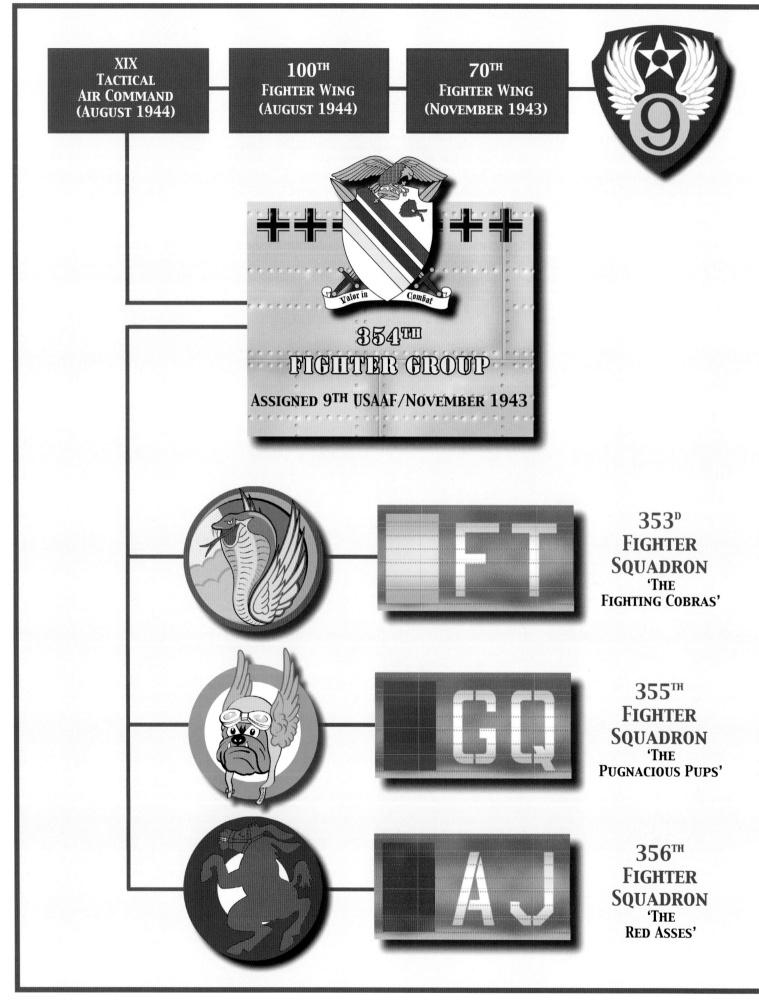

XIX
TACTICAL
AIR COMMAND
(AUGUST 1944)

100TH
FIGHTER WING
(AUGUST 1944)

70TH
FIGHTER WING
(NOVEMBER 1943)

Valor in Combat

354TH
FIGHTER GROUP

ASSIGNED 9TH USAAF/NOVEMBER 1943

FT

353D
FIGHTER
SQUADRON
'THE
FIGHTING COBRAS'

GQ

355TH
FIGHTER
SQUADRON
'THE
PUGNACIOUS PUPS'

AJ

356TH
FIGHTER
SQUADRON
'THE
RED ASSES'

P-51 'MUSTANG' / P-47 'THUNDERBOLT'

354th Fighter Group:

motto: *Valor In Combat*
Sobriquet: *The Pioneer Mustang Group*
Campaign Streamers:
Air Offensive, Europe; Normandy; Northern France;
Rhineland; Ardennes-Alsace; Central Europe.
Unit Decorations:
Distinguished Unit Citation - ETO, Dec-43 thru 15-May-44;
France, 25-Aug-44.
French Croix de Guerre with Palm, 1-Dec-43 thru 31-Dec-44.
Overseas Combat Commanders:
Col.Kenneth R. Martin, 25-Nov-42
Col. James H. Howard, 12-Feb-44
Col. George R. Bickell, c.Apr -44
Overseas Stations:
No.486 Greenham Common, Berkshire; c.Nov -43
No.150 Boxted, Essex; c.Nov-43
No.410 Lashenden, Kent; c.Apr-44
A-2 Criqueville, Basse-Normandiec.Jun-44
A-31 Gael, Bretagne; c.Aug-44
A-66 Orconte, Champagne-Ardennec; Sep-44
A-98 Rosieres en Haye
    (aka. Meurthe-en-Moselle), Lorraine; 1-Dec-44
Y-64 Ober Olm, Hessen; 8-Apr-45
R-45 Ansbach, Bavaria Bayern; 30-Apr-45
R-29 Herzogenaurach, Bavaria Bayern; c.May-45

Insignia / Markings:

Group Insignia:
officially replaced 18-Oct-57
Squadron Insignia:
353d FS; officially replaced 27-Aug-57
355th FS; officially replaced 25-Jun-57
365th FS; officially replaced 25-Jun-57
Squadron Codes:
353d FS - **FT** • *355th FS* - **CQ** • *346th FS* - **AJ**
Squadron Colors:
353d FS - Yellow • *355th FS* - Blue • *356th FS* - Red
Aircraft Markings:

Photographic evidence would indicate that the 354th Fighter Group initially relied solely upon two-letter RAF style SD-110 tactical codes for squadron identification during that units early deployment in Great Britain. The first twelve inches of the forward engine cowling, spinner, as well as the fuselage call letter and squadron code were painted in accordance with the Allied Quick Identification Markings present on each respective aircraft, i.e., White on two-color camouflaged airframes, Black on natural metal finishes. The use of colors and nose patterns as an additional means of squadron identification does not seem to have come into widespread use until the 354th's conversion to the Thunderbolts (see pages 26-27).

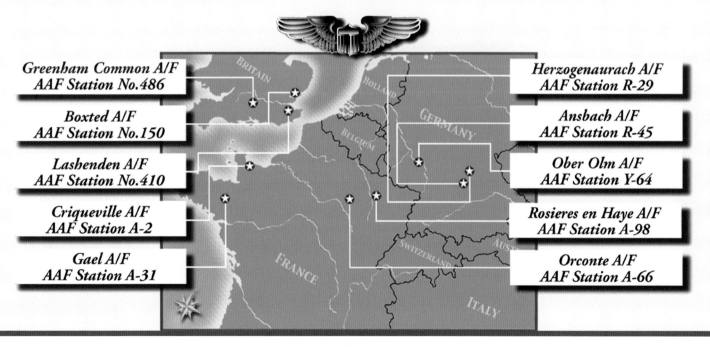

Greenham Common A/F
AAF Station No.486

Boxted A/F
AAF Station No.150

Lashenden A/F
AAF Station No.410

Criqueville A/F
AAF Station A-2

Gael A/F
AAF Station A-31

Herzogenaurach A/F
AAF Station R-29

Ansbach A/F
AAF Station R-45

Ober Olm A/F
AAF Station Y-64

Rosieres en Haye A/F
AAF Station A-98

Orconte A/F
AAF Station A-66

353ᴰ FIGHTER SQUADRON

In November 1944 the 354th Fighter Group was notified that the entire unit was to convert from their much loved P-51 Mustangs to the P-47 Thunderbolt. Disgruntled, but obedient to orders, the entire group undertook transitional training and soon took to the air with their replacement aircraft. For whatever reason this conversion was not to last long and by February 1945 the pilots of all three squadrons were once again behind the controls of their beloved P-51 Mustangs.

Below are two variations of 353dFS tactical nose markings which appeared on that squadrons P-47's during the brief period which they were flown. The image on the cowling of the lower aircraft was not an official squadron designator.

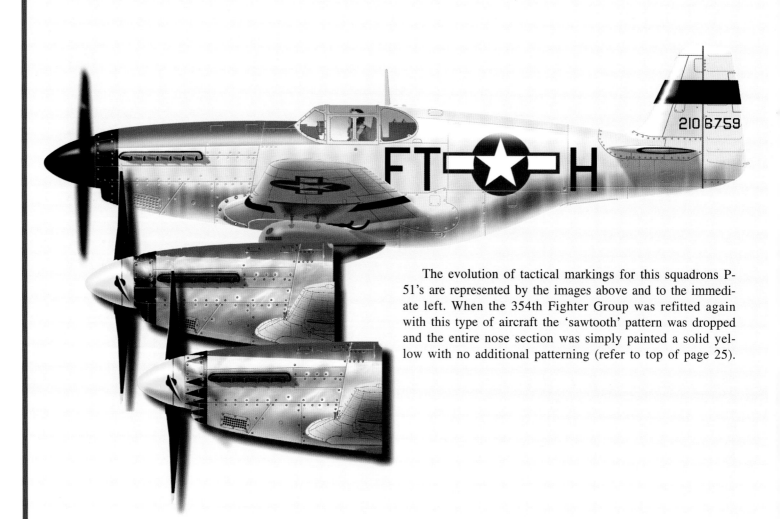

The evolution of tactical markings for this squadrons P-51's are represented by the images above and to the immediate left. When the 354th Fighter Group was refitted again with this type of aircraft the 'sawtooth' pattern was dropped and the entire nose section was simply painted a solid yellow with no additional patterning (refer to top of page 25).

355ᵗʰ FIGHTER SQUADRON

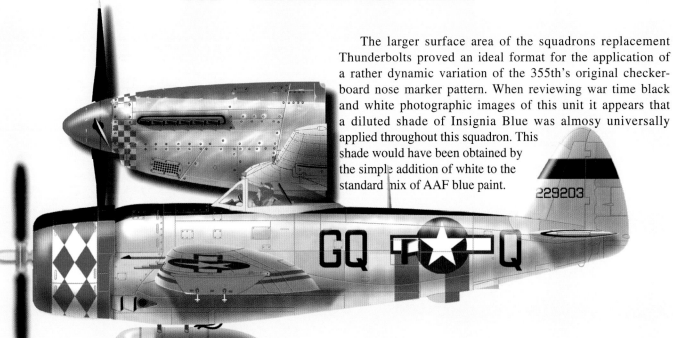

The larger surface area of the squadrons replacement Thunderbolts proved an ideal format for the application of a rather dynamic variation of the 355th's original checkerboard nose marker pattern. When reviewing war time black and white photographic images of this unit it appears that a diluted shade of Insignia Blue was almosy universally applied throughout this squadron. This shade would have been obtained by the simple addition of white to the standard mix of AAF blue paint.

356ᵗʰ FIGHTER SQUADRON

As near as can be determined it appears that when all three squadrons of the 354th Fighter Group transitioned back to their original P-51 Mustangs, the more complex tactical markings as seen on these pages were discarded in favor of a simple solid color application. This would have consisted of a respective squadron color being applied as a solid to both spinner and forward engine cowling areas. This was undoubtedly due to the mobile nature of this unit during the final months of the war. Like so many other tactical fighter groups comprising the Ninth AAF, the 354th found itself shuffled from one Advanced Landing Ground (ALG) after another from D-Day to V-E Day. A lack of both time and resources inherent in many of these forward bases dictated a policy of relative simplicity.

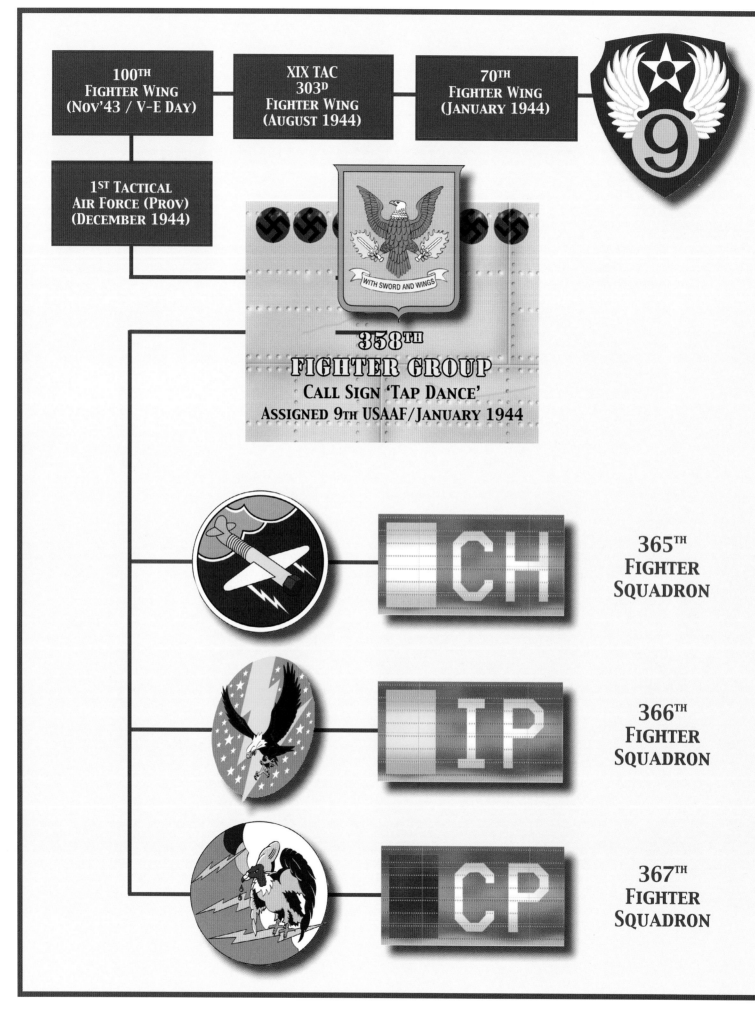

100TH
FIGHTER WING
(NOV'43 / V-E DAY)

XIX TAC
303D
FIGHTER WING
(AUGUST 1944)

70TH
FIGHTER WING
(JANUARY 1944)

1ST TACTICAL
AIR FORCE (PROV)
(DECEMBER 1944)

WITH SWORD AND WINGS

358TH
FIGHTER GROUP
CALL SIGN 'TAP DANCE'
ASSIGNED 9TH USAAF/JANUARY 1944

365TH
FIGHTER
SQUADRON

366TH
FIGHTER
SQUADRON

367TH
FIGHTER
SQUADRON

358th Fighter Group:

Motto: *With Sword And Wings*
Sobriquet: *Orange Tails*
Campaign Streamers:
American Theater; Air Offensive, Europe; Normandy;
Northern France; Rhineland; Ardennes-Alsace; Central Europe.
Unit Decorations:
Distinguished Unit Citation - Ardennes, 24-Dec-44 thru 2-Jan-45;
ETO. 19 thru 20-Mar-45; Germany, 8 thru 25-Apr-45; *French
Croix de Guerre with Palm.*
Overseas Combat Commanders:
Col.Cecil L.Wells, 1-Jan-43
Col. James B. Tipton, 20-Jan-44
Overseas Stations:
*No.345 Goxhill, Lincolnshire; 20-Oct-43
*No.373 Leiston, Suffolk; c.Nov -43
*No.157 Raydon, Suffolk; 31-Jan-44
No.411 High Halden, Kent; 13-Apr-44
A-14 Crettesville, Basse-Normandie; 3-Jul-44
A-28 Pontorson, Bretagne; 14-Aug-44
A-67 Vitry-le-Francois, Champagne-Ardenne; 14-Sep-44
A-80 Mourmelon, Chanpagne-Ardenne; 16-Oct-44
A-90 Toul, Lorraine; 9-Nov-44
Y-79 Mannheim-Sandhoven, Baden-Wuerttemberg; 2-Apr-45
*Duty stations with Eighth AAF.

Insignia / Markings:

Group Insignia:
officially replaced 28-Jul-54
Squadron Insignia:
365th FS; no documentation located.
366th FS; officially approved 6-Sep-43.
367th FS; officially approved 1-Mar-44.
Squadron Codes:
355th FS - **CH** • *366th FS* - **IP** • *347th FS* - **CP**
Squadron Colors:
365th FS - White • *366th FS* - Yellow • *367th FS* - Red
Aircraft Markings:

In the latter part of 1944 the 358thFG adopted their distinctive tactical marking. By combining what appears to be equal parts Insignia Red and White paint the resulting highly visual orange color was applied to the entire rear tail section which included both upper and lower horizontal tail surfaces.

The results leave absolutely no speculation as to why the 358th Fighter Group came to be known as the Orange Tails. The aircraft canopy frame was often similarly painted.

The red cowling was followed by the respective squadron color. Any decorative application to the cowling flaps were an individual application with no official tactical significance.

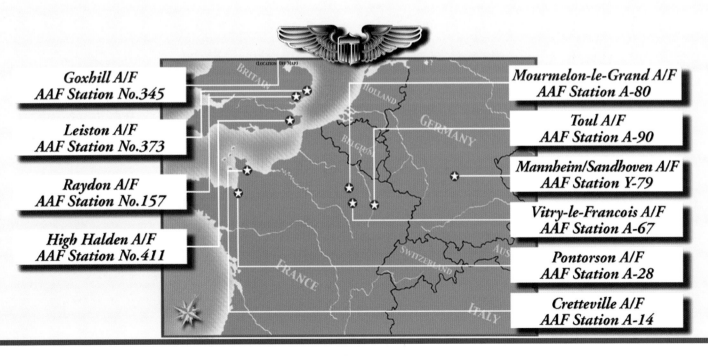

XIX TAC
100TH
FIGHTER WING
(AUGUST 1944)

IX TAC
70TH
FIGHTER WING
(DECEMBER 1943)

NO KNOWN
INSIGNIA

362D
FIGHTER GROUP

ASSIGNED 9TH USAAF/NOVEMBER 1943

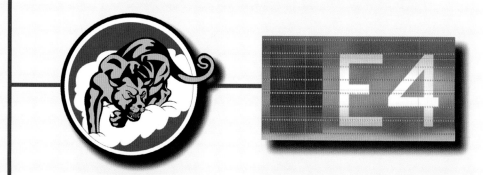

377TH
FIGHTER
SQUADRON

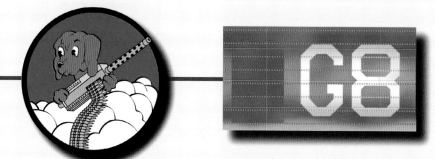

378TH
FIGHTER
SQUADRON

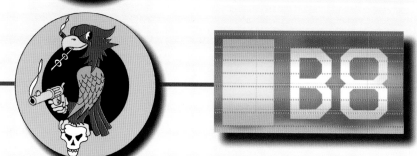

379TH
FIGHTER
SQUADRON

P-47 'THUNDERBOLT'

362d Fighter Group:

Motto: unknown

Sobriquet: *Mogin's Maulers*

Campaign Streamers:

American Theater; Air Offensive, Europe; Normandy; Northern France; Rhineland; Ardennes-Alsace; Central Europe.

Unit Decorations:

Distinguished Unit Citation - Brest, 25Aug44; Moselle-Rhine River Triangle, 16-Mar-45.

Overseas Combat Commanders:

Col.Morton D. Magoffin, 1-Mar-43

Col. Joseph L Laughlin, 10-Aug-44

Overseas Stations:

No.159 / Wormingford, Essex; 30-Nov-43

No.412 / Headcorn, Kent; 13-Apr-44

A-12 / Lignerolles, Basse-Normandie; 2-Jul-44

A-27 / Rennes, Bretagne; 10-Aug-44

A-79 / Prosnes, Champagne-Ardenne; 19-Sep-44

A-82 (No.393) / Verdun (Rouvres), Lorraine; 5-Nov-44

Y-73 / Frankfurt/Rhine-Main, Hessen; 8-Apr-45

R-28 / Furth, Bavaria Bayern; 30-Apr-45

R-10 / Illesheim, Bavaria Bayern; 3-May-45

Insignia / Markings:

Group Insignia:

No wartime insignia known to exist

Squadron Insignia:

377th FS; officially approved 25-Aug-43

378th FS; unofficial

379th FS; unofficial.

The image at right was developed for the 321st FS and is believed to have been designed by Cpt. George Rarey. A commercial artist before the war, Rarey flew with the 379th FS and was killed in action in late 1944. Information concerning this design would be appreciated.

Squadron Codes:

377th FS - **E4** • *378th FS* - **G8** • *379th FS* - **B8**

Squadron Colors:

377th FS - Red • *378th FS* - Green • *379th FS* - Yellow

Aircraft Markings:

Initially the 362d FS displayed no identifying markings other than their individual squadron codes and the standard QIM's. Later, squadron colors were applied to the central cowling area, the leading edge and tail tip were painted red. Patterns on cowling flaps were individual, not tactical in nature.

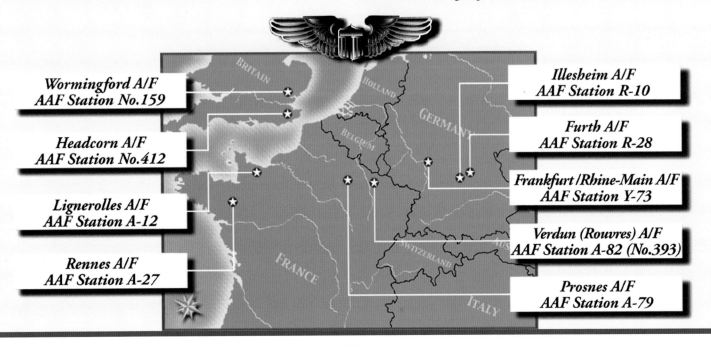

Wormingford A/F
AAF Station No.159

Headcorn A/F
AAF Station No.412

Lignerolles A/F
AAF Station A-12

Rennes A/F
AAF Station A-27

Illesheim A/F
AAF Station R-10

Furth A/F
AAF Station R-28

Frankfurt /Rhine-Main A/F
AAF Station Y-73

Verdun (Rouvres) A/F
AAF Station A-82 (No.393)

Prosnes A/F
AAF Station A-79

XXIX TACTICAL AIR COMMAND (OCTOBER 1944)	XIX TAC 100TH FIGHTER WING (AUGUST 1944)	IX ASC 70TH FIGHTER WING (DECEMBER 1943)

NO KNOWN INSIGNIA

363D FIGHTER GROUP

*REDESIGNATED 363D TACTICAL RECONNAISSANCE GROUP (4 SEPTEMBER 1944)

ASSIGNED 9TH USAAF/JANUARY 1944

NO KNOWN INSIGNIA

A9 — **380TH FIGHTER SQUADRON**

NO KNOWN INSIGNIA

B3 — **381ST FIGHTER SQUADRON**

NO KNOWN INSIGNIA

C3 — **382D FIGHTER SQUADRON**

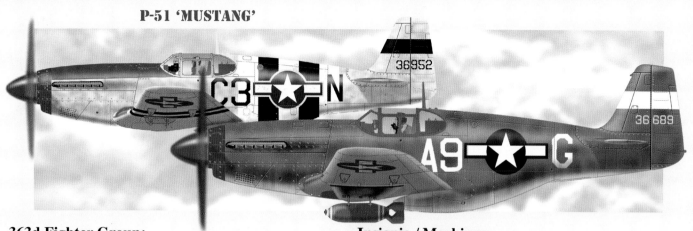

P-51 'MUSTANG'

363d Fighter Group:

Motto: unknown
Sobriquet: unknown
Campaign Streamers:
Air Offensive, Europe; Normandy; Northern France;
Rhineland; Ardennes-Alsace; Central Europe.
Unit Decorations:
Order of the Day, Belgian Army: 1-Oct-44, 18-Dec-44 thru
15-Jan-45, *Belgian Fourragere*.
Overseas Combat Commanders:
Col. John R, Ulricson, 5-Jun-43
Col. James B. Tipton, 7-May-44
Lt.Col. James M. Smelley, 1-Sep-44
Overseas Stations:
No.471 Keevil, Wiltshire; 23-Dec-43
No.128 Rivenhall, Essex; Jan-44
No,418 Staplehurst, Kent; Apr-44
A-15 Maupertus, Basse Normandie; 4-Jul-44
A-7 Azeville, Basse Normandie; Aug-44
A-35 Le Mans, Pay-de-la-Loire; Sep-44
(Refer to pages 134-135 for additional duty stations as the
redesignated 363d Tactical Reconnaissance Group)
Combat Operations:
23-Feb-44 - 3-Sep-44

Insignia / Markings:

Group Insignia:
unknown; officially replaced 16-Jun-52
Squadron Insignia:
380th FS; unknown
381st FS; unknown
382d FS; unknown
Squadron Codes:
380th FS **- A9** • *381st* **- B3** • *382d FS* **- C3**
Squadron Colors:
380th FS **- Blue**
371st FS **- Yellow**
383d FS **- Red**
Aircraft Markings:

Squadron colors were adopted by the 363rd but the use of these colors as tactical markings were confined to the propeller spinner and the forward 12 inches of the engine cowling. The standard British style squadron codes and aircraft call letters were of a standard location, White on camouflaged paint schemes, Black on natural metal finishes, with a height of approximately 24 inches.

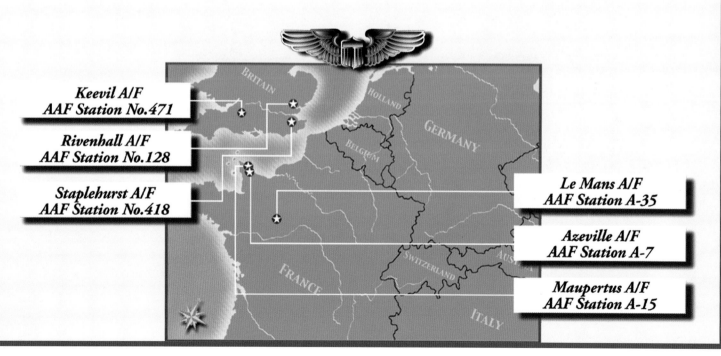

Keevil A/F
AAF Station No.471

Rivenhall A/F
AAF Station No.128

Staplehurst A/F
AAF Station No.418

Le Mans A/F
AAF Station A-35

Azeville A/F
AAF Station A-7

Maupertus A/F
AAF Station A-15

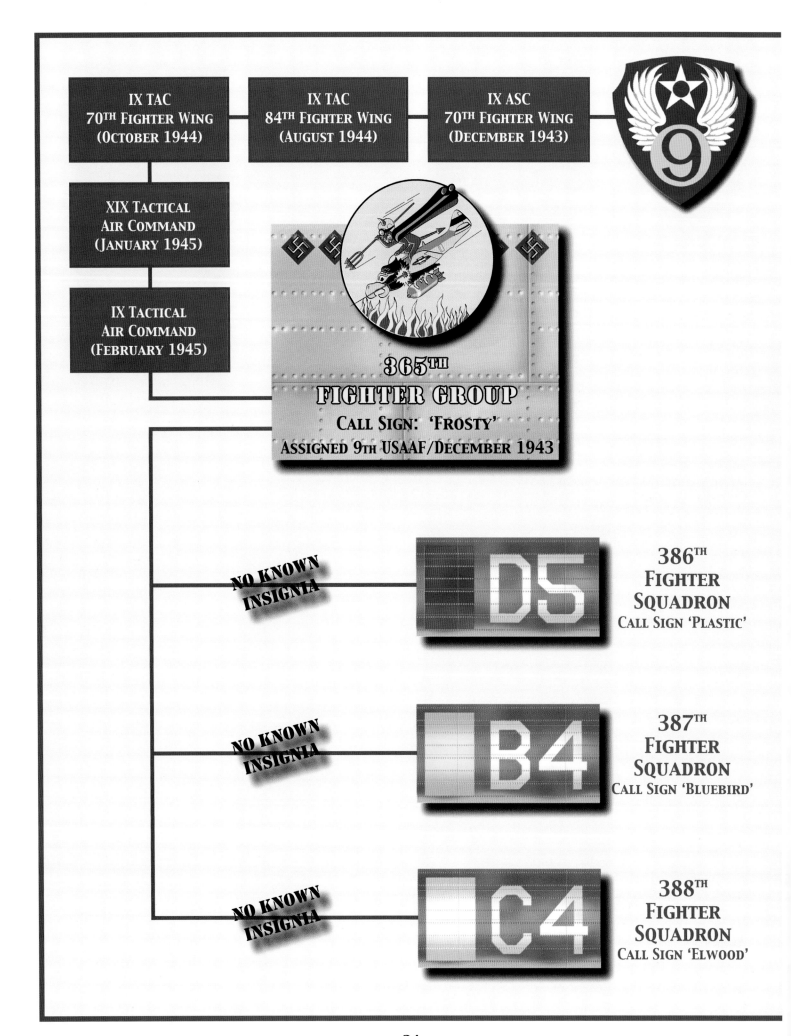

IX TAC
70TH FIGHTER WING
(OCTOBER 1944)

IX TAC
84TH FIGHTER WING
(AUGUST 1944)

IX ASC
70TH FIGHTER WING
(DECEMBER 1943)

XIX TACTICAL
AIR COMMAND
(JANUARY 1945)

IX TACTICAL
AIR COMMAND
(FEBRUARY 1945)

365TH
FIGHTER GROUP
CALL SIGN: 'FROSTY'
ASSIGNED 9TH USAAF/DECEMBER 1943

NO KNOWN INSIGNIA

D5

386TH
FIGHTER
SQUADRON
CALL SIGN 'PLASTIC'

NO KNOWN INSIGNIA

B4

387TH
FIGHTER
SQUADRON
CALL SIGN 'BLUEBIRD'

NO KNOWN INSIGNIA

C4

388TH
FIGHTER
SQUADRON
CALL SIGN 'ELWOOD'

P-47 'THUNDERBOLT'

365th Fighter Group:

Moto: unknown
Sobriquet: *The Hell Hawks*
Campaign Streamers:
American Theater; Air Offensive, Europe; Normandy;
Northern France; Rhineland; Ardennes-Alsace; Central Europe.
Unit Decorations:
Distinguished Unit Citation: Germany, 21-Oct-44 and 20-Apr-45.
Order of the Day, Belgium Army: 6-Jun-44 thru 30-Sep-44 and
16-Dec-44 thru 25-Jan-45. *Belgian Fourragere*.
Overseas Combat Commanders:
Col. Lance Call, 15-May-43
Col. Ray J.Stecker, 26-Jun-44
Lt.Col. Robert C. Richardson III, 26-Apr-45
Overseas Stations:
No.154 Gosfield, Essex; 22-Dec-43
No.408 Beaulieu, Hampshire; 5-Mar-44
A-7 Azeville, Basse Normandie; 28-Jun-44
[1.)]*A-12* Lignerolles, Basse Normandie; 2-Jul-44
A-48 Bretigny, Ile-de-France; 3-Sep-44
A-68 Juvincourt, Champagne-Ardenne; 15-Sep-44
A-84 Chievres, Province de Hainaut; 4-Oct-44
Y-34 Mentz, Lorraine; 27-Dec-44
A-78 Florennes/Juzaine, Province de Namur; 30-Jan-45
Y-46 Aachen, Nordrhein-Westphalia; 16-Mar-45
Y-86 Fritzlar, Hessen; 13-Apr-45
[1.)] reconnaissance detachment only

Insignia / Markings:

Group Insignia:
officially replaced 6-Oct-54
Although not officially approved, the Hell Hawks group insignia was widely used within all three squadrons of this unit.
Squadron Insignia:
386th FS; unknown
387th FS; unknown
388th FS; unknown
Squadron Codes:
386th FS - **D5** • *387th* - **B4** • *388th FS* - **C4**
Squadron Colors:
386th FS - Red • *387th FS* - Yellow • *388th FS* - White
Aircraft Markings:

Tactical aircraft recognition markings within this unit appear to have been limited to the application of the respective squadron color to the leading 12 inch surface area of the engine cowling with an accompanying red band of approximately the same width applied with red paint just forward of the cowling flaps. This latter device apparently served as the group color indicator.

Squadron codes were applied in the standard prescribed manner i.e., white letters / numerals on camouflaged airframe surfaces and black on natural metal finishes.

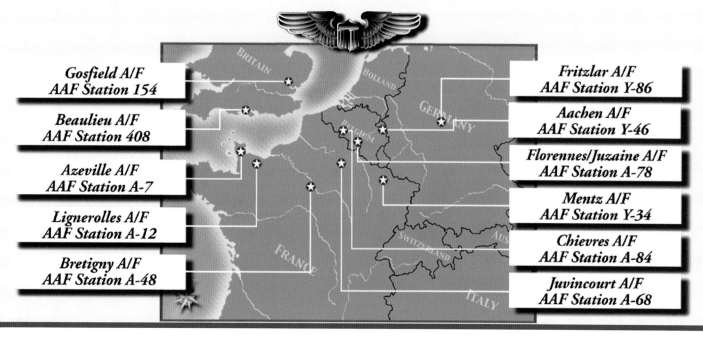

Gosfield A/F AAF Station 154	**Fritzlar A/F** AAF Station Y-86
Beaulieu A/F AAF Station 408	**Aachen A/F** AAF Station Y-46
Azeville A/F AAF Station A-7	**Florennes/Juzaine A/F** AAF Station A-78
Lignerolles A/F AAF Station A-12	**Mentz A/F** AAF Station Y-34
Bretigny A/F AAF Station A-48	**Chievres A/F** AAF Station A-84
	Juvincourt A/F AAF Station A-68

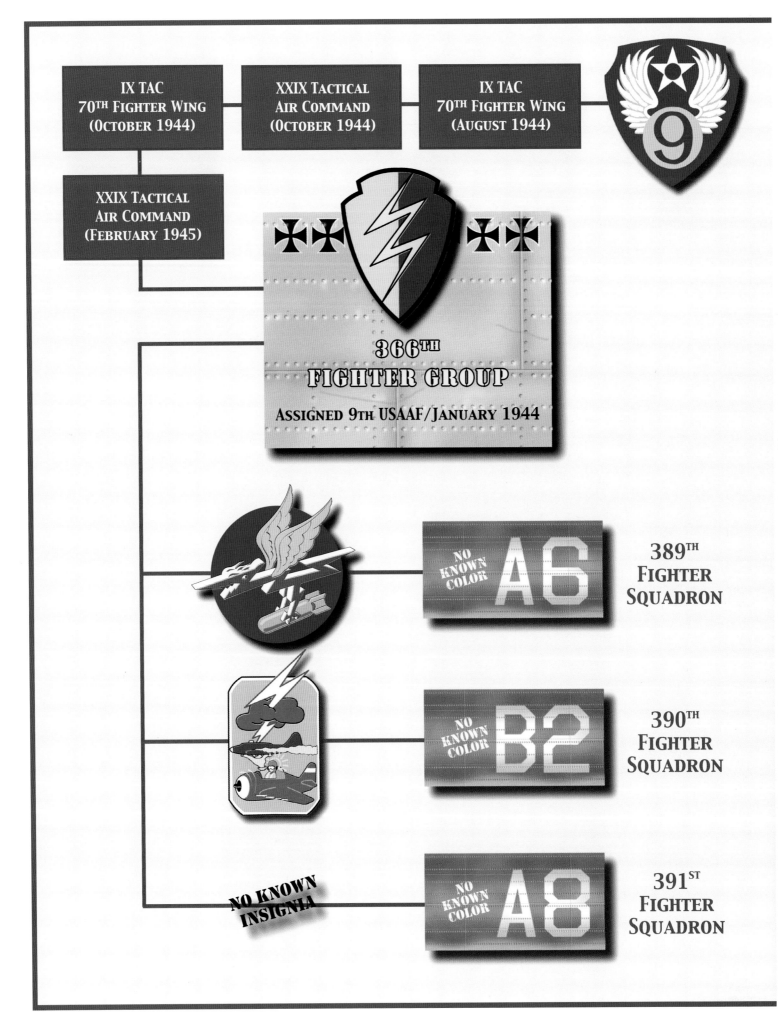

IX TAC
70TH FIGHTER WING
(OCTOBER 1944)

XXIX TACTICAL
AIR COMMAND
(OCTOBER 1944)

IX TAC
70TH FIGHTER WING
(AUGUST 1944)

XXIX TACTICAL
AIR COMMAND
(FEBRUARY 1945)

366TH
FIGHTER GROUP

ASSIGNED 9TH USAAF/JANUARY 1944

NO KNOWN
COLOR
A6

389TH
FIGHTER
SQUADRON

NO KNOWN
COLOR
B2

390TH
FIGHTER
SQUADRON

NO KNOWN
INSIGNIA

NO KNOWN
COLOR
A8

391ST
FIGHTER
SQUADRON

P-47 'THUNDERBOLT'

366th Fighter Group:

Motto: unknown

Sobriquet: unknown

Campaign Streamers:
Air Offensive, Europe; Normandy; Northern France; Rhineland; Ardennes-Alsace; Central Europe.

Unit Decorations:
Distinguished Unit Citation: Normandy, 11-Jul-44. *Order of the Day, Belgium Army*: 6-Jun-44 thru 30-Sep-44 and 18-Dec-44 thru 15-Jan-45. *Belgian Fourragere.*

Overseas Combat Commanders:
Col. Dyke F. Meyer, 11-Jul-43
Lt.Col. James P. Tipton, 19-Apr-44
Lt.Col. Donald K. Bennett, 30-Apr-44
Co. Harold N. Holt, 22-May-44
Lt.Col. Ansel J. Wheeler, 28-Apr-45

Overseas Stations:
No.466 Membury, Berkshire; 10-Jan-44
No.407 Thruxton, Hampshire; 1-Mar-44
A-1 St.Pierre du Mont, Basse Normandie; 17-Jun-44
A-41 Dreux, Centre-Val-de-Loire; 24-Aug-44
A-70 Laon / Couvron, Picardie; 8-Sep-44
Y-29 Asch, Province Limburg; 19-Nov-44
A-94 Munster / Handorf, Nordrhein-Westphalia; 4-Oct-44

Insignia / Markings:

Group Insignia:
officially replaced 6-Oct-54

Squadron Insignia:
389th FS; officially approved 13-Feb-45
390th FS; officially replaced 6-Oct-55
391st FS; unknown

Squadron Codes:
389th FS - **A6** • *390th FS* - **B2** • *391st FS* - **A8**

Squadron Colors:
386th FS - none
3787th FS - none
388th FS - none

Aircraft Markings:

Research to date indicates that the 366th Fighter Groups tactical aircraft markings consisted solely of the standard Allied Quick Identification Markings accompanied by the respective squadron code applied with white paint on camouflaged surfaces and black on natural metal finishes. Many of the P-47's within this group, however, did display a quite impressive assortment of well designed and executed nose art which unfortunately falls outside the scope and confines of this text.

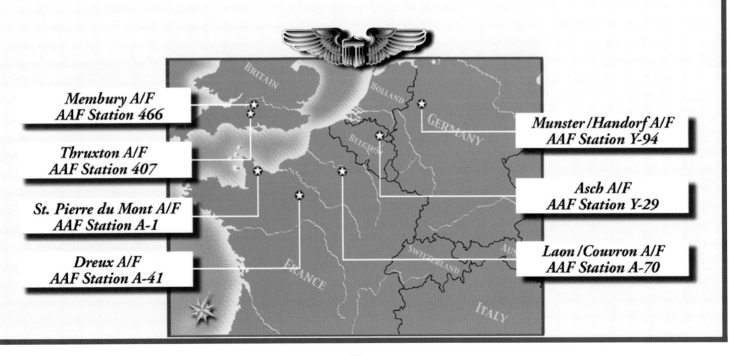

XIX Tactical Air Command (January 1945)	IX TAC 70th Fighter Wing (August 1944)	

NO KNOWN INSIGNIA

367th FIGHTER GROUP

ASSIGNED 9th USAAF/MARCH 1944

392d FIGHTER SQUADRON
Call Sign 'Nobhole'

NO KNOWN INSIGNIA

393d FIGHTER SQUADRON
Call Sign 'Decco'

394th FIGHTER SQUADRON
Call Sign 'Casket'

P-38 'LIGHTNING' / P-47 'THUNDERBOLT'

367th Fighter Group:

Motto: unknown

Sobriquet: *The Dynamite Gang*

Campaign Streamers:

Air Offensive, Europe; Normandy; Northern France; Rhineland; Ardennes-Alsace; Central Europe.

Unit Decorations:

Distinguished Unit Citation - France, 25-Aug-44; Germany, 19-Mar-45: *Order of the Day, Belgium Army*, 6-Jun-44 thru 30-Sep-44, 16-Dec thru 25-Jan-45: *Belgian Fourragere.*

Overseas Combat Commanders:

Col. Charles M. Young, 22-Jan-44

Col. Edwin S. Chickering, 9-Nov-44

Overseas Stations:

No.452 Stony Cross, Hampshirs; 5-Apr-44

No.347 Lbsley, Hampshire; 6-Jul-44

A-6 Beuzeville, Basse-Normandie; 22-Jul-44

A-2 Criqueville, Basse-Normandie; 14-Aug-44

A-44 Peray, Basse-Normandie; 4-Sep-44

A-71 Clastres, Picardie; 8-Sep-44

A-68 Juvincourt, Champagne-Ardenne; 28-Oct-44

A-64 St. Dizier, Champagne-Ardenne; 1-Feb-45

A-94 Conflans, Lorraine; 14-Mar-45

Y-74 Frankfurt / Eschborn, Hessen; 10-Apr-45

Insignia / Markings:

Group Insignia:

unknown.

Squadron Insignia:

392d FS; unofficial.

393d FS; unknown.

394th FS; officially approved 25-Feb-44.

Squadron Codes:

392d FS - H5 • *393d FS* - 8L • *394th FS* - 4N

Squadron Colors:

392d FS - Red • *393d FS* - Blue • *394th FS* - Yellow

Aircraft Markings:

Most of the original P-38's within the 367th FG displayed the last three digits of each aircrafts respective serial number on the cupola nose section. The stencil lines inherent with these applications were rarely filled in. Use of the original squadron geometric symbols in squadron colors was continued even after the 367th FG had converted to P-47's. The entire engine cowling, including flaps, was similarly painted with each squadrons color.

A bar *under* a call letter was used to denote if a particular aircraft was a second in series within any given squadron.

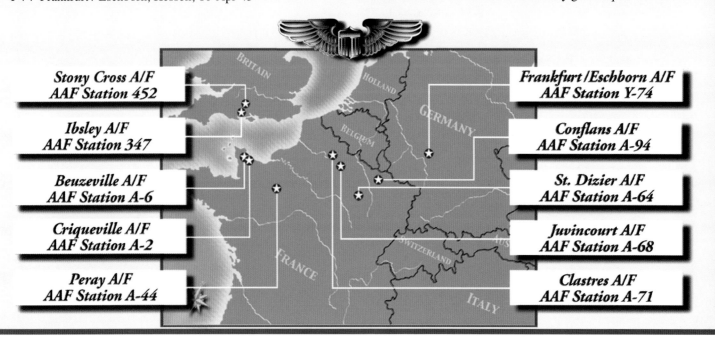

Stony Cross A/F AAF Station 452	**Frankfurt/Eschborn A/F** AAF Station Y-74
Ibsley A/F AAF Station 347	**Conflans A/F** AAF Station A-94
Beuzeville A/F AAF Station A-6	**St. Dizier A/F** AAF Station A-64
Criqueville A/F AAF Station A-2	**Juvincourt A/F** AAF Station A-68
Peray A/F AAF Station A-44	**Clastres A/F** AAF Station A-71

XIX TACTICAL AIR COMMAND (JANUARY 1945)	IX TAC 70TH FIGHTER WING (OCTOBER 1944)	IX TAC 71ST FIGHTER WING (MARCH 1944)

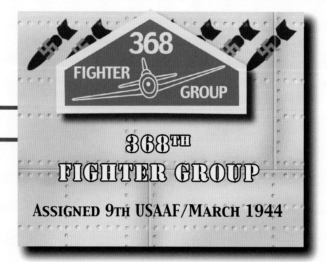

368TH FIGHTER GROUP

ASSIGNED 9TH USAAF/MARCH 1944

395TH FIGHTER SQUADRON

396TH FIGHTER SQUADRON

397TH FIGHTER SQUADRON

P-47 'THUNDERBOLT'

368th Fighter Group:

Motto: unknown

Sobriquet: unknown

Campaign Streamers:

Air Offensive, Europe; Normandy; Northern France; Rhineland; Ardennes-Alsace; Central Europe.

Unit Decorations:

Distinguished Unit Citation - France, 3-Sep-44: *Order of the Day, Belgium Army* - 6-Jun-44 thru 30-Sep-44, 16-Dec thru 25-Jan-45: *Belgian Fourragere.*

Overseas Combat Commanders:

Col. Gilbert L. Meyers, 3-Jun-43

Col. Frank S. Perego, 1-Nov-44

Overseas Stations:

No.486 Greenham Common, Berkshire; 13-Jan-44

No.404 Chilbolton, Hampshire; 15-Mar-44

A-3 Cardonville, Basse-Normandie; 20-Jun-44

A-40 Chartes, Centre-Val-de-Loire; 23-Aug-44

A-69 Laon / Athies, Picardie; 11-Sep-44

A-84 Chievres, Province de Hainaut; 2-Oct-44

A-68 Juvincourt, Champagne-Ardenne; 27-Dec-44

Y-34 Metz / Frescathy, Lorraine; 5-Jan-45

Y-73 Frankfurt-Rhein-Main, Hessen; 15-Apr-45

Insignia / Markings:

Group Insignia:

unknown. (The image depicted on the facing page was actually signage posted over the entrance of 368th FG Headquarters and not an insignia per se).

Squadron Insignia:

395th FS; unofficial. (sobriquet; *Panzer Dusters*).

396th FS; unknown. This image may well be post war in origin but is included within this text as there are conflicting claims at this time. (sobriquet; *Thunder Bums*).

397th FS; Approved 13-Apr-44. (sobriquet; *Jabo Angles*).

Squadron Codes:

395th FS - A7 • 396th FS - C2 • 397th FS - D3

Squadron Colors:

395th FS - Red • *396th FS* - Yellow • *397th FS* - Blue

Aircraft Markings:

The 398thFG does not appear to have employed squadron colors on any camouflaged P-47 assigned to that unit, relying instead on standard white QIM's. Engine cowlings as well as propeller spinners were painted in squadron colors on virtually all of the 368th FG's natural metal finished Thunderbolts. Additionally, canopies & tail braces were sometimes painted in squadron colors. The top area of the tail fins were painted with the groups yellow identification color.

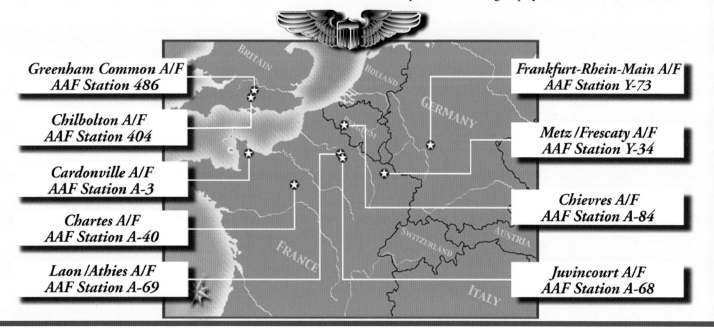

| XXIX TACTICAL AIR COMMAND (FEBRUARY 1945) | IX TAC 70TH FIGHTER WING (OCTOBER 1944) | IX TAC 71ST FIGHTER WING (AUGUST 1944) |

NO KNOWN INSIGNIA

370TH FIGHTER GROUP

ASSIGNED 9TH USAAF/JANUARY 1944

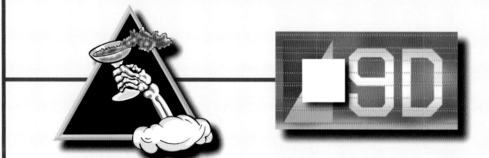

401ST FIGHTER SQUADRON

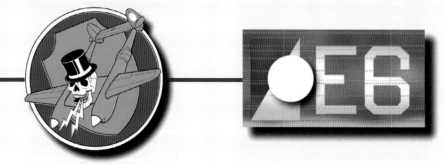

402D FIGHTER SQUADRON

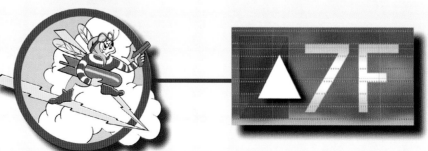

485TH FIGHTER SQUADRON

P-38 'LIGHTNING' / P-51 'MUSTANG'

370th Fighter Group:
Motto: unknown
Sobriquet: unknown
Campaign Streamers:
Air Offensive, Europe; Normandy; Northern France;
Rhineland; Ardennes-Alsace; Central Europe.
Unit Decorations:
Distinguished Unit Citation Hurtgen Forest, Germany, 2-Dec-44;
Order of the Day, Belgium Army 6-Jun-44 thru 30-Sep-44,
1-Oct -44 and 16-Dec-44 thru 25-Jan-45; *Belgian Fourragere.*
Overseas Combat Commanders:
Col. Howard F. Nichols, 1-Jul-43
Lt. Col. Seth J. McGee, 6-Nov-44
Col. Morgan A. Griffin, 22-Feb-45
Overseas Stations:
No. 467 Aldermaston, Berkshire; 12-Feb-44
No. 406 Andover, Hampshire; 29-Feb-44
A-3 Cardonville, Basse Normandie; 24-Jul-44
A-19 La Vielle, Basse Normandie; 15-Aug-44
A-45 Lonray, Basse Normandie; 6-Sep-44
A-73 Roye / Amy, Picardie; 11-Sep-44
A-78 Florennes / Juxaine, Province de Namur; 26-Sep-44
Y-32 Ophoven / Zwartberg, Province Limburg; 27-Jan-45
Y-99 Gutersloh, Nordrhein-Westphalia; 20-Apr-45

Insignia / Markings:
Group Insignia: unknown.
Squadron Insignia:
401st FS; unofficial.
402d FS; unofficial.
485th FS; officially approved 20-Mar-45.
      402d FS (1st design):
The 370th FG first arrived in England
equipped with P-47 Thunderbolts but
these were immediately replaced with
P-38 Lightnings. The insignia shown
at right was displayed by the 402d FS
prior to the conversion of the entire
group to the Lightning and reflects the
Thunderbolts characteristic four prop assembly.
Squadron Codes:
401st FS - **9D** • *402d FS* - **E6** • *485th FS* - **7F**
Squadron Colors:
492d FS - Red / Yellow
493d FS - Red / White
494th FS - Red / Blue
Aircraft Markings:
 P-38 markings were standard for ETO. The 370thFG did not
transition to the P-51 Mustang until the final weeks of the war.

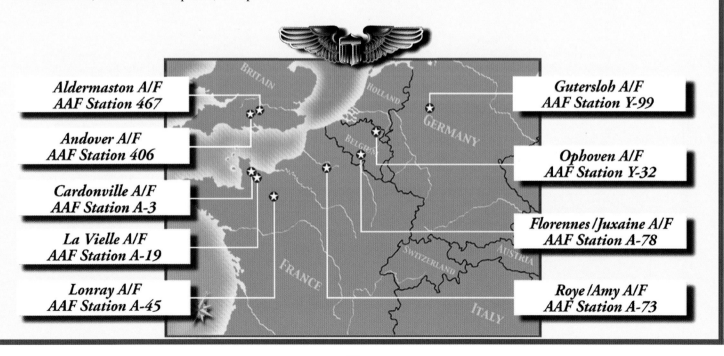

Aldermaston A/F
AAF Station 467

Andover A/F
AAF Station 406

Cardonville A/F
AAF Station A-3

La Vielle A/F
AAF Station A-19

Lonray A/F
AAF Station A-45

Gutersloh A/F
AAF Station Y-99

Ophoven A/F
AAF Station Y-32

Florennes / Juxaine A/F
AAF Station A-78

Roye / Amy A/F
AAF Station A-73

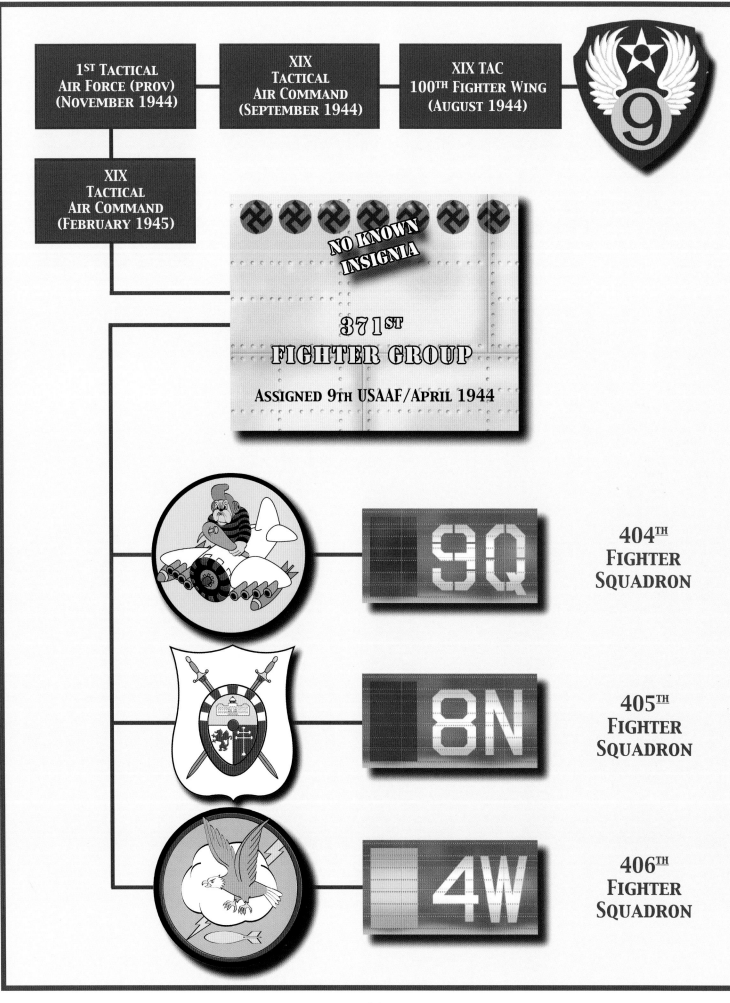

1ST TACTICAL
AIR FORCE (PROV)
(NOVEMBER 1944)

XIX
TACTICAL
AIR COMMAND
(SEPTEMBER 1944)

XIX TAC
100TH FIGHTER WING
(AUGUST 1944)

XIX
TACTICAL
AIR COMMAND
(FEBRUARY 1945)

NO KNOWN
INSIGNIA

371ST
FIGHTER GROUP

ASSIGNED 9TH USAAF/APRIL 1944

9Q

404TH
FIGHTER
SQUADRON

8N

405TH
FIGHTER
SQUADRON

4W

406TH
FIGHTER
SQUADRON

44

P-47 'THUNDERBOLT'

371st Fighter Group

Motto: unknown

Sobriquet: unknown

Campaign Streamers:

Air Offensive, Europe; Normandy; Northern France; Rhineland; Ardennes-Alsace; Central Europe.

Unit Decorations:

Distinguished Unit Citation- Germany, 15-Mar-44 thru 21-Mar-44; *Order of the Day, Belgium Army*-6-Jun-44 thru 30-Sep-44.

Overseas Combat Commanders:

Col. Bingham T. Kleine, 27-Jul-43

Overseas Stations:

No.415 Bisterne Close, Hampshire; Mar-44

A-6   Beuzeville, Basse Normandie; Jun-44

A-65 Perthes, Lorraine; 18-Sep-44

Y-7   Dole / Tavaux, Franche-Comte; 1-Oct-44

Y-1   Tantonville, Lorraine; 20-Dec-44

Y-34 Metz, Lorraine; 15-Feb-45

Y-74 Frankfurt / Eschborn, Hessen; 7-Apr-45

R-10 Furth, Bavaria Bayern; 5-May-45

Insignia / Markings:

Group Insignia: unknown.

Squadron Insignia:

404th FS; unofficial.

405th FS; unofficial.

406th FS; unofficial

The design shown at right is reputed to be the unofficial insignia belonging to *Headquarters Squadron, 371st Fighter Group*. The art work has all the earmarks of Disney Studios, however additional research is needed to determine its actual origins.

Squadron Codes:

404tht FS - **9Q** • *405th FS* - **8N** • *406th FS* - **4W**

Squadron Colors:

404th FS - Red

405th FS - Blue, medium

406th FS - Yellow

Aircraft Markings:

All squadrons of the 371st FG applied their respective color to the entire cowling area of their Thunderbolts. Some wartime photographs exist which show that various paints were additionally applied to the cowling flaps. Documentation is currently lacking however that would determine the extent and specific tactical purpose of such applications, if any at all.

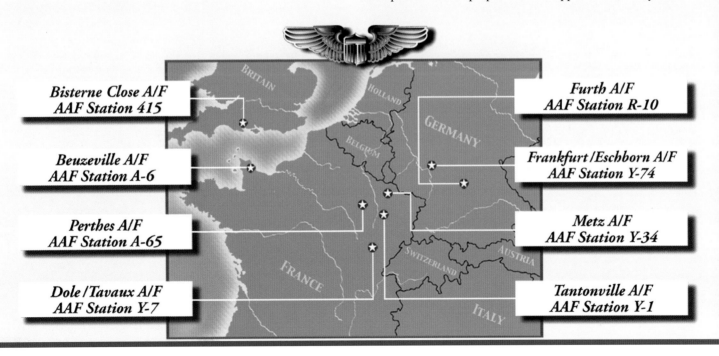

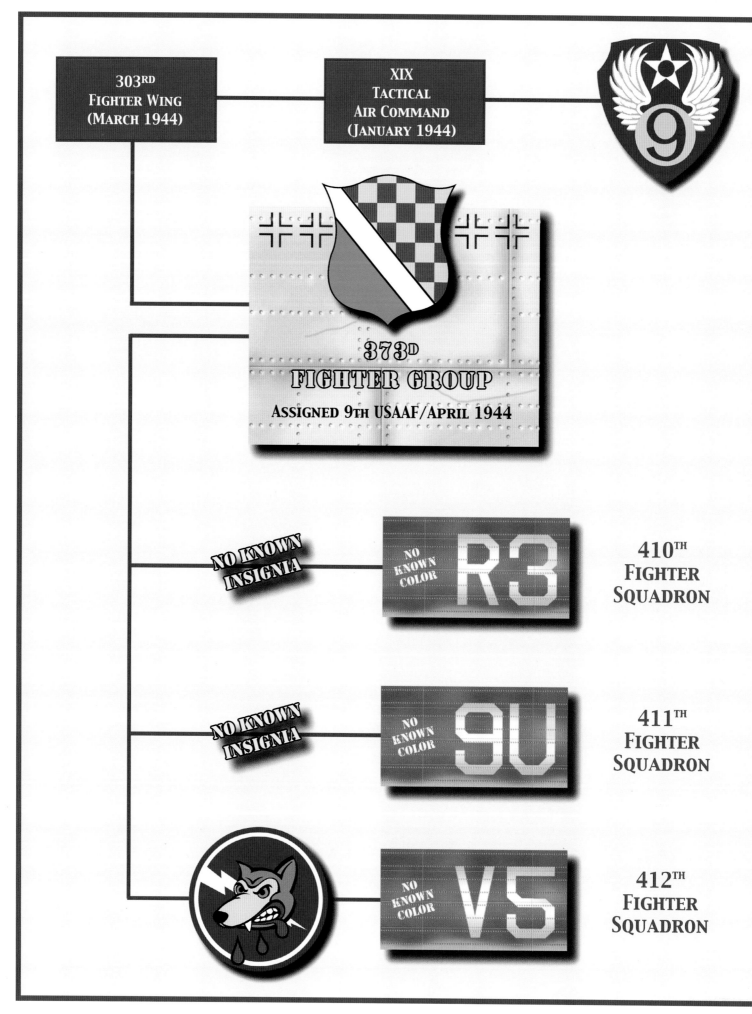

303RD
FIGHTER WING
(MARCH 1944)

XIX
TACTICAL
AIR COMMAND
(JANUARY 1944)

373D
FIGHTER GROUP
ASSIGNED 9TH USAAF/APRIL 1944

NO KNOWN
INSIGNIA

NO
KNOWN
COLOR

R3

410TH
FIGHTER
SQUADRON

NO KNOWN
INSIGNIA

NO
KNOWN
COLOR

9U

411TH
FIGHTER
SQUADRON

NO
KNOWN
COLOR

V5

412TH
FIGHTER
SQUADRON

P-47 'THUNDERBOLT'

373d Fighter Group:

Motto: unknown

Sobriquet: unknown

Campaign Streamers:

Air Offensive, Europe; Normandy; Northern France; Rhineland; Ardennes-Alsace; Central Europe.

Unit Decorations:

Distinguished Unit Citation, Rhine River, 2-Mar-45;

French Croix de Guerre with Palm, Aug-44;

Order of the Day, Belgium Army - 1-Oct-44 and 18-Dec-44 thru 15-Jan-45: *Belgian Fourragere.*

Overseas Combat Commanders:

Col. William H. Schwartz Jr., 25-Aug-43

Col. James C. McGehee, 17Nov44

Overseas Stations:

No.419 Woodchurch, Kent; 4-Apr-44

A-13 Tour en Bassin, Basse-Normandie; 19-Jul-44

A-29 St. James, Pays-de-la-Loire; 19-Aug-44

A-62D Reims, Champagne Ardenne; 19-Sept-44

Y-10 Le Culot, Province de Brabant; 22-Oct-44

Y-55 Venlo, Provincie Limburg; 11-Mar-45

Y-98 Lippstadt, Nordrhein-Westphalia; 20-Apr-45

Insignia / Markings:

Group Insignia: unofficial.

Squadron Insignia:

410th FS; unknown.

411th FS; unknown.

412th FS; unofficial and in need of corroboration. Little is known about this design. This is an example of the type of image that surfaces while in the process of researching 'visually' obscure units such as the 373rd Fighter Group. It is included herein because it *appears* to be of WWII vintage but could conceivably fall into the post war era.

Squadron Codes:

410th FS - **R3** • *411th FS* - **9U** • *412th FS* - **V5**

Squadron Colors:

410th FS - unknown

411th FS - unknown

412th FS - unknown

Aircraft Markings:

Other than the obligatory squadron codes and the Allied Quick Identification Markings, research into the 373d FG has failed to reveal any additional tactical markings of any kind.

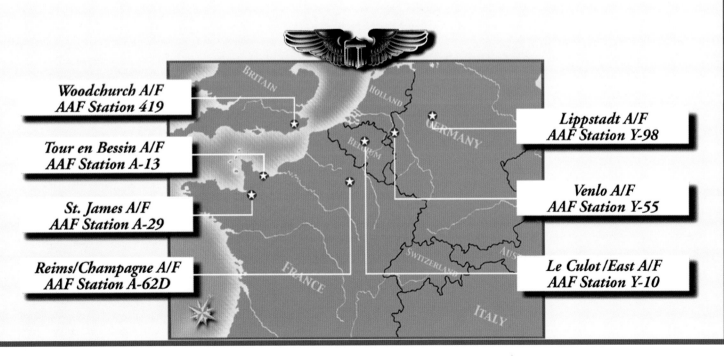

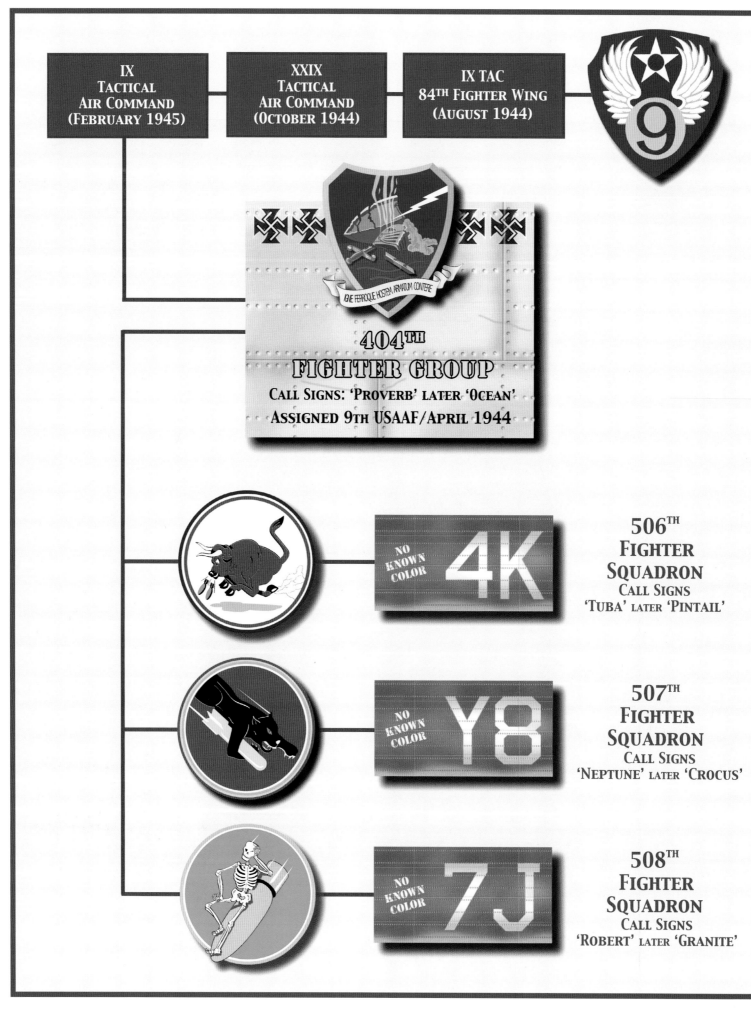

IX
TACTICAL
AIR COMMAND
(FEBRUARY 1945)

XXIX
TACTICAL
AIR COMMAND
(OCTOBER 1944)

IX TAC
84TH FIGHTER WING
(AUGUST 1944)

404TH
FIGHTER GROUP
CALL SIGNS: 'PROVERB' LATER 'OCEAN'
ASSIGNED 9TH USAAF/APRIL 1944

IGNE FERROQUE HOSTEM ARMATUM CONTERE

NO KNOWN COLOR
4K

506TH
FIGHTER
SQUADRON
CALL SIGNS
'TUBA' LATER 'PINTAIL'

NO KNOWN COLOR
Y8

507TH
FIGHTER
SQUADRON
CALL SIGNS
'NEPTUNE' LATER 'CROCUS'

NO KNOWN COLOR
7J

508TH
FIGHTER
SQUADRON
CALL SIGNS
'ROBERT' LATER 'GRANITE'

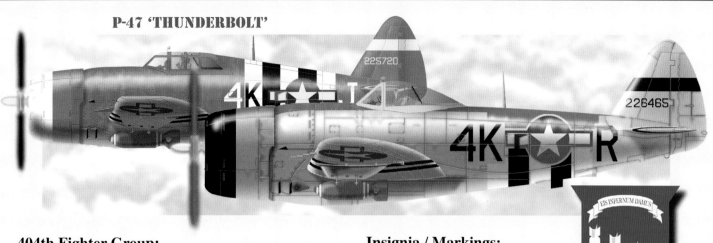

P-47 'THUNDERBOLT'

404th Fighter Group:

Motto: unknown

Sobriquet: unknown

Campaign Streamers:

American Theater: Air Offensive, Europe; Normandy; Northern France; Rhineland; Ardennes-Alsace; Central Europe.

Unit Decorations:

Distinguished Unit Citation - Germany, 10-Sep-44; *French Croix de Guerre with Palm*, 29 thru 31-Jul-44; *Order of the Day, Belgium Army* - 6-Jun-44 thru 30-Sep-44, 1-Oct-44 and 18-Dec-44 thru 15-Jan-45: *Belgian Fourragere.*

Overseas Combat Commanders:

Col. Carrol W. McColpin, 27 Jan 44

Lt. Col. Leo C. Moon, 25-Nov-44

Lt. Col. John R. Murphy, 23-Apr-45

Overseas Stations:

No.414 Winkton, Hampshire; 4-Apr-44

A-5 Chippelle, Basse Normandie; 6-Jul-44

A-48 Bretigny, Ile-de-France; 29-Aug-44

A-68 Juvincourt, Champagne-Ardenne; 13-Sept-44

A-92 St. Trond, 1-Oct-44

Y-54 Kelz, Province Limburg; 30-Mar-45

Y-86 Fritzlar, Hessen; 12-Apr-45

Insignia / Markings:

Group Insignia: unofficial

Originally constituted as the 404th Bombardment Group (Dive), the design at top right was the original group insignia prior to the unit being redesignated. The image immediately below the group insignia once belonged to the 623d BS(D) and had been approved 17-May-43. This squadron was disbanded when the group was reorganized and deployed to Great Britain as a fighter unit.

Squadron Insignia:

506th FS; unofficial

507th FS; unofficial

508th FS; approved 22-Jun-43

Squadron Codes:

506th FS - **4K** • *507th FS* - **Y8** • *508th FS* - **7J**

Squadron Colors:

506th FS - unknown

507th FS - unknown

508th FS - unknown

Aircraft Markings:

The 404th FG was yet another unit within the Ninth AAF that displayed little more than the squadron codes, call letter and Allied Quick Identification Markings. The vast majority of P-47's within this group were of a natural metal finish variety.

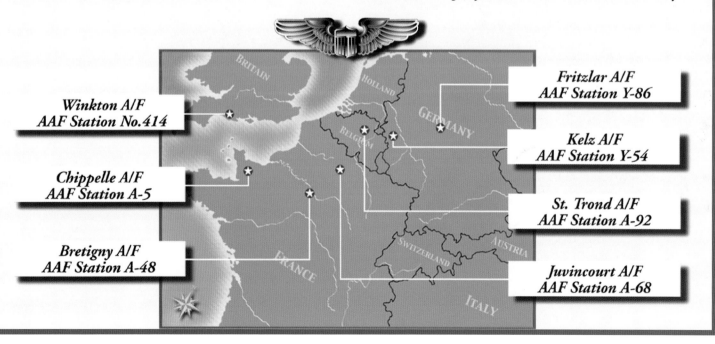

XXIX TAC
(FEBRUARY 1945)

XIX TAC
100TH FIGHTER WING
(OCTOBER 1944)

XIX TAC
303D FIGHTER WING
(AUGUST 1944)

NO KNOWN INSIGNIA

405TH
FIGHTER GROUP

ASSIGNED 9TH USAAF/MARCH 1944

G9

509TH
FIGHTER
SQUADRON

2Z

510TH
FIGHTER
SQUADRON

K4

511TH
FIGHTER
SQUADRON

P-47 'THUNDERBOLT'

405th Fighter Group:

Motto: unknown

Sobriquet: unknown

Campaign Streamers:

Air Offensive, Europe; Normandy; Northern France; Rhineland; Ardennes-Alsace; Central Europe.

Unit Decorations:

Distinguished Unit Citation - France, 24-Sep-44; *Order of the Day, Belgium Army* - 6-Jun-44 thru 30-Sep-44.

Overseas Combat Commanders:

Col. James Ferguson, 5-Nov-43

Col. Robert L. Delashaw, 26-Apr-44

Lt. J. Garrett Jackson, 22-Oct-44

Overseas Stations:

No.416 Christchurch, Hampshire; 7-Mar-44

A-8N Picauville, Basse Normandie; 30-Jul-44

A-64 St. Dizier, Champange-Ardenne; 14-Sep-44

Y-32 Ophoven, Province Limburg; 9-Feb-45

R-6 Kitzingen, Bavaria Bayern; 30-Apr-45

Combat Operations:

11-Apr-44 thru 8-May-45

Insignia / Markings:

Group Insignia: unknown

Originally constituted as the 405th Bombardment Group (Dive), redesignated 405th Fighter-Bomber Group, August 1944. A third and final redesignation to the 405th Fighter Group occurred in May, 1944.

Squadron Insignia:

509th FS; unofficial - officially replaced 30-Jan-57

510th FS; unofficial - officially replaced 14-Feb-57

511th FS; oficially approved 12-Feb-45

Squadron Codes:

509th FS - **G9** • *510th FS* - **2Z** • *511th FS* - **K4**

Squadron Colors:

509th FS - **Red**

510th FS - **Blue**

511th FS - **Yellow**

Aircraft Markings:

The 405th FG began applying color tactical markings to their aircraft sometime in the latter part of 1944. These markings were at first little more than the painting of each respective squadron color to the leading edge of the engine cowling. By wars end many of the groups P-47's had expanded the color tactical markings to include the canopy frame, anti-glare panels and even the black horizontal Allied Quick Identification tail band sometimes received an overcoat of squadron color.

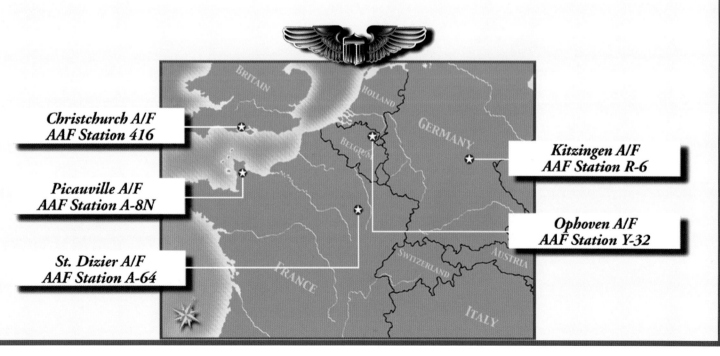

Christchurch A/F
AAF Station 416

Picauville A/F
AAF Station A-8N

St. Dizier A/F
AAF Station A-64

Kitzingen A/F
AAF Station R-6

Ophoven A/F
AAF Station Y-32

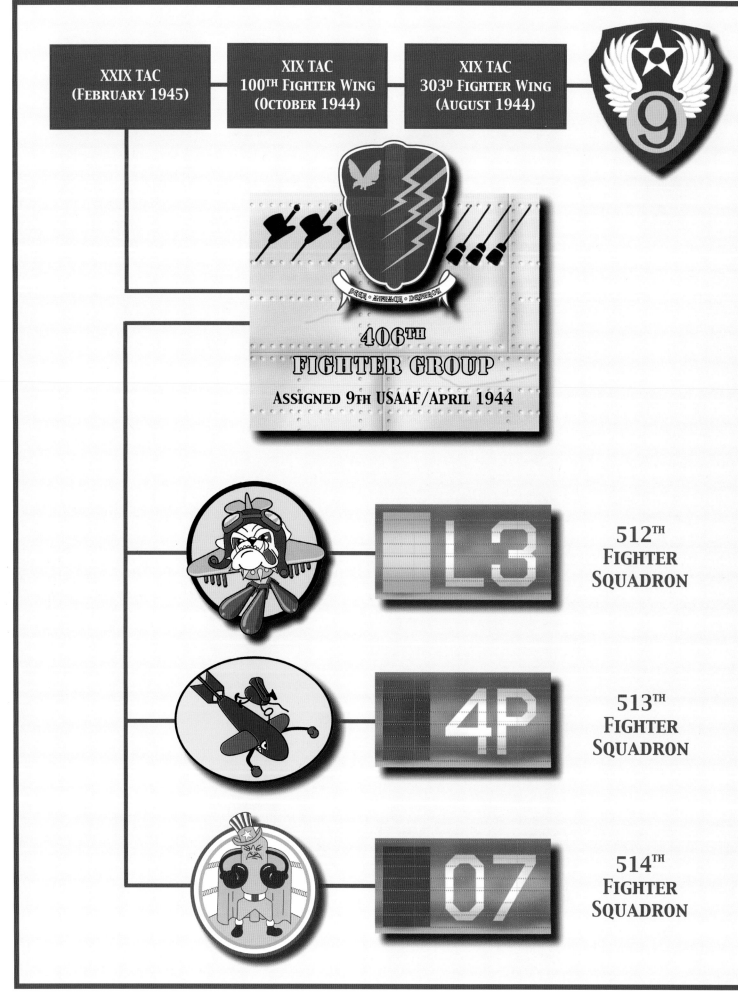

XXIX TAC
(FEBRUARY 1945)

XIX TAC
100TH FIGHTER WING
(OCTOBER 1944)

XIX TAC
303D FIGHTER WING
(AUGUST 1944)

9

406TH
FIGHTER GROUP

ASSIGNED 9TH USAAF/APRIL 1944

L3

512TH
FIGHTER
SQUADRON

4P

513TH
FIGHTER
SQUADRON

07

514TH
FIGHTER
SQUADRON

P-47 'THUNDERBOLT'

406th Fighter Group:

Motto: *Seek-Attack-Destroy*

Sobriquet: *The Raider Group*

Campaign Streamers:

American Theater; Air Offensive, Europe; Normandy;
Northern France; Rhineland; Ardennes-Alsace; Central Europe.

Unit Decorations:

Distinguished Unit Citation - France, 7-Sep-44;
Belgium, 23 thru 27 December, 1944

Overseas Combat Commanders:

Col. Anthony V. Grosetta, 6-Nov-43

Overseas Stations:

No. 417 Ashford, Kent; 4-Apr-44

A-13 Tour-en-Basin, Basse Normandie; 5-Aug-44

A-14 Cretteville, Basse Normandie; 17-Aug-44

A-36 St. Lenoard, Pays-de-la-Loire; 4-Sep-44

Y-34 Metz, Lorraine; 2-Feb-45

Y-29 Asch, Province Limburg; 8-Feb-45

Y-94 Handorf, Nordrhein-Westphalia; 15-Apr-45

Combat Operations:

First sortie 9-May-44

Insignia / Markings:

Group Insignia: unofficial

This was yet another outfit originally constituted as a Bombardment Group (Dive), the 406th. It too was redesignated as a Fighter-Bomber Group, in August, 1943 and finally again redesignation as the 406th Fighter Group in May, 1944.

Squadron Insignia:

512th FS; unofficial - officially replaced 9-Sep-55

513th FS; unofficial - officially replaced 28-Apr-55
Sobriquet *The Rocketeers* or *Rocket Squadron*, so named because this was the first AAF unit to be equipped with the 5 in. HVRA (High Velocity Rocket, Aircraft), unguided air to ground 'tank busting' ordnance.

514th FS; unofficial - officially replaced 1-Mar-55

Squadron Codes:

512th FS - **L3** • *513th FS* - **4P** • *514th FS* - **O7**

Squadron Colors:

512th FS -**Yellow**

513th FS - **Red**

514th FS - **Blue**

Aircraft Markings:

Late in the war the 406th Fighter Group adopted some rather very striking tactical markings. Of special note was the replacement of the tail Allied Quick Identification Markings with a wide horizontal band incorporating all three of the groups squadron colors.

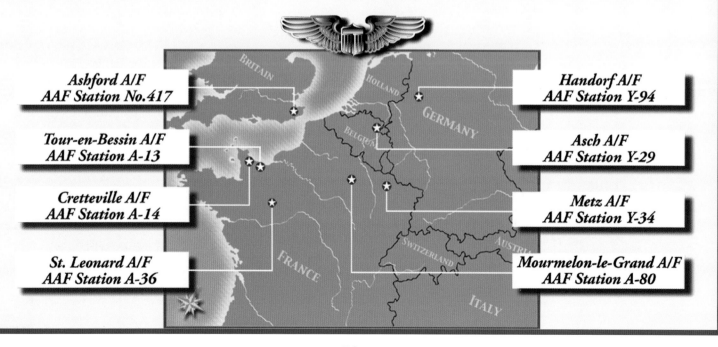

Ashford A/F
AAF Station No.417

Tour-en-Bessin A/F
AAF Station A-13

Cretteville A/F
AAF Station A-14

St. Leonard A/F
AAF Station A-36

Handorf A/F
AAF Station Y-94

Asch A/F
AAF Station Y-29

Metz A/F
AAF Station Y-34

Mourmelon-le-Grand A/F
AAF Station A-80

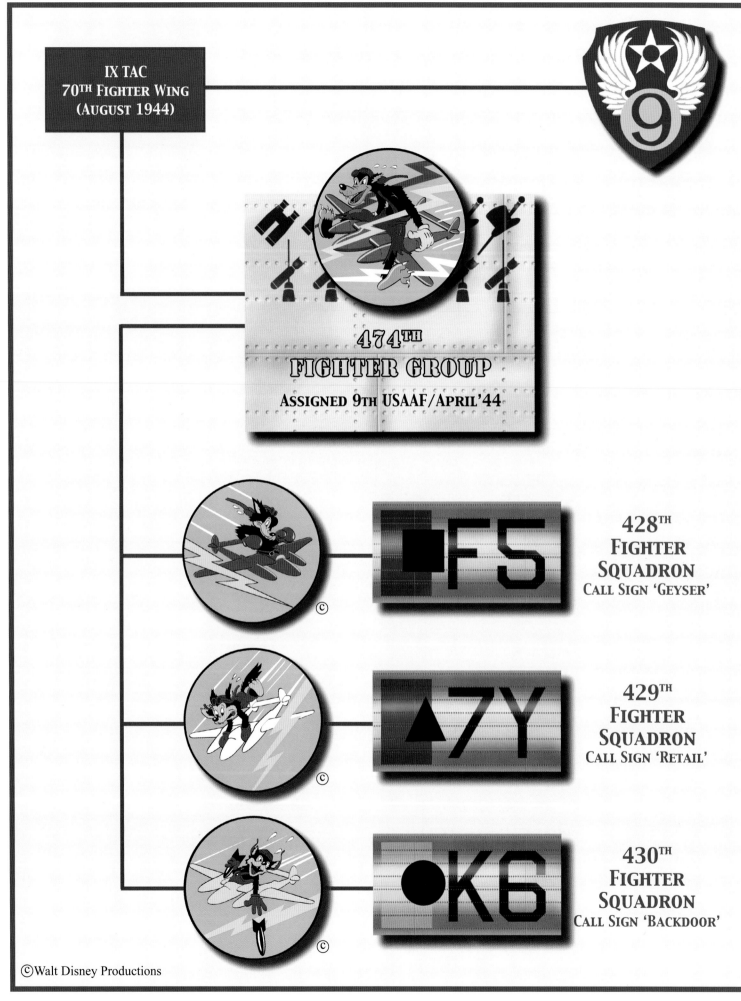

IX TAC
70TH FIGHTER WING
(AUGUST 1944)

474TH
FIGHTER GROUP
ASSIGNED 9TH USAAF/APRIL '44

428TH
FIGHTER
SQUADRON
CALL SIGN 'GEYSER'

429TH
FIGHTER
SQUADRON
CALL SIGN 'RETAIL'

430TH
FIGHTER
SQUADRON
CALL SIGN 'BACKDOOR'

P-38 'LIGHTNING'

474th Fighter Group:

Motto: unknown

Sobriquet: unknown

Campaign Streamers:

Air Offensive, Europe; Normandy; Northern France; Rhineland; Ardennes-Alsace; Central Europe.

Unit Decorations:

Distinguished Unit Citation - France, 23-Aug-44;

Order of the Day, Belgian Army, 6-Jun-44 thru 30-Sep-44 and 16-Dec-44 thru 25-Jan-45; *Belgium Fourragere*.

Overseas Combat Commanders:

Col. Clinton C. Wasem, 1-Aug-43

Overseas Stations:

1.) Moreton, Essex; 12-Mar-44

No. 454 Warmwell, Dorset; Apr-44

A-11 St. Lambert / Neuilly, Basse Normandie; 6-Aug-44

A-43 St. Marceau, Pays-de-la-Loire; 29-Aug-44

Y-72 Peronne, Picardy; 6-Sep-44

A-78 Florennes / Juzaine, Province de Namur; 1-Oct-44

Y-59 Strassfeld, Nordrhein-Westphalia; 22-Mar-45

R-2 Langensalza, Thuringia; 22-Apr-45

* there is no RAF or AAF numerical listing for this station.

Combat Operations:

25-Apr-44 thru 8-May-45

Insignia / Markings:

Group Insignia: unofficial; officially replaced 22-Jun-55

Squadron Insignia:

428th FS; unofficial - officially replaced 3-Jun-54

429th FS; unofficial - officially replaced 7-Jul-55

430th FS; unofficial - officially replaced 15-Jul-54

Squadron Codes:

428th FS - **F5** • *429th FS* - **7Y** • *430th FS* - **K6**

Squadron Colors:

428th FS - **Red**

429th FS - **Blue** (formerly **White**)

430th FS - **Yellow**

Aircraft Markings:

Virtually all P-38's within the 474thFG reversed the color order of the fuselage Invasion Stripes from White to Black to Black to White. Wing applications however remained consistent with the original SHAEF directive. Spinners, and in some cases, the nacelle nose and frontal air intake cowlings received a coat of squadron color. The tactical geometric symbols were normally applied with Black paint, occasionally however Black was substituted with a squadron color. The tail serial numbers were often simply over painted by the squadron tactical symbol with the last three digits of this number stenciled to both sides of the nacelle with stencil breaks normally remaining unfilled. Although frowned upon, the use of squadron colors would sometimes find their way onto the fuselage codes as well.

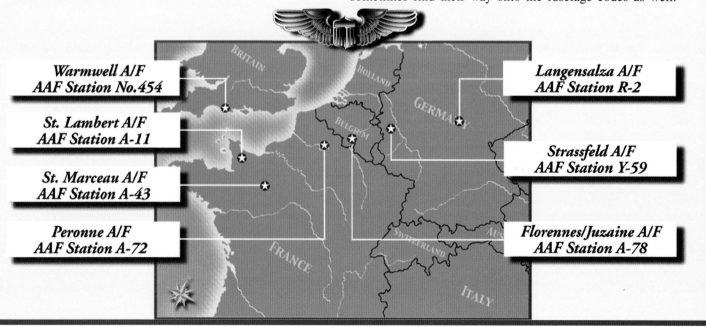

Warmwell A/F
AAF Station No.454

St. Lambert A/F
AAF Station A-11

St. Marceau A/F
AAF Station A-43

Peronne A/F
AAF Station A-72

Langensalza A/F
AAF Station R-2

Strassfeld A/F
AAF Station Y-59

Florennes/Juzaine A/F
AAF Station A-78

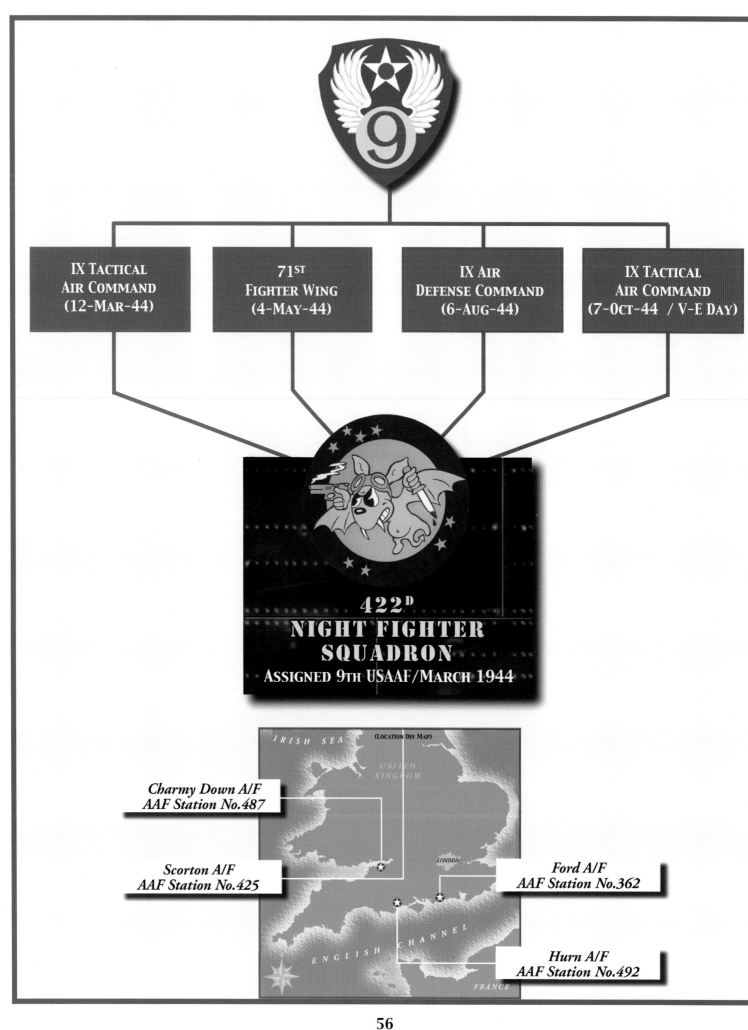

IX TACTICAL
AIR COMMAND
(12-MAR-44)

71ST
FIGHTER WING
(4-MAY-44)

IX AIR
DEFENSE COMMAND
(6-AUG-44)

IX TACTICAL
AIR COMMAND
(7-OCT-44 / V-E DAY)

422D
NIGHT FIGHTER
SQUADRON
ASSIGNED 9TH USAAF/MARCH 1944

Charmy Down A/F
AAF Station No.487

Scorton A/F
AAF Station No.425

Ford A/F
AAF Station No.362

Hurn A/F
AAF Station No.492

422d Night Fighter Squadron:

Motto: unknown

Sobriquet: unknown

Campaign Streamers:

Normandy; Northern France; Rhineland; Ardennes-Alsace; Central Europe: Air Combat, EAME Theater

Unit Decorations:

Distinguished Unit Citation - Ardennes Salient, 16, 17, 27, and 28 of December, 1944.

Overseas Stations:

No. 487 Charmy Down, Somerset; 7-Mar-44

No. 425 Scorton, Yorkshirs; 6-May-44

[1.)] *No.492* Hurn, Hampshire; 28-Jun-44

[1.)] *No.362* Ford, Sussex, 6-Jul-44

A-15 Maupertus, Basse Normandie; 25-Jul-44

A-39 Chateaudun, Centre-Val-de-Loire; 28-Aug-44

A-78 Florennes / Juzaine, Province de Namur; 16-Sep-44

Y-59 Strassfeld, Nordrhein-Westphalia; 6-Apr-45

R-2 Langensalza, Thuringia; 24-Apr-45

[1.)] detachments only at these stations

Combat Operations:

3-Jul-44 thru 4-May-45

Insignia / Markings:

Squadron Insignia:

422d NFS; officially approved 29-Dec-43

Squadron Code:

none

Squadron Color:

none

Aircraft Markings:

Originally flew combat operations with a standard AAF Olive Drab over Neutral Gray paint scheme as per ANA Directive No.157. Following experiments conducted at Elgin Field in Florida it was recommended that this standard two-color paint scheme be replaced with gloss black for all aircraft conducting nighttime operations. On 19-Feb-44 General Brereton commanding the Ninth Air Force requested that henceforth all P-61 and P-70 Night Fighters destined for his command receive a factory paint scheme of gloss black as per the Eligin Field test results. In the meantime the AAF Engineering Division at Wright Field in Ohio directed that a gloss black, designated as Jet No. 62, be added to the existing ANA Bulletin No.157. By wars end all night fighters of the Ninth would bear this color.

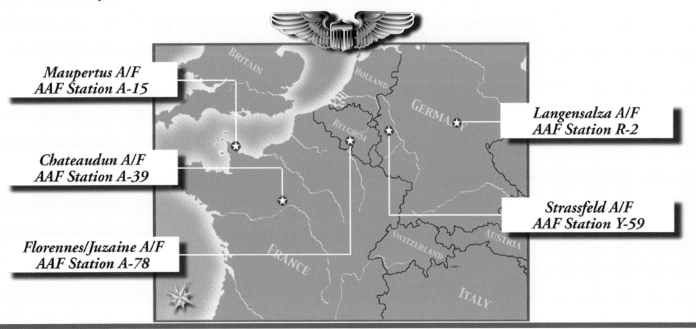

Maupertus A/F
AAF Station A-15

Chateaudun A/F
AAF Station A-39

Florennes/Juzaine A/F
AAF Station A-78

Langensalza A/F
AAF Station R-2

Strassfeld A/F
AAF Station Y-59

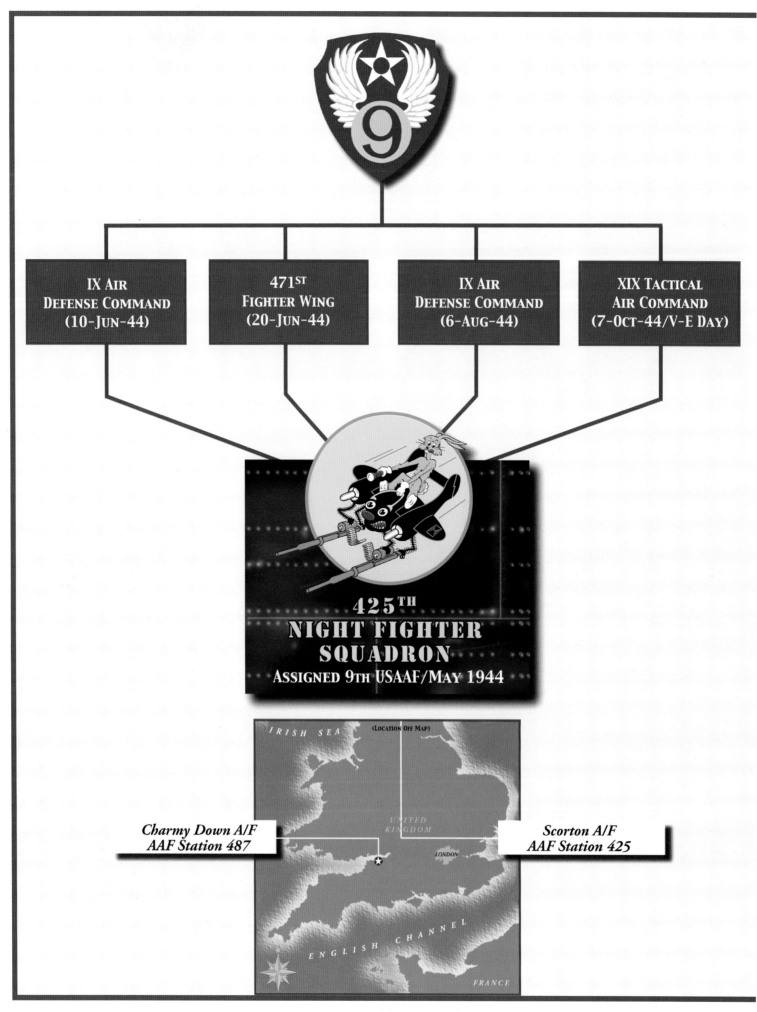

IX AIR
DEFENSE COMMAND
(10-JUN-44)

471ST
FIGHTER WING
(20-JUN-44)

IX AIR
DEFENSE COMMAND
(6-AUG-44)

XIX TACTICAL
AIR COMMAND
(7-OCT-44/V-E DAY)

425TH
NIGHT FIGHTER
SQUADRON
ASSIGNED 9TH USAAF/MAY 1944

IRISH SEA

(LOCATION OFF MAP)

UNITED KINGDOM

LONDON

Charmy Down A/F
AAF Station 487

Scorton A/F
AAF Station 425

ENGLISH CHANNEL

FRANCE

425th Night Fighter Squadron:

Motto: unknown

Sobriquet: unknown

Campaign Streamers:

Normandy; Northern France; Rhineland; Ardennes-Alsace; Central Europe: Air Combat, EAME Theater

Unit Decorations: *none.*

Overseas Stations:

No.487 Charmy Down, Somerset; 26-May-44

No.425 Scorton, Yorkshire; 12-Jun-44

[1.)] Stoneman Park, 12-Aug-44

A-33 Vannes, Bretagne; 18-Aug-44

[1.)] Le Mousloiris, 1-Sep-44

A-58 Coulommiers, Ile-de-France; 11-Sep-44

A-79 Prosnes, Champagne-Ardenne; 13-Oct-44

A-82 Verdun (No.393-Etain), Lorraine; 9-Nov-44

Y-73 Frankfurt-Rhine-Main, Hessen; 12-Apr-45

R-30 Furth-Industriehafen, Bavaria Bayern; 2-May-45

[1.)] there are no RAF or AAF numerical listings for this station.

Combat Operations:

July 1944 thru 8-May-45

Insignia / Markings:

Squadron Insignia:

425th NFS; officially approved 5-May-45

Squadron Code:

Squadron Color:

Aircraft Markings:

Due to the unusual airframe configuration of the P-61 the fuselage national insignia was smaller than that normally displayed on other AAF combat aircraft. On 29-May-44 these were directed to be reduced proportionately and conform to a height hot exceeding 75% of the overall fuselage height at the point of insignia application. In September of the previous year all AAF P-61 radio call numbers (aircraft serial numbers) were ordered reduced in height and applied to the lower outside tail surfaces using Insignia Red No.45. Both the 422d and 425th NFS were given the option by Gen. Spaatz to substitute gray for the white within the U.S. National Insignia on all surfaces. Article 2, section (a) of the SHAEF directive regarding the application of Invasion, or D-Day Stripes, specifically exempted all Night Fighters from compliance with this directive. Interestingly, both the 422d and 425th NFS opted not to avail themselves of this exemption.

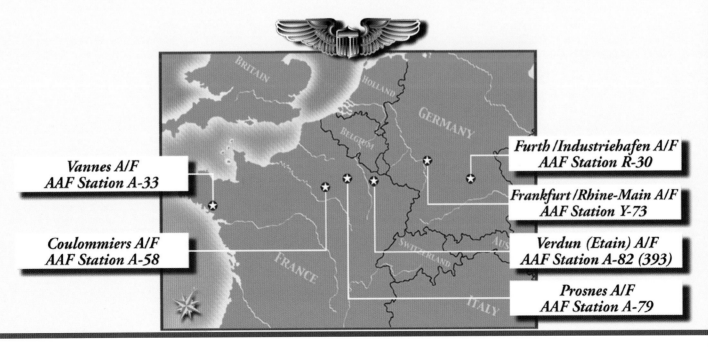

Vannes A/F
AAF Station A-33

Coulommiers A/F
AAF Station A-58

Furth /Industriehafen A/F
AAF Station R-30

Frankfurt /Rhine-Main A/F
AAF Station Y-73

Verdun (Etain) A/F
AAF Station A-82 (393)

Prosnes A/F
AAF Station A-79

TROOP CARRIER
UNITS OF THE
NINTH U.S.A.A.F.

The Troop Carrier pilots who flew countless sorties on behalf of the Allied war effort are deserving of much more praise than they have been accorded in post war histories. Contemporary documentaries tend to focus on the major airborne campaigns of the war such as the Normandy Invasion or Operation Market Garden. While there can be no argument that events of this magnitude were major milestones in the history of World War II, they only illustrate one aspect of the full scope of missions that were conducted by this branch of the Army Air Force.

Insertion of OSS operatives, countless supply drops behind enemy lines, often at night, were additional duties carried out by the Troop Transport crews. These supply missions were vital to Allied ground forces and resistance fighters operating deep within German occupied territory. The timely evacuation of wounded personnel to rear areas was yet another invaluable contribution made by the Troop Carrier service.

The total makeup of the troop carrier structure within the Ninth AAF was massive, The largest such collective effort the world has ever seen consisted of the following three major elements which together comprised the IX Troop Carrier Command, Ninth U.S. Army Air Force.

IX TROOP CARRIER COMMAND

50TH TROOP CARRIER WING
(Insignia officially approved 22-Sep-42)

52D TROOP CARRIER WING
(Insignia officially approved 22-Sep-42)

53D TROOP CARRIER WING
(Insignia officially approved 6-Apr-43)

The combat deployment of a large contingent of airborne assault troops would require a multiple grouping of a standard AAF three aircraft 'V' formation. These would group to form a Serial which consisted of a predetermined number of aircraft from a designated TC Group. The total number of 'V's comprising each Serial varied greatly in direct proportion to the respective mission. Each pilot was responsible for maintaining his proper position and interval within a formation and this was accomplished totally by means visual orientation.

Transports were devoid of the more elaborate tactical markings such as those utilized by the fighter and bomber units. The only visual reference to aid a pilot with his formation flying were the large squadron codes painted on the forward section of all Ninth AAF Troop Transports and the individual aircraft's call letter located on the vertical stabilizer.

The only additional tactical markings affixed to the troop transports were the now familiar Invasion Stripes which were hastily applied immediately prior to D-Day. With many Allied aircraft, especially the larger ones, these were seldom the precision paint jobs so often depicted in movies, as evidenced by the accompanying photos.

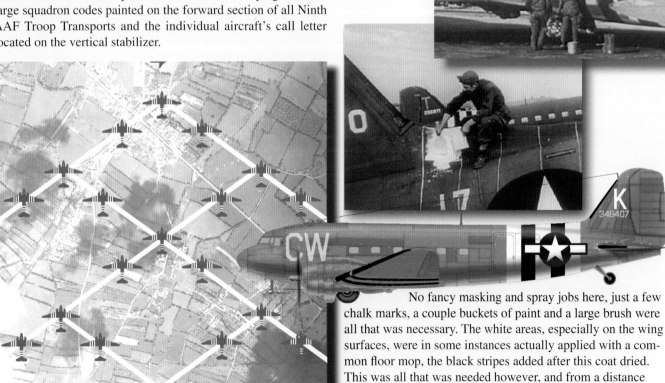

No fancy masking and spray jobs here, just a few chalk marks, a couple buckets of paint and a large brush were all that was necessary. The white areas, especially on the wing surfaces, were in some instances actually applied with a common floor mop, the black stripes added after this coat dried. This was all that was needed however, and from a distance most of these applications looked almost professional.

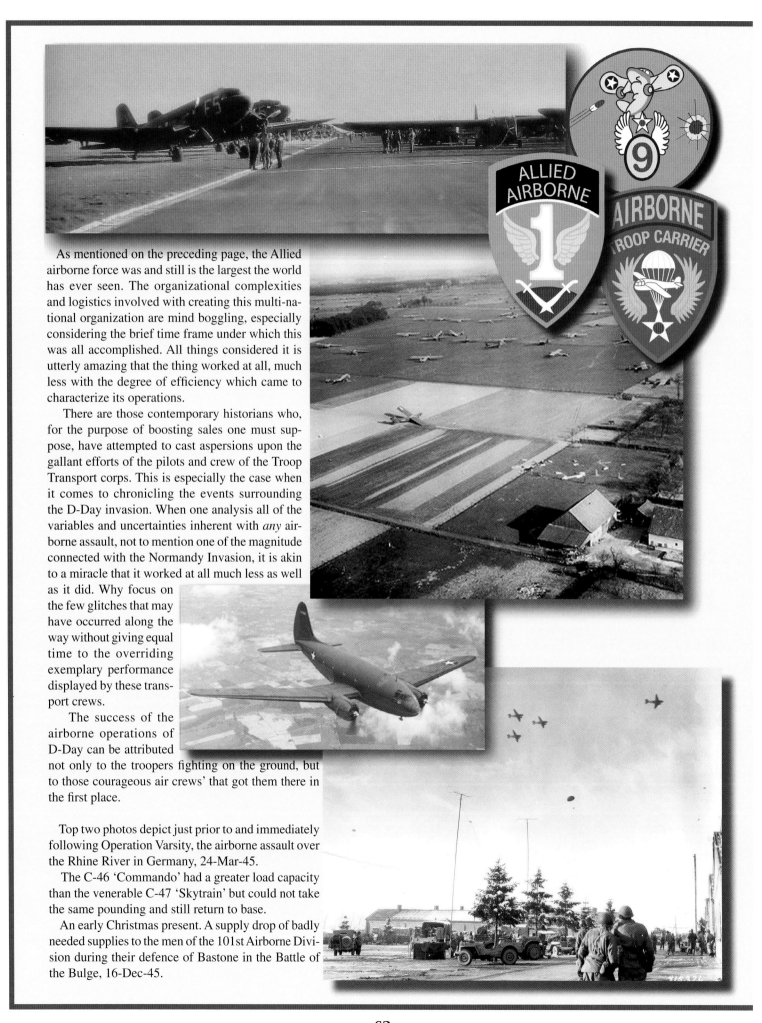

As mentioned on the preceding page, the Allied airborne force was and still is the largest the world has ever seen. The organizational complexities and logistics involved with creating this multi-national organization are mind boggling, especially considering the brief time frame under which this was all accomplished. All things considered it is utterly amazing that the thing worked at all, much less with the degree of efficiency which came to characterize its operations.

There are those contemporary historians who, for the purpose of boosting sales one must suppose, have attempted to cast aspersions upon the gallant efforts of the pilots and crew of the Troop Transport corps. This is especially the case when it comes to chronicling the events surrounding the D-Day invasion. When one analysis all of the variables and uncertainties inherent with *any* airborne assault, not to mention one of the magnitude connected with the Normandy Invasion, it is akin to a miracle that it worked at all much less as well as it did. Why focus on the few glitches that may have occurred along the way without giving equal time to the overriding exemplary performance displayed by these transport crews.

The success of the airborne operations of D-Day can be attributed not only to the troopers fighting on the ground, but to those courageous air crews' that got them there in the first place.

Top two photos depict just prior to and immediately following Operation Varsity, the airborne assault over the Rhine River in Germany, 24-Mar-45.

The C-46 'Commando' had a greater load capacity than the venerable C-47 'Skytrain' but could not take the same pounding and still return to base.

An early Christmas present. A supply drop of badly needed supplies to the men of the 101st Airborne Division during their defence of Bastone in the Battle of the Bulge, 16-Dec-45.

52ND TROOP CARRIER WING (FEBRUARY 1944)

IX TROOP CARRIER COMMAND

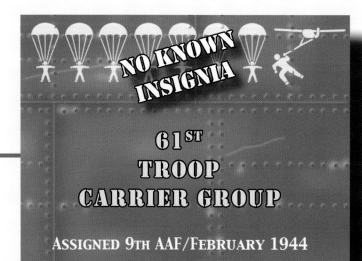

NO KNOWN INSIGNIA

61ST TROOP CARRIER GROUP

ASSIGNED 9TH AAF/FEBRUARY 1944

14TH TRCRSQDN

15TH TRCRSQDN

NO KNOWN INSIGNIA

NO KNOWN INSIGNIA

53RD TRCRSQDN

59TH TRCRSQDN

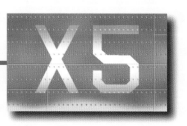

C-47 'SKYTRAIN'

61st Troop Carrier Group:

Motto: unknown

Sobriquet: unknown

Campaign Streamers:
American Theater; Sicily; Rome-Arno; Normandy; Northern France; Rhineland; Central Europe.

Unit Decorations:
Distinguished Unit Citation - Sicily, 11-Jul-43 and France, 6 thru 7 June, 1944

Overseas Combat Commanders:
Col. Willis W. Mitchell, 11-Mar-43

[1.] **Overseas Stations:**
No.483 Barkston Heath, Lincolnshire; 18-Feb-44
[2.] *B-92* Abbeville / Drucat, Alsace; 13-Mar-45

Combat Operations:
June 1944 thru May 1945

[1.] This list does not reflect the actual combat roll of this group which experienced extensive operations with the Twelfth AAF prior to transferring to the Ninth.

[2.] B-92 was an RAF airfield used by the AAF as a staging area for troop carrier units supporting the First Allied Airborne Army.

Insignia / Markings:

Group Insignia: unknown

Squadron Insignia:
14th TCS; officially approved 28-Dec-42
15th TCS; unknown
53d TCS; unofficial
59th TCS; unknown

Squadron Codes:
14th TCS - **3I**
15th TCS - **Y9**
53d TCS - **3A**
59th TCS - **X5**

Squadron Colors:
14th TCS - none
15th TCS - none
53d TCS - none
59th TCS - none

Aircraft Markings:
Standard USAAF two-color camouflage with White or Sky squadron code located on forward fuselage, with the a/c call letter positioned on the tail just above the aircraft call number.

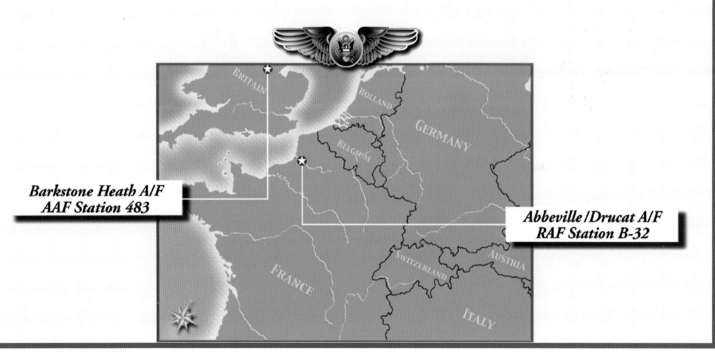

Barkstone Heath A/F
AAF Station 483

Abbeville/Drucat A/F
RAF Station B-32

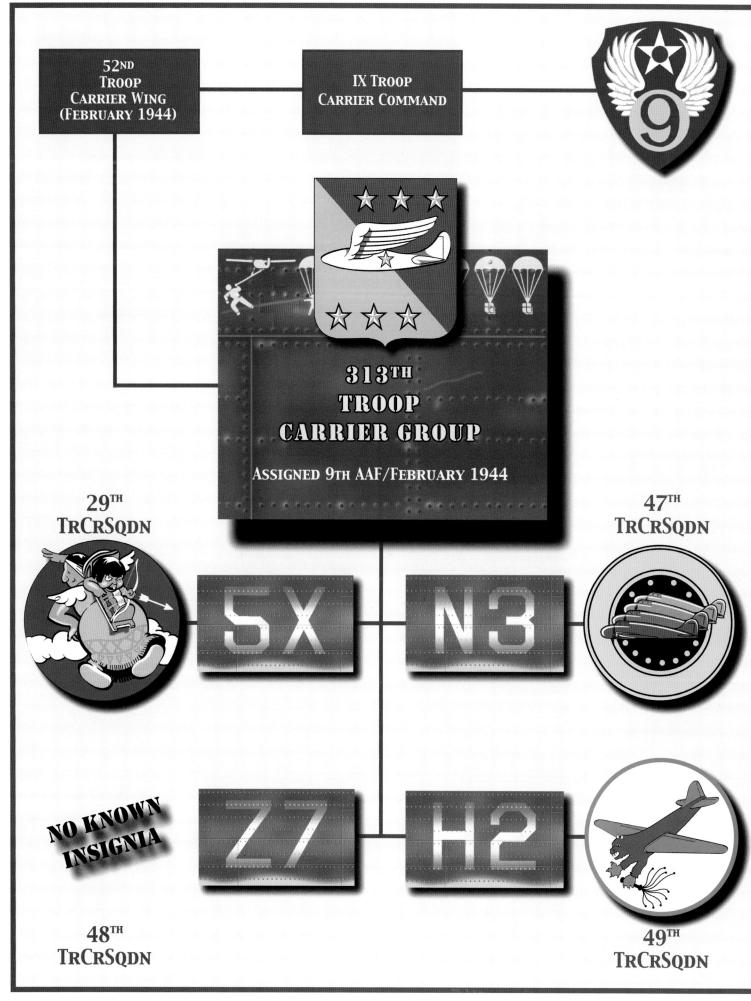

52ND TROOP CARRIER WING (FEBRUARY 1944)

IX TROOP CARRIER COMMAND

313TH TROOP CARRIER GROUP

ASSIGNED 9TH AAF/FEBRUARY 1944

29TH TRCRSQDN

47TH TRCRSQDN

5X

N3

NO KNOWN INSIGNIA

Z7

H2

48TH TRCRSQDN

49TH TRCRSQDN

313th Troop Carrier Group:

Motto: unknown

Sobriquet: unknown

Campaign Streamers:
American Theater; Sicily; Rome-Arno; Normandy; Northern France; Rhineland; Central Europe.

Unit Decorations:
Distinguished Unit Citation - Sicily, 11-Jul-43 and France, 6 thru 7 June, 1944

Overseas Combat Commanders:
Col. Clayton Stiles, 9-Apr-43

[1] **Overseas Stations:**
No.484 Folkingham, Lincolnshire; 4-Feb-44
[2] *B-54* Achiet, Alsace; 28-Feb-45

Combat Operations:
9-Jul-44 thru 8-May-45

[1] This list does not reflect the actual combat roll of this group which experienced extensive operations with the Twelfth AAF prior to transferring to the Ninth.

[2] B-32 was an RAF airfield used by the AAF as a staging area for troop carrier units supporting the First Allied Airborne Army.

Insignia / Markings:

Group Insignia: officially approved 3-Feb-43

Squadron Insignia:
29th TCS; officially approved 24-Aug-43
47th TCS; officially approved 27-Feb-43
48th TCS; unknown
49th TCS; officially approved 13-Jan-43

Squadron Codes:
29th TCS - **5 X**
47th TCS - **N 3**
48th TCS - **Z 7**
49th TCS - **H 2**

Squadron Colors:
29th TCS - none
47th TCS - none
48th TCS - none
49th TCS - none

Aircraft Markings:
Standard USAAF two-color camouflage with White or Sky squadron code located on forward fuselage, with the a/c call letter positioned on the tail just above the aircraft call number.

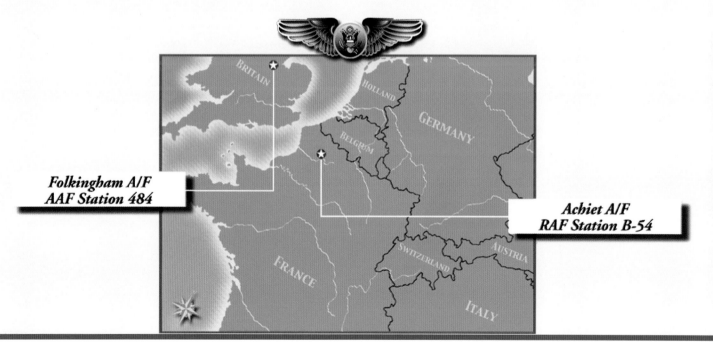

Folkingham A/F
AAF Station 484

Achiet A/F
RAF Station B-54

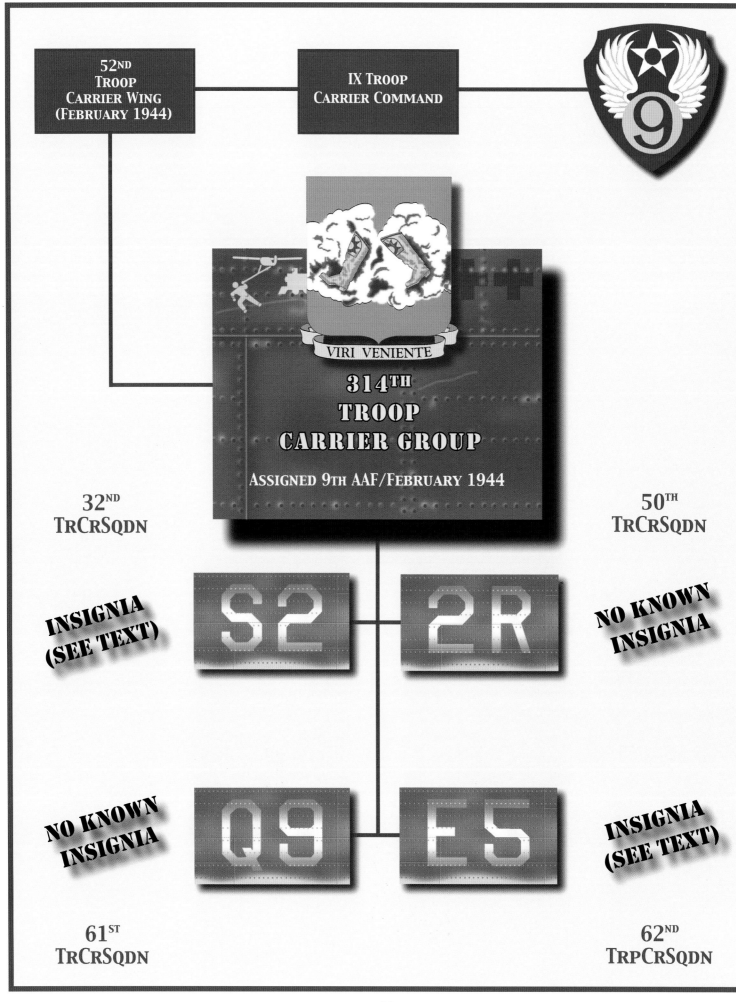

52ND TROOP CARRIER WING (FEBRUARY 1944)

IX TROOP CARRIER COMMAND

VIRI VENIENTE

314TH TROOP CARRIER GROUP

ASSIGNED 9TH AAF/FEBRUARY 1944

32ND TrCrSqdn

INSIGNIA (SEE TEXT)

S2

2R

NO KNOWN INSIGNIA

50TH TrCrSqdn

NO KNOWN INSIGNIA

Q9

E5

INSIGNIA (SEE TEXT)

61ST TrCrSqdn

62ND TrpCrSqdn

314th Troop Carrier Group:

Motto: *Viri Veniente (Men Will Come)*

Sobriquet: unknown

Campaign Streamers:

American Theater; Sicily; Naples-Foggia; Normandy; Northern France; Rhineland; Central Europe.

Unit Decorations:

Distinguished Unit Citation - France, 6-Jun-44

Overseas Combat Commanders:

Col. Clayton Stiles, 9-Apr-43

[1.] **Overseas Stations:**

No.538 Saltby, Lincolnshire; Feb-44

[2.] *B-44* Poix, Alsace; Feb-45

Combat Operations:

July 1943 thru 8-May-45

[1.] This list does not reflect the actual combat roll of this group which experienced extensive operations with the Twelfth AAF prior to transferring to the Ninth.

[2.] B-44 was an RAF airfield used by the AAF as a staging area for troop carrier units supporting the First Allied Airborne Army.

Insignia / Markings:

Group Insignia:

officially approved 17-Aug-42

Squadron Insignia:

32d TCS; (see text)

50th TCS; unknown

61st TCS; unknown

62d TCS; (see text)

Squadron Codes:

32d TCS - **S 2**

50th TCS - **2 R**

61st TCS - **Q 9**

62d TCS - **E 5**

Squadron Colors:

32d TCS - none

50th TCS - none

61st TCS - none

62d TCS - none

Aircraft Markings:

The two designs above have been attributed to the 32d (top) and 62d (bottom) TCS's but additional corroboration is needed before either is confirmed as WWII era.

Standard USAAF two-color camouflage with White or Sky squadron code located on forward fuselage, and the a/c call letter positioned on the tail just above the aircraft call number.

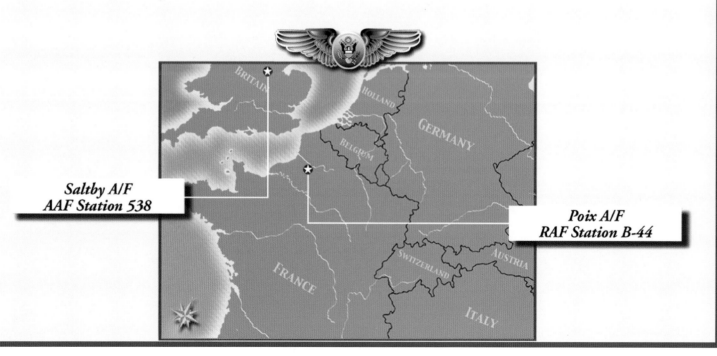

Saltby A/F
AAF Station 538

Poix A/F
RAF Station B-44

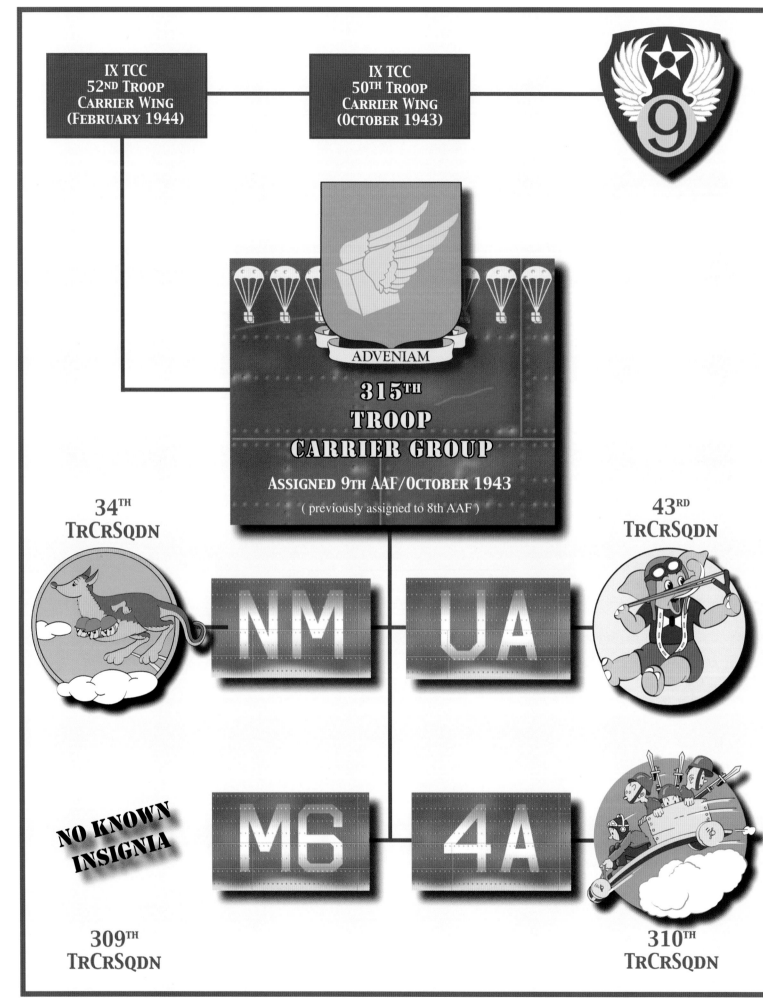

IX TCC
52ND TROOP
CARRIER WING
(FEBRUARY 1944)

IX TCC
50TH TROOP
CARRIER WING
(OCTOBER 1943)

ADVENIAM

315TH
TROOP
CARRIER GROUP

ASSIGNED 9TH AAF/OCTOBER 1943

(previously assigned to 8th AAF)

34TH
TRCRSQDN

43RD
TRCRSQDN

NM

UA

NO KNOWN
INSIGNIA

M6

4A

309TH
TRCRSQDN

310TH
TRCRSQDN

315th Troop Carrier Group:

Motto: *Adveniam (I Will Arrive)*

Sobriquet: unknown

Campaign Streamers:
American Theater; Sicily; Naples-Foggia; Normandy; Northern France; Rhineland; Central Europe.

Unit Decorations:
Distinguished Unit Citation - France, 6-Jun-44

Overseas Combat Commanders:
Col. Hamish McLelland, 17-Apr-42
Col. Howard B. Lyon, 27-Sep-44
Lt.Col. Robert J. Gibbons, 27-Mar-45

[1.] **Overseas Stations:**
No.467 Alderston, Berkshire; 1-Dec-42
[1.] *No.474* Welford Park, Berkshire; 6-Nov-43
No.493 Spanhoe / Wakerly, Northamptonshire; 7-Feb-44
[2.] *B-48* Amiens / Glisy, Alsace; 6-Apr-45

Combat Operations:
July 1943 thru 8-May-45

[1.] In May 1943 a detachment was temporarily posted to Algeria to assist in the Allied invasion of Sicily and later Italy. This detachment rejoined the rest of the Group in March 1944.
[2.] B-48 was an RAF airfield used by the AAF as a staging area for troop carrier units supporting the First Allied Airborne Army.

Insignia / Markings:

Group Insignia:
officially approved 22-May-42

Squadron Insignia:
34th - TCS; (see text)
43d - TCS; officially replaced 3-Dec-53
309th TCS; unknown
310th TCS; approved 23-Oct-44

Squadron Codes:
34th - TCS - **N M**
43d - TCS - **U A**
309th TCS - **M 6**
310th TCS - **4 A**

Squadron Colors:
34th - TCS - none
43d - TCS - none
309th TCS - none
310th TCS - none

Aircraft Markings:

The insignia above was officially approved for the 34thTCS 24-Mar-54. It is included here because it has been proposed that this was actually a late war replacement for the image on the opposite page. As of press time however, corroboration of this claim is pending.

Standard USAAF two-color camouflage with White or Sky squadron code located on forward fuselage, and the a/c call letter positioned on the tail just above the aircraft call number.

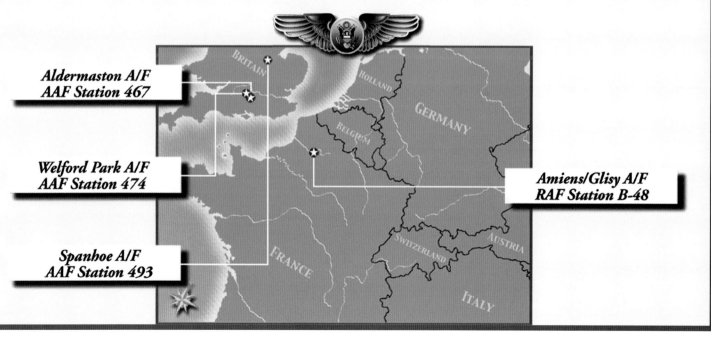

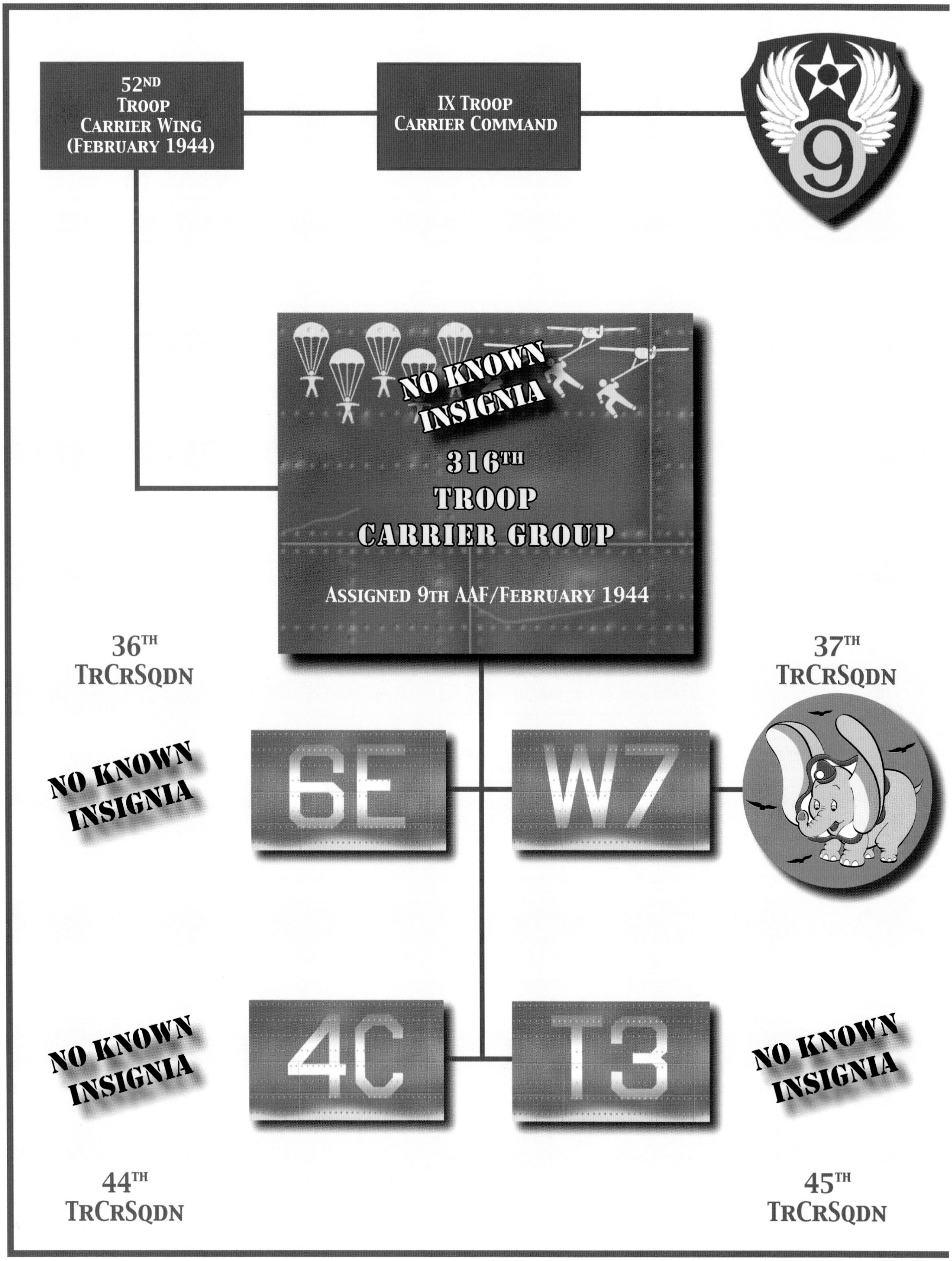

52ND
TROOP
CARRIER WING
(FEBRUARY 1944)

IX TROOP
CARRIER COMMAND

NO KNOWN
INSIGNIA

316TH
TROOP
CARRIER GROUP

ASSIGNED 9TH AAF/FEBRUARY 1944

36TH
TRCRSQDN

NO KNOWN
INSIGNIA

6E

W7

37TH
TRCRSQDN

NO KNOWN
INSIGNIA

4C

T3

NO KNOWN
INSIGNIA

44TH
TRCRSQDN

45TH
TRCRSQDN

316th Troop Carrier Group:

Motto: *Valor Without Arms*

Sobriquet: unknown

Campaign Streamers:

American Theater; Egypt-Libya; Tunisia; Sicily; Naples-Foggia; Rome-Arno; Normandy; Northern France; Rhineland; Central Europe.

Unit Decorations:

Distinguished Unit Citation - Egypt / Libya / Tunisia / Sicily, 25-Nov-42 thru 25-Aug-43; Sicily, 11-Jul-43: France, 6 thru 7 June, 1944.

Overseas Combat Commanders:

Col. Jerome B. McCauley, 14-Feb-42

Lt.Col. Burton R. Fleet, 12-Aug-43

Col. Harvey A. Berger, 13-May-44

[1.] **Overseas Stations:**

No.489 Cottesmore, Rutland; 15-Feb-44

Combat Operations:

November 1942 thru 8-May-45

[1.] Posted to numerous other airfields while serving in the Mediterranean Theater with both the Ninth and Twelfth AAF's.

Insignia / Markings:

Group Insignia: unknown

Squadron Insignia:

36th - TCS; unknown

37th - TCS; unofficial

44th - TCS; unknown

45th - TCS; unknown

Squadron Codes:

36th - TCS - **6 E**

37th - TCS - **W 7**

44th - TCS - **4 C**

45th - TCS - **T 3**

Squadron Colors:

36th - TCS - none

37th - TCS - none

44th - TCS - none

45th - TCS - none

Aircraft Markings:

Standard USAAF two-color camouflage with White or Sky squadron code located on forward fuselage, and the a/c call letter positioned on the tail just above the aircraft call number.

The insignia above once represented the 38thTCS which was assigned to the 316thTCG until 19-May-42. Cross referencing unit histories can often provide clues that sometimes lead to the discovery of long forgotten images. The insignia of the 37thTCS on the facing page has all the earmarks of a Disney design, however, this image is still being researched.

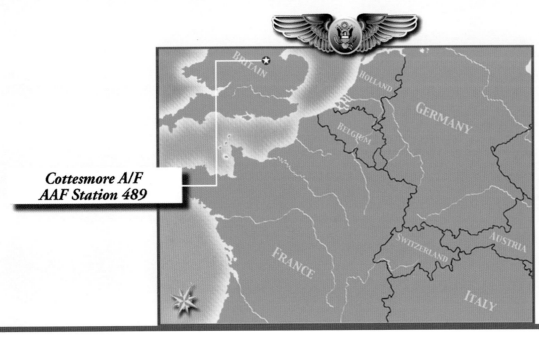

Cottesmore A/F
AAF Station 489

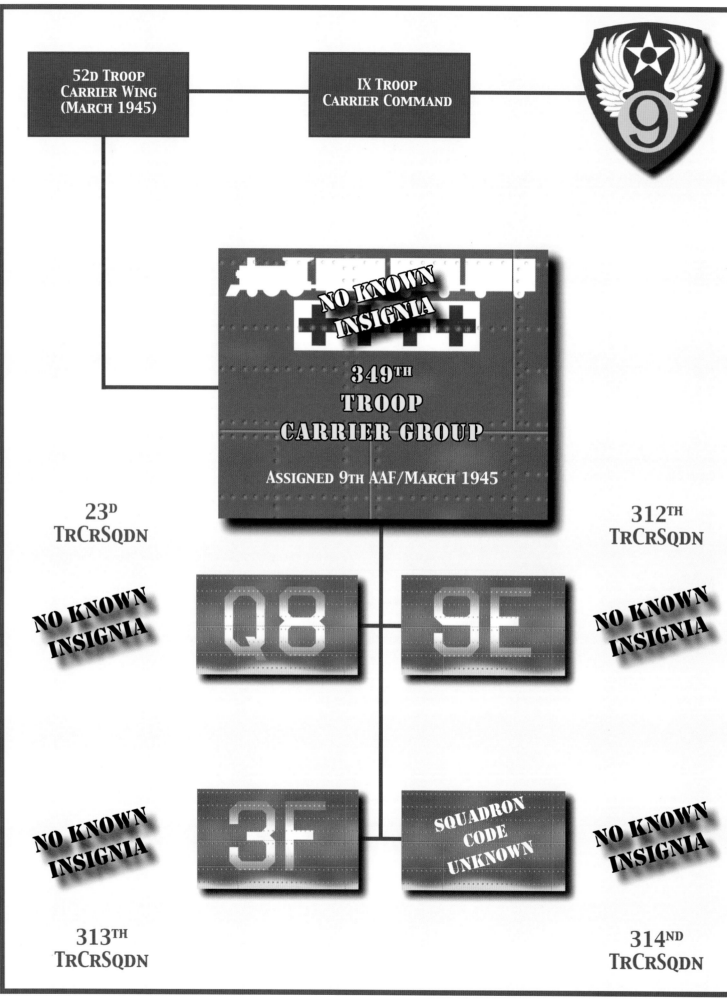

52D TROOP CARRIER WING (MARCH 1945)

IX TROOP CARRIER COMMAND

NO KNOWN INSIGNIA

349TH TROOP CARRIER GROUP

ASSIGNED 9TH AAF/MARCH 1945

23D TrCrSqdn

NO KNOWN INSIGNIA

Q8

9E

312TH TrCrSqdn

NO KNOWN INSIGNIA

NO KNOWN INSIGNIA

3F

SQUADRON CODE UNKNOWN

NO KNOWN INSIGNIA

313TH TrCrSqdn

314ND TrCrSqdn

C-46 'COMMANDO'

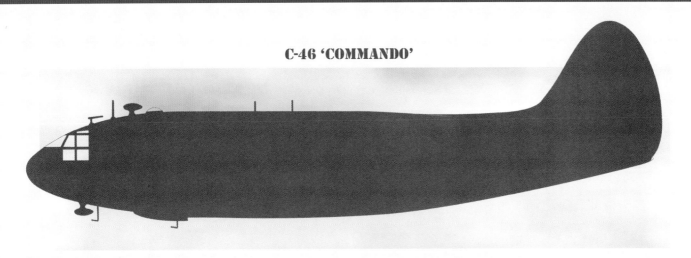

349th Troop Carrier Group:

Motto: unknown

Sobriquet: unknown

Campaign Streamers:
American Theater; EAME Theater

Unit Decorations: none

Overseas Combat Commanders:
Col. Leonard J. Barrow Jr., 26-Nov-43

Overseas Stations:
No.483 Barkstone Heath, Lincolnshire; 30-Mar-45
A-73 Roye /Amy, Alsace; 18-Apr-45

Operations:

There is very little information readily available regarding the war time deployment of this outfit, in fact tracing the history of this unit is somewhat of a challenge in itself as it has undergone no fewer than ten redesignations since its' original formation in 1943. As of this writing it is currently known as the 349th Air Mobility Wing. The 349thTCG came very late to the conflict in the ETO and although it made an important contribution with the delivery of badly needed supplies and medical evacuations throughout Western Europe, it does not appear to have engaged in any combat operations per.

Insignia / Markings:

Group Insignia: unknown

Squadron Insignia:
23d TCS; unknown
312th TCS; unknown
313th TCS; unknown
314th TCS; unknown

Squadron Codes:
23d TCS - **Q 8**
312th TCS - **9 E**
313th TCS - **3 F**
314th TCS - unknown

Squadron Colors:
23d TCS; none
312th TCS; none
313th TCS; none
314th TCS; none

Aircraft Markings:

As of press time no definitive documentation or photographic evidence has surfaced pertaining to any of the specifics relating to airframe finishes during overseas deployment. Similarly, virtually nothing is known as to the size, placement or colors used in the application of both the squadron codes and individual aircraft call letters.

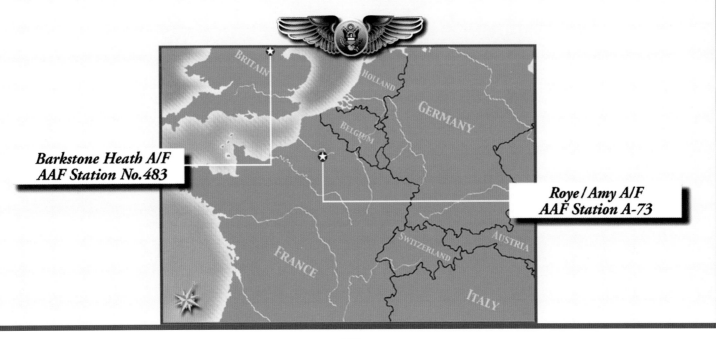

Barkstone Heath A/F
AAF Station No.483

Roye / Amy A/F
AAF Station A-73

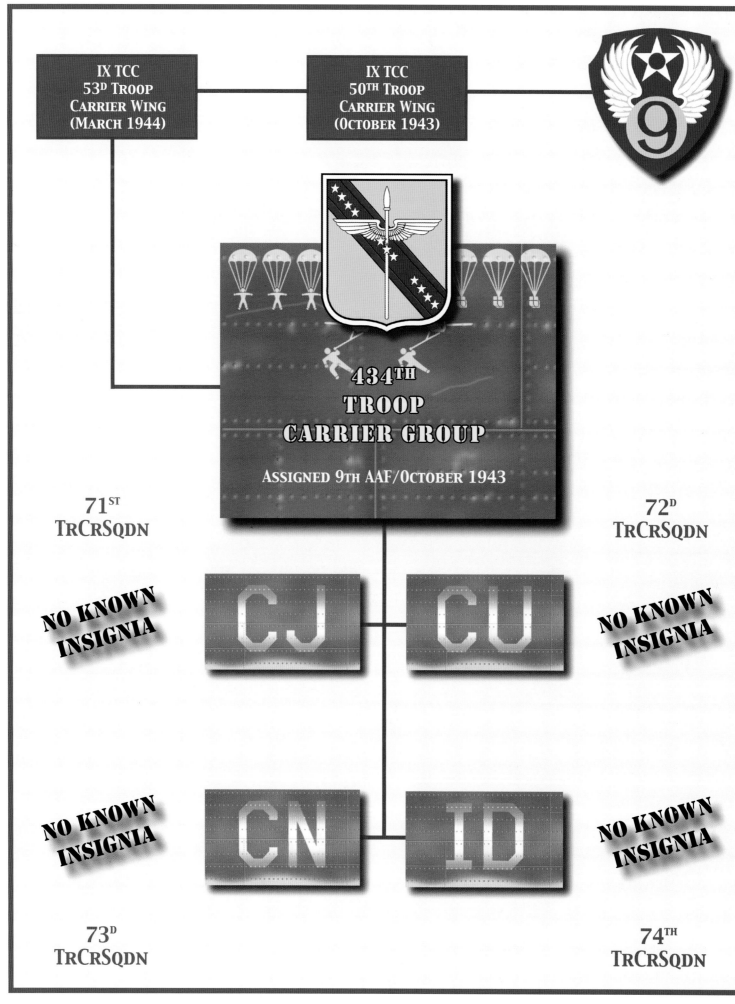

IX TCC
53D TROOP
CARRIER WING
(MARCH 1944)

IX TCC
50TH TROOP
CARRIER WING
(OCTOBER 1943)

434TH
TROOP
CARRIER GROUP

ASSIGNED 9TH AAF/OCTOBER 1943

71ST
TRCRSQDN

72D
TRCRSQDN

NO KNOWN
INSIGNIA

NO KNOWN
INSIGNIA

CJ

CU

NO KNOWN
INSIGNIA

NO KNOWN
INSIGNIA

CN

ID

73D
TRCRSQDN

74TH
TRCRSQDN

C-47 'SKYTRAIN' / C-53 'SKYTROOPER'

434th Troop Carrier Group:

Motto: unknown

Sobriquet: unknown

Campaign Streamers:
American Theater; Normandy; Northern France; Rhineland; Ardennes-Alsace; Central Europe.

Unit Decorations:
Distinguished Unit Citation: France, 6 thru 7 June, 1944; *French Croix de Guerre with Palm:* 6 thru 7 June, 1944 and 20 thru 28 August, 1944; *French Fourragere.*

Overseas Combat Commanders:
Lt.Col. Fred D. Stevens, 18-Aug-43
Col. William B. Whitacre, 29-Nov-43
Lt.Col. Ben A. Garland, 17-Dec-44

Overseas Stations:
No.488 Fulbeck, Lincolnshire; 7-Oct-43
No.474 Welford Park, Berkshire; 10-Dec-43
No.467 Aldermaston, Berkshire; 3-Mar-44
A-10 Mourmelon-le-Grand, Alsace; Feb-45

Combat Operations:
6-Jun-44 thru 8-May-45

Insignia / Markings:

Group Insignia:
The design on the facing page was officially replaced 10-Oct-52

Squadron Insignia:
71st TCS; unknown
72d TCS; unknown
73d TCS; unknown
74th TCS; unknown

Squadron Codes:
71st TCS - **C J**
72d TCS - **C U**
73d TCS - **C N**
74th TCS - **I D**

Squadron Colors:
71st TCS; none
72d TCS; none
73d TCS; none
74th TCS; none

Aircraft Markings:
  Standard USAAF two-color camouflage with White or Sky squadron code located on forward fuselage, and the a/c call letter positioned on the tail just above the aircraft call number.

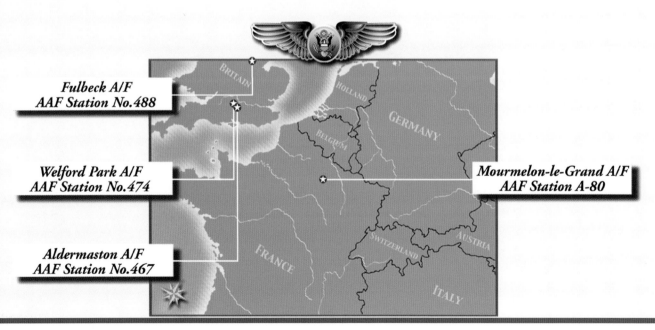

Fulbeck A/F
AAF Station No.488

Welford Park A/F
AAF Station No.474

Aldermaston A/F
AAF Station No.467

Mourmelon-le-Grand A/F
AAF Station A-80

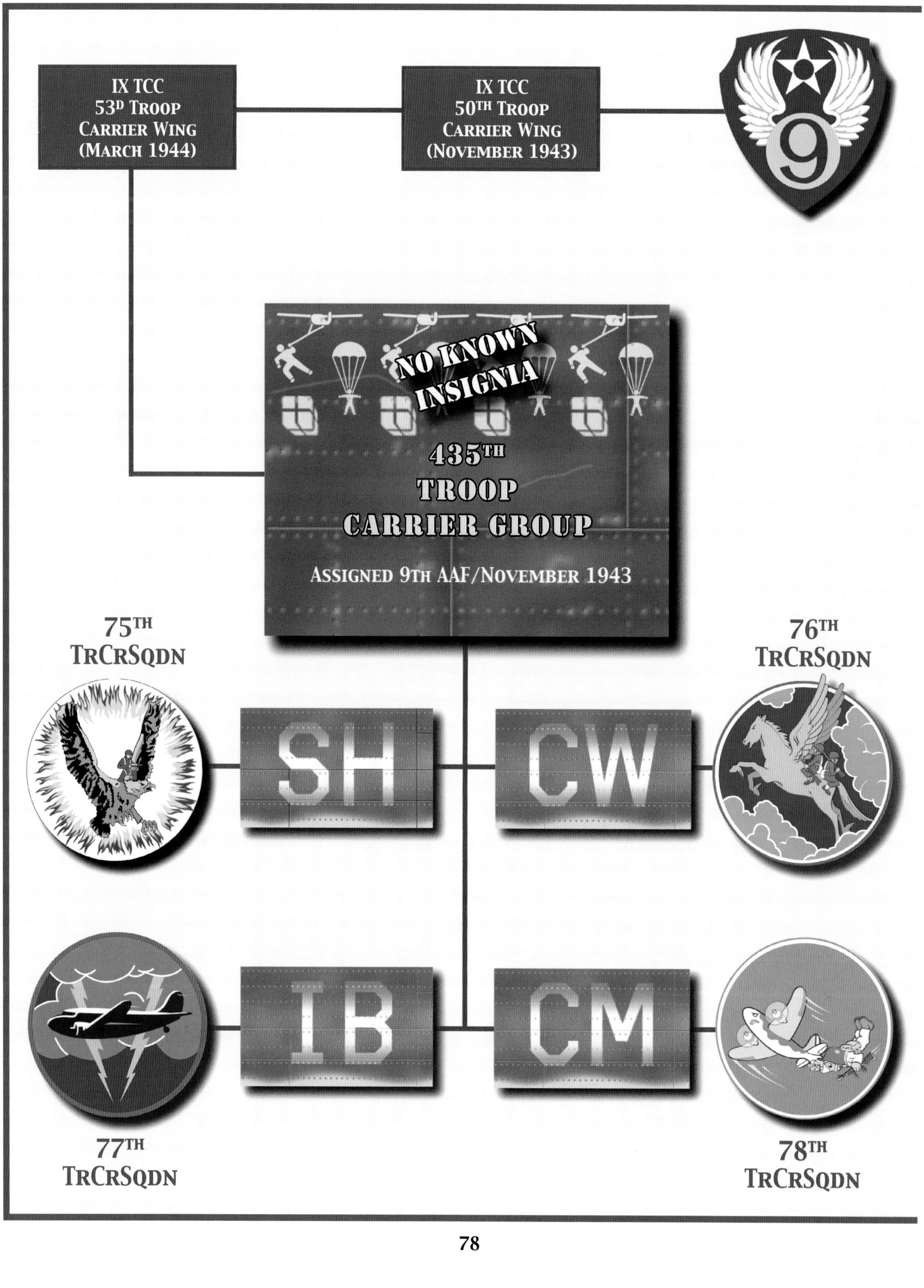

IX TCC
53D TROOP
CARRIER WING
(MARCH 1944)

IX TCC
50TH TROOP
CARRIER WING
(NOVEMBER 1943)

NO KNOWN INSIGNIA

**435TH
TROOP
CARRIER GROUP**

ASSIGNED 9TH AAF/NOVEMBER 1943

75TH
TrCrSqDN

SH

CW

76TH
TrCrSqDN

77TH
TrCrSqDN

IB

CM

78TH
TrCrSqDN

435th Troop Carrier Group:

Motto: unknown

Sobriquet: unknown

Campaign Streamers:

Rome-Arno; Normandy;

Northern France; Southern France;

Rhineland; Ardennes-Alsace; Central Europe.

Unit Decorations:

Distinguished Unit Citation: France, 6 thru 7 June, 1944

Overseas Combat Commanders:

Col. Frank J. MacNees, 25-Feb-43

[1.] **Overseas Stations:**

No.490 Langar, Nottinghamshire; 3-Nov-43

No.474 Welford Park, Berkshire; 25-Jan-44

A-48 Bretigny, Alsace; 13-Feb-45

Combat Operations:

6-Jun-44 thru 8-May-45

[1.] A contingent was detached to the Twelfth AF in Italy to assist in the invasion of Southern France in August 1944.

Insignia / Markings:

Group Insignia:

The design on the facing page was officially replaced 10-Oct-52.

Squadron Insignia:

75th TCS; officially approved 6-Sep-43

76th TCS; officially approved 30-Mar-44

77th TCS; design shown officially replaced 4-May-60

78th TCS; officially approved 26-Oct-43

Squadron Codes:

75th TCS - **S H**

76th TCS - **C W**

77th TCS - **I B**

78th TCS - **C M**

Squadron Colors:

75th TCS; none

76th TCS; none

77th TCS; none

78th TCS; none

Aircraft Markings:

Standard USAAF two-color camouflage with White or Sky squadron code located on forward fuselage, and the a/c call letter positioned on the tail just above the aircraft call number.

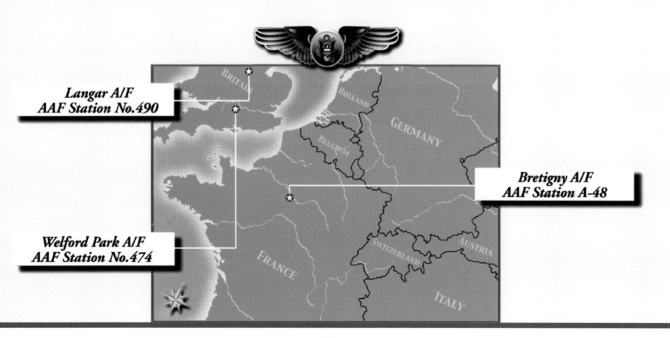

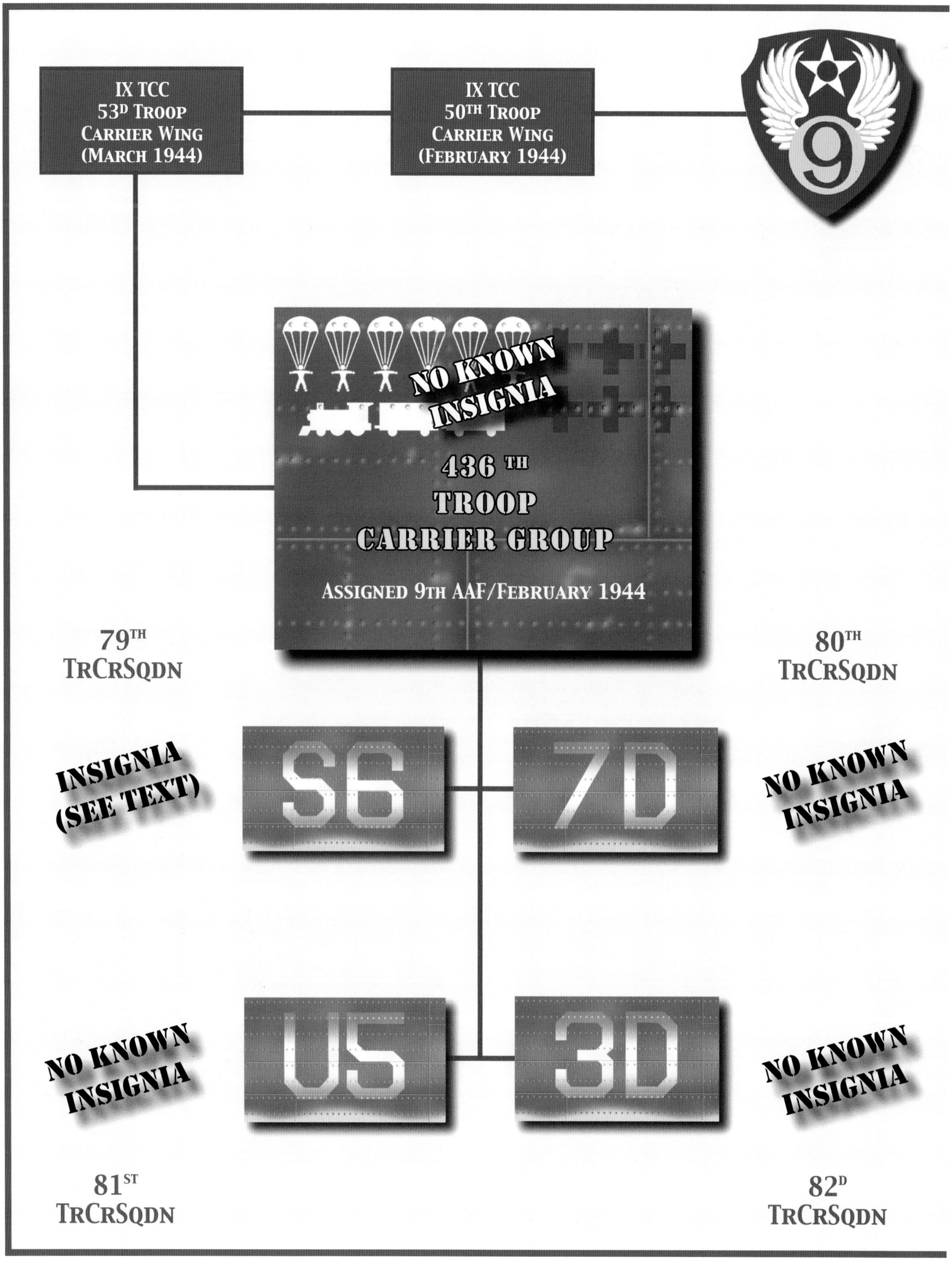

IX TCC
53D TROOP
CARRIER WING
(MARCH 1944)

IX TCC
50TH TROOP
CARRIER WING
(FEBRUARY 1944)

NO KNOWN
INSIGNIA

436TH
TROOP
CARRIER GROUP

ASSIGNED 9TH AAF/FEBRUARY 1944

79TH
TrCrSqdn

80TH
TrCrSqdn

INSIGNIA
(SEE TEXT)

S6

7D

NO KNOWN
INSIGNIA

NO KNOWN
INSIGNIA

U5

3D

NO KNOWN
INSIGNIA

81ST
TrCrSqdn

82D
TrCrSqdn

436th Troop Carrier Group:

Motto: unknown

Sobriquet: unknown

Campaign Streamers:

American Theater; Rome-Arno; Normandy;
Northern France; Southern France; Rhineland; Central Europe.

Unit Decorations:

Distinguished Unit Citation: France, 6 thru 7 June 1944.

Overseas Combat Commanders:

Col. Adriel N. Williams, 4-Feb-44

[1.] **Overseas Stations:**

No.481 Bottesford, Leicestershire; Jan-44

No.466 Membury, Berkshire; 3-Mar-44

A-55 Melun, Alsace; 26-Feb-45

Combat Operations:

6-Jun-44 thru 8-May-45

[1.] Detachment sent to Italy for temporary duty with the Twelfth AF to assist in the invasion of Southern France in August 1944.

Insignia / Markings:

Group Insignia: unknown

Squadron Insignia:

79th TCS; see text

80th TCS; unknown

81st TCS; unknown

82d TCS; unknown

Squadron Codes:

79th TCS - **S 6**

80th TCS - **7 D**

81st TCS - **U 5**

82d TCS - **3 D**

Squadron Colors:

79th TCS; none

80th TCS; none

81st TCS; none

82d TCS; none

Aircraft Markings:

The design above represents a typical problem inherent with many unit insignia from the WWII era. This image was found painted on the wall of one of the buildings at Membury AF used by the 436th TCG. Unfortunately, by the time this design came to anyone's attention, the war had been long over. Although it is believed by some to be the insignia of the 79th TCS, there are others that attribute it to the 436th TCG itself. Obviously more research is necessary in order to confirm this designs actual origin.

Standard USAAF two-color camouflage with White, Identification Yellow or Sky squadron code letters located on forward section of the fuselage, with the a/c call letter positioned on the tail just above the aircraft call number.

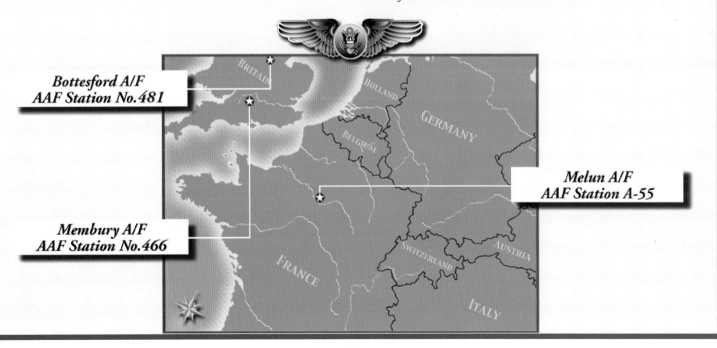

Bottesford A/F
AAF Station No.481

Membury A/F
AAF Station No.466

Melun A/F
AAF Station A-55

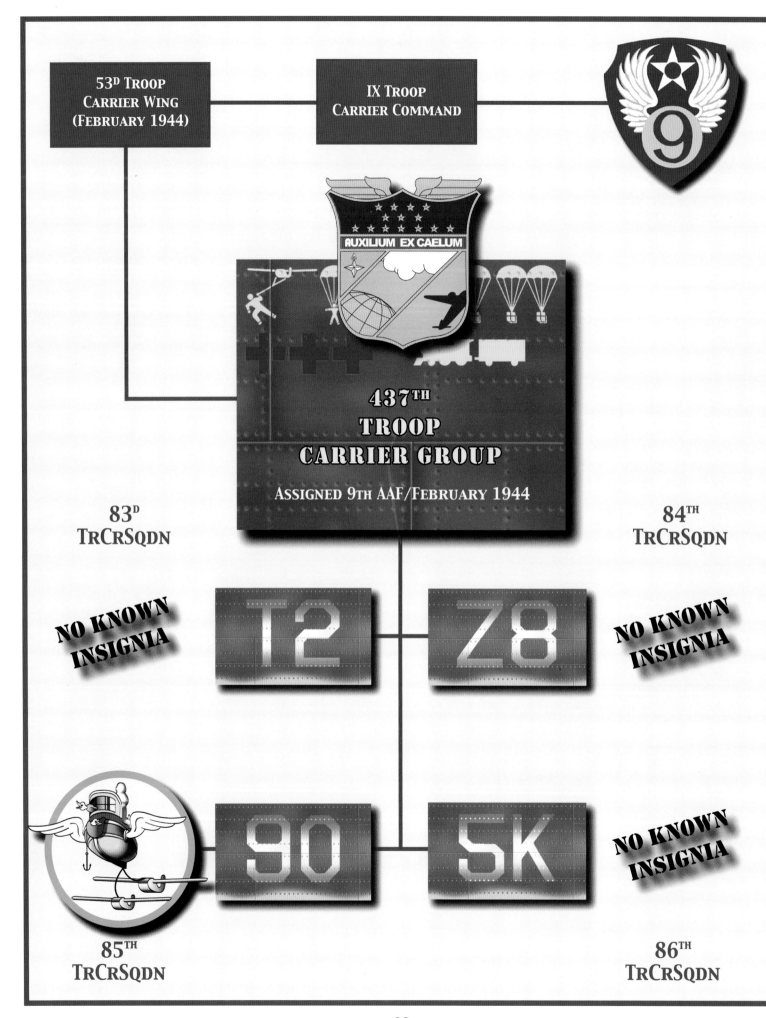

53D TROOP CARRIER WING (FEBRUARY 1944)

IX TROOP CARRIER COMMAND

437TH TROOP CARRIER GROUP

AUXILIUM EX CAELUM

ASSIGNED 9TH AAF/FEBRUARY 1944

83D TRCRSQDN

NO KNOWN INSIGNIA

T2

Z8

84TH TRCRSQDN

NO KNOWN INSIGNIA

90

5K

85TH TRCRSQDN

86TH TRCRSQDN

NO KNOWN INSIGNIA

C-47 'SKYTRAIN' / C-53 'SKYTROOPER'

437th Troop Carrier Group:

Motto: *Support from the Sky*

Sobriquet: unknown

Campaign Streamers:

American Theater; Rome-Arno; Normandy; Northern France; Southern France; Rhineland; Ardennes-Alsace; Central Europe.

Unit Decorations:

Distinguished Unit Citation: France, 6 thru 7 June, 1944

Overseas Combat Commanders:

Col. Cedric E. Hudgens, 1-May-43

Col. Donald J. French, 12-Jun-44

[1.] **Overseas Stations:**

No.482 Balderton, Lincolnshire; Jun-44

No.469 Ramsbury, Wiltshire; 5-Feb-44

A-58 Coulommiers / Voisins, Alsace; 25-Feb-45

Combat Operations:

6-Jun-44 thru 8-May-45

[1.] Deployed a detachment to Italy for temporary duty with the Twelfth AF to participate in the pending Allied invasion of Southern France in August 1944.

Insignia / Markings:

Group Insignia: officially replaced 24-Nov-53

Squadron Insignia:

83d TCS; unknown

84th TCS; unknown

85th TCS; unofficial

86th TCS; unknown

Squadron Codes:

83d TCS - **T 2**

84th TCS - **Z 8**

86th TCS - **9 0**

86th TCS - **5 K**

Squadron Colors:

83d TCS; none

84th TCS; none

85th TCS; none

86th TCS; none

Aircraft Markings:

Standard USAAF two-color camouflage with White, Identification Yellow or Sky squadron code letters located on forward section of the fuselage, with the a/c call letter positioned on the tail just above the aircraft call number.

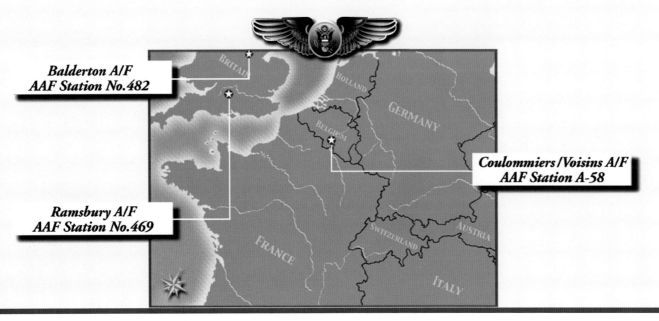

Balderton A/F
AAF Station No.482

Coulommiers / Voisins A/F
AAF Station A-58

Ramsbury A/F
AAF Station No.469

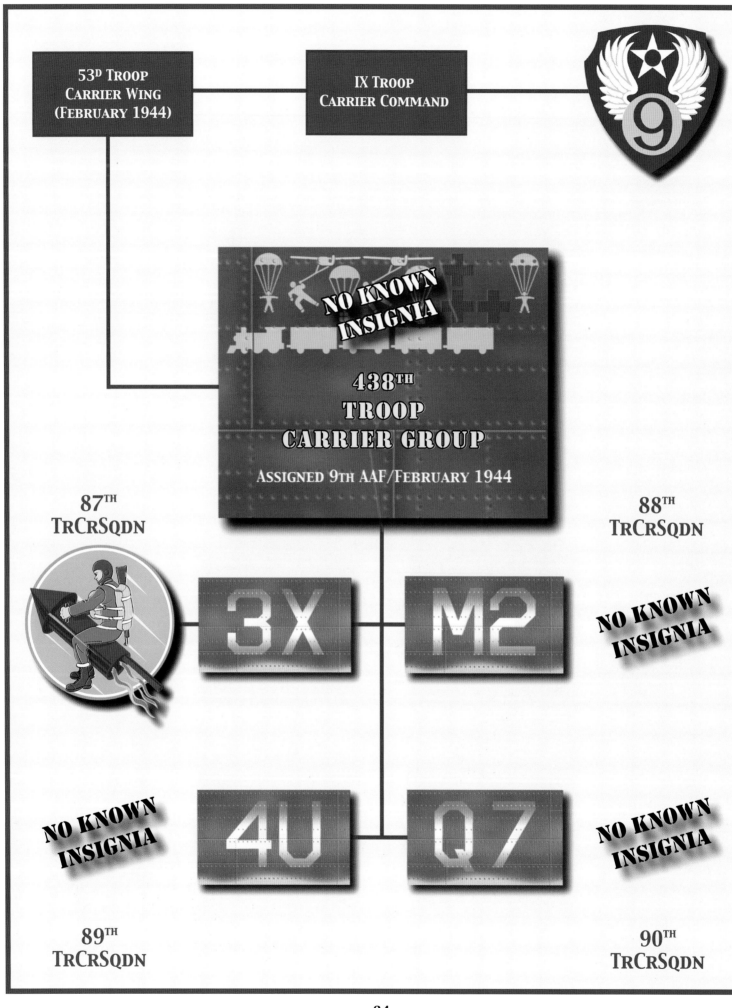

53D TROOP
CARRIER WING
(FEBRUARY 1944)

IX TROOP
CARRIER COMMAND

NO KNOWN
INSIGNIA

438TH
TROOP
CARRIER GROUP

ASSIGNED 9TH AAF/FEBRUARY 1944

87TH
TrCrSqdn

88TH
TrCrSqdn

3X

M2

NO KNOWN
INSIGNIA

NO KNOWN
INSIGNIA

4U

Q7

NO KNOWN
INSIGNIA

89TH
TrCrSqdn

90TH
TrCrSqdn

438th Troop Carrier Group:

Motto: unknown

Sobriquet: unknown

Campaign Streamers:

Rome-Arno; Normandy; Northern France;
Southern France; Rhineland; Ardennes-Alsace; Central Europe.

Unit Decorations:

Distinguished Unit Citation: France, 6 thru 7 June, 1944

Overseas Combat Commanders:

Col. John M. Donalson, 13-Jul-43

[1.] **Overseas Stations:**

No.474 Welford Park,Berkshire; Feb-44

No.486 Greenham Common,Berkshire; Feb-44

A-79 Prosnes, Alsace; Feb-45

Combat Operations:

6-Jun-44 thru 8-May-45

[1.] Deployed a detachment to Italy for temporary duty with the Twelfth AF to participate in the pending Allied invasion of Southern France in August 1944.

Insignia / Markings:

Group Insignia: unknown

Squadron Insignia:

87th TCS; officially approved 3-Apr-44

88th TCS; unknown

89th TCS; unknown

90th TCS; unknown

Squadron Codes:

87th TCS - **3 X**

88th TCS - **M 2**

89th TCS - **4 U**

90th TCS - **Q 7**

Squadron Colors:

87th TCS; none

88th TCS; none

89th TCS; none

90th TCS; none

Aircraft Markings:

Standard USAAF two-color camouflage with White or Sky squadron code letters located on forward section of the fuselage, with the a/c call letter positioned on the tail just above the aircraft call number.

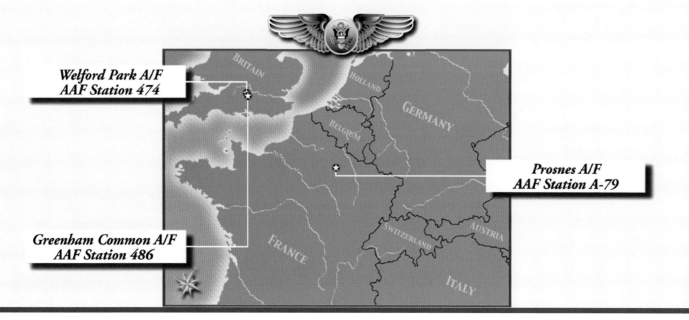

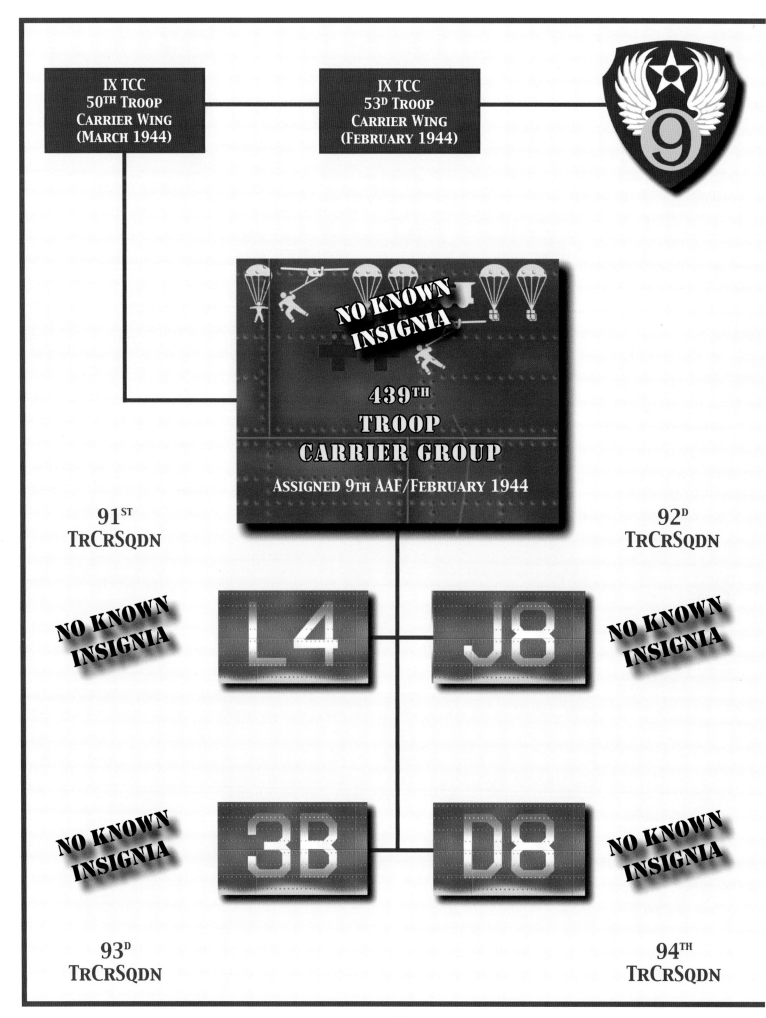

IX TCC
50TH TROOP
CARRIER WING
(MARCH 1944)

IX TCC
53D TROOP
CARRIER WING
(FEBRUARY 1944)

NO KNOWN
INSIGNIA

439TH
TROOP
CARRIER GROUP

ASSIGNED 9TH AAF/FEBRUARY 1944

91ST
TRCRSQDN

92D
TRCRSQDN

NO KNOWN
INSIGNIA

L4

J8

NO KNOWN
INSIGNIA

NO KNOWN
INSIGNIA

3B

D8

NO KNOWN
INSIGNIA

93D
TRCRSQDN

94TH
TRCRSQDN

C-47 'SKYTRAIN' / C-53 'SKYTROOPER'

439th Troop Carrier Group:

Motto: unknown

Sobriquet: unknown

Campaign Streamers:

American Theater; Rome-Arno; Normandy; Northern France; Southern France; Rhineland; Ardennes-Alsace; Central Europe.

Unit Decorations:

Distinguished Unit Citation: France, 6 thru 7 June, 1944; *French Croix de Guerre with Palm*, 6 thru 7 June, 1944 and 15-Aug-44; *French Fourragere*.

Overseas Combat Commanders:

Col. Charles H. Young, 21-Jan-44

[1.]**Overseas Stations:**

No.482 Balderton, Lincolnshire; 21-Feb-44

No.462 Upottery, Devon; 26-Apr-44

A-68 Juvincourt, Champagne-Ardenne; 8-Sep-44

A-45 Lonray, Basse Normandie; 28-Sep-44

A-39 Chateaudun, Alsace; 4-Nov-44

Combat Operations:

6-Jun-44 thru 8-May-45

[1.] Deployed a detachment to Italy for temporary duty with the Twelfth AF to participate in the pending Allied invasion of Southern France in August 1944.

Insignia / Markings:

Group Insignia: unknown

Squadron Insignia:

91st TCS; unknown

92d TCS; unknown

93d TCS; unknown

94th TCS; unknown

Squadron Codes:

91st TCS - **L 4**

92d TCS - **J 8**

93d TCS - **3 B**

94th TCS - **D 8**

Squadron Colors:

91st TCS; none

92d TCS; none

93d TCS; none

94th TCS; none

Aircraft Markings:

Standard USAAF two-color camouflage with White or Sky squadron code letters located on forward section of the fuselage, with the a/c call letter positioned on the tail just above the aircraft call number.

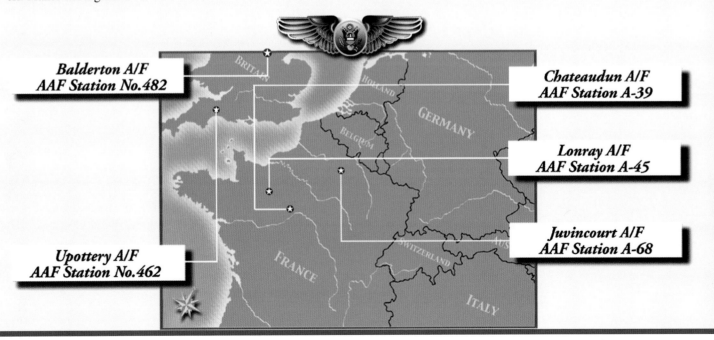

Balderton A/F
AAF Station No.482

Chateaudun A/F
AAF Station A-39

Lonray A/F
AAF Station A-45

Juvincourt A/F
AAF Station A-68

Upottery A/F
AAF Station No.462

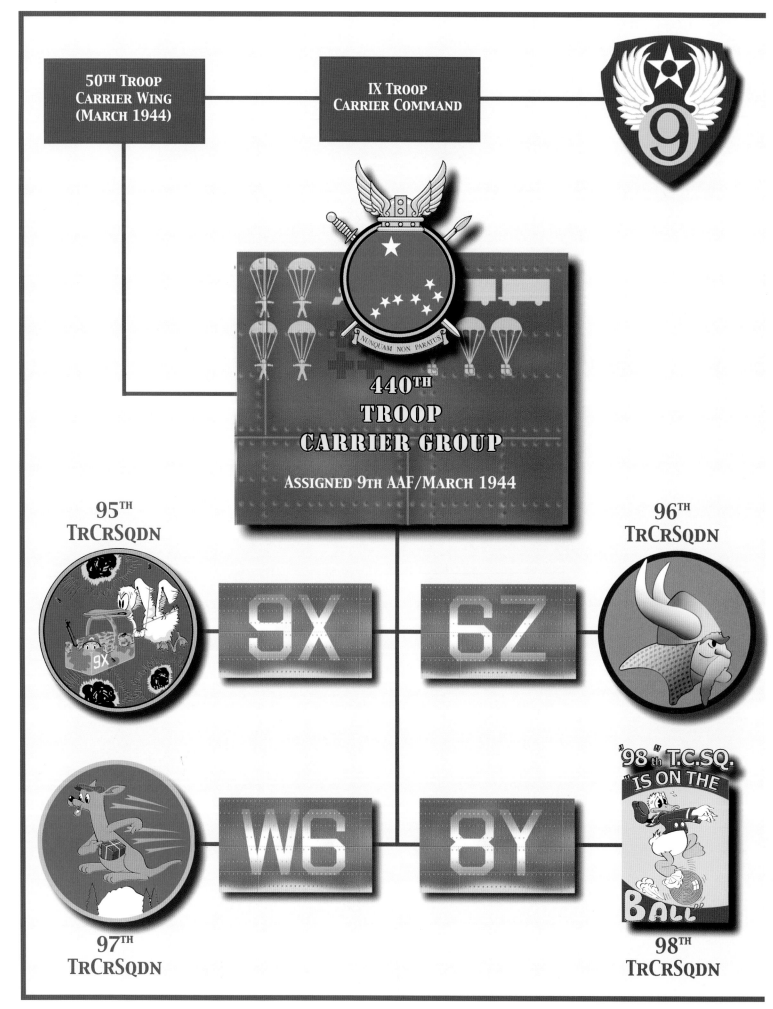

50TH TROOP
CARRIER WING
(MARCH 1944)

IX TROOP
CARRIER COMMAND

440TH
TROOP
CARRIER GROUP

ASSIGNED 9TH AAF/MARCH 1944

NUNQUAM NON PARATUS

95TH
TrCrSqdn

96TH
TrCrSqdn

9X

6Z

97TH
TrCrSqdn

98TH
TrCrSqdn

W6

8Y

"98"TH T.C.SQ.
"IS ON THE
BALL"

C-47 'SKYTRAIN' / C-53 'SKYTROOPER'

440th Troop Carrier Group:

Motto: *Nunquam Non Paratus (Never Unprepared)*

Sobriquet: unknown

Campaign Streamers:

Rome-Arno; Normandy; Northern France;
Southern France; Rhineland; Ardennes-Alsace; Central Europe.

Unit Decorations:

Distinguished Unit Citation: France, 6 thru 7 June, 1944;

Overseas Combat Commanders:

Col. Frank X. Kerbs, 7-Jul-43 / 29-Oct-44

Lt.Col. Loyd C. Waldorf, 18-Sep-44

[1.] **Overseas Stations:**

No.481 Bottesford, Leicestershire; 11-Mar-44

No.463 Exeter, Devon; 26-Apr-44

A-62D Reims/Champagne, Alsace; 11-Sep-44

A-35 Le Mans, Pays-de-la-Loire; 30-Sep-44

A-50 Orleans/Bricy, Centre-Val-de-Loire; 2-Nov-44

Combat Operations:

6-Jun-44 thru 8-May-45

[1.] Deployed a detachment to Italy for temporary duty with the Twelfth AF to participate in the pending Allied invasion of Southern France in August 1944.

Insignia / Markings:

Group Insignia: modified and readopted 14-Nov-58

Squadron Insignia:

95th TCS; unofficial

96th TCS; unofficial

97th TCS; unofficial

98th TCS; unofficial

Squadron Codes:

95th TCS - **9 X**

96th TCS - **6 Z**

97th TCS - **W 6**

98th TCS - **8 Y**

Squadron Colors:

95th TCS; none

96th TCS; none

97th TCS; none

98th TCS; none

Special Note:
The 97thTCS insignia depicted is reported to have been the unofficial WWII squadron design which was subsequently officially adopted by that unit in 1960. The 96thTCS insignia was obtained from a poor quality b&w photo submitted by a squadron veteran and developed relying on verbal description for details and color break. 98thTCS design was also an unofficial squadron insignia for which the squadron reportedly obtained written permission from Walt Disney for the use of the Donald Duck image.

Aircraft Markings:

Standard USAAF two-color camouflage with White or Sky squadron code letters located on forward section of the fuselage, with the a/c call letter positioned on the tail just above the aircraft call number.

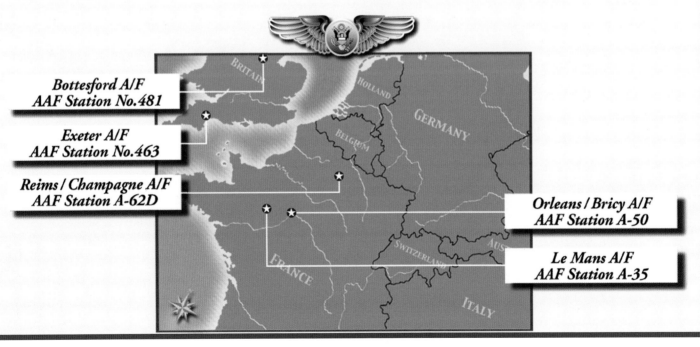

Bottesford A/F
AAF Station No.481

Exeter A/F
AAF Station No.463

Reims / Champagne A/F
AAF Station A-62D

Orleans / Bricy A/F
AAF Station A-50

Le Mans A/F
AAF Station A-35

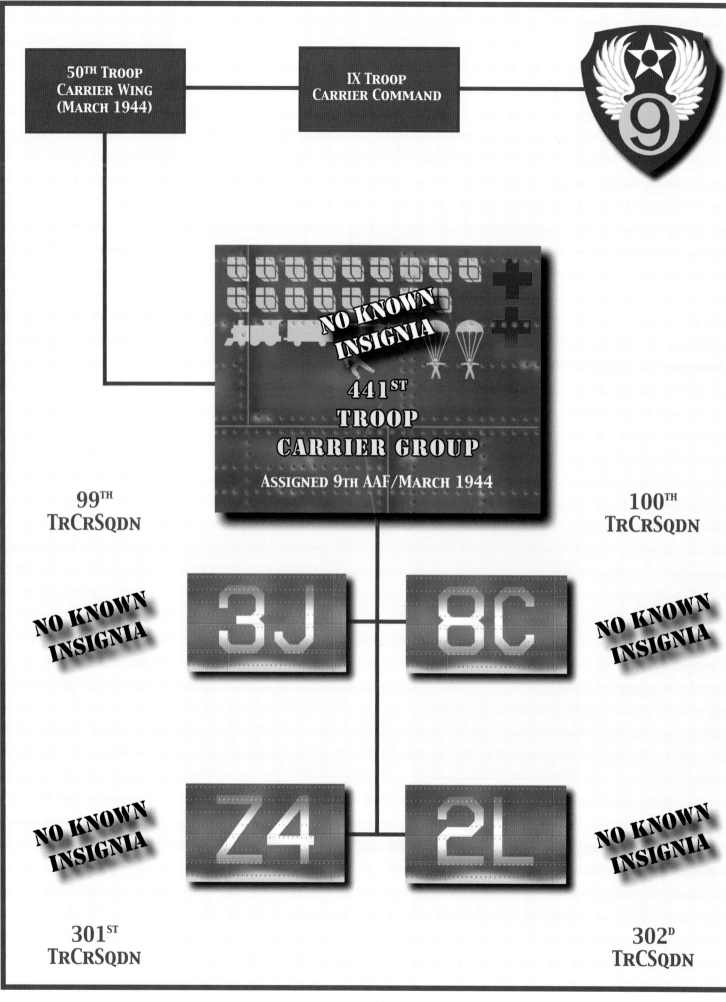

50TH TROOP CARRIER WING (MARCH 1944)

IX TROOP CARRIER COMMAND

NO KNOWN INSIGNIA

441ST TROOP CARRIER GROUP

ASSIGNED 9TH AAF/MARCH 1944

99TH TrCrSqdn

NO KNOWN INSIGNIA

3J

8C

NO KNOWN INSIGNIA

100TH TrCrSqdn

NO KNOWN INSIGNIA

Z4

2L

NO KNOWN INSIGNIA

301ST TrCrSqdn

302D TrCSqdn

C-47 'SKYTRAIN' / C-53 'SKYTROOPER'

441st Troop Carrier Group:

Motto: unknown

Sobriquet: unknown

Campaign Streamers:

Rome-Arno; Normandy; Northern France;

Southern France; Rhineland; Ardennes-Alsace; Central Europe.

Unit Decorations:

Distinguished Unit Citation: France, 6 thru 7 June, 1944

Overseas Combat Commanders:

Col. Theodore G. Kershaw, 8-Aug-43

Col. William H. Parkhill, 24-Nov-44

[1.] **Overseas Stations:**

No.490 Langer, Nottinghamshire; 17-Mar-44

No.464 Merryfield, Somerset; 27-Apr-44

A-63 Villeneuve / Vetrus, Champagne-Ardenne; 8-Sep-44

A-43 St. Marceau, Pay-de-la-Loire; 2-Oct-44

A-41 Dreux, Centre-Val-de-Loire; 3-Nov-44

Combat Operations:

6Jun-44 thru 8-May-45

[1.] Deployed a detachment to Italy for temporary duty with the Twelfth AF to participate in the pending Allied invasion of Southern France in August 1944.

Insignia / Markings:

Group Insignia: unknown

Squadron Insignia:

99th TCS; unknown

100th TCS; unknown

301st TCS; unknown

302d TCS; unknown

Squadron Codes:

99th TCS - **3 J**

100th TCS - **B C**

301st TCS - **Z 4**

302d TCS - **2 L**

Squadron Colors:

99th TCS; none

100th TCS; none

301st TCS; none

302d TCS; none

Aircraft Markings:

Standard USAAF two-color camouflage with White or Sky squadron code letters located on forward section of the fuselage, with the a/c call letter positioned on the tail just above the aircraft call number.

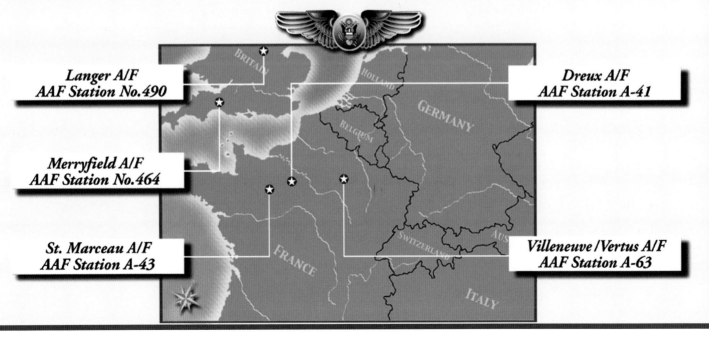

Langer A/F
AAF Station No.490

Merryfield A/F
AAF Station No.464

St. Marceau A/F
AAF Station A-43

Dreux A/F
AAF Station A-41

Villeneuve /Vertus A/F
AAF Station A-63

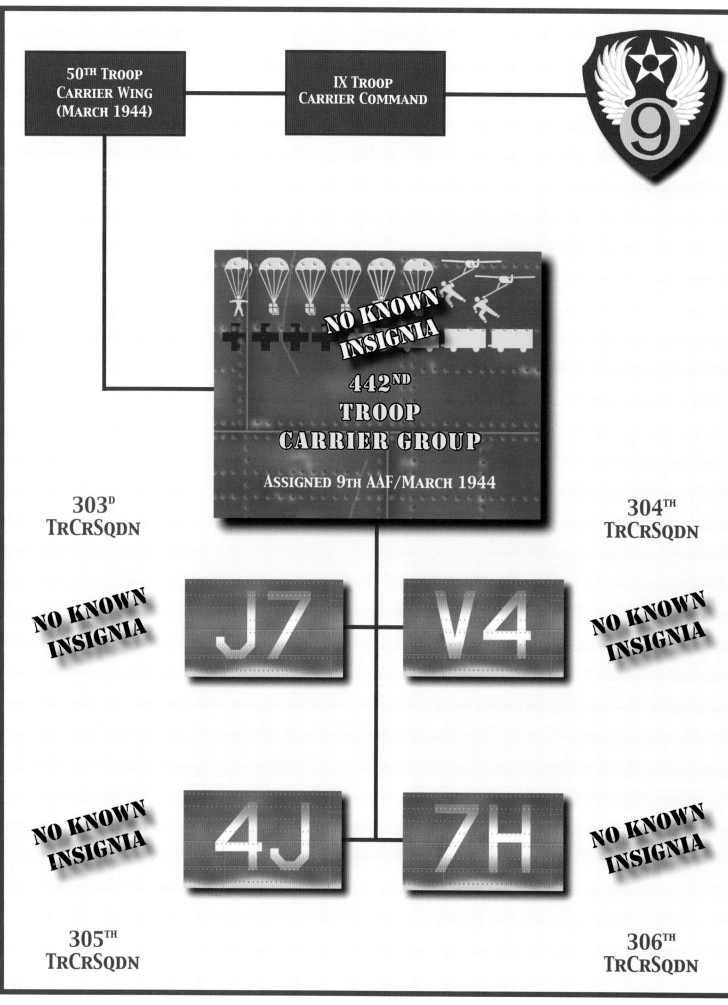

50TH TROOP CARRIER WING (MARCH 1944)

IX TROOP CARRIER COMMAND

NO KNOWN INSIGNIA

442ND TROOP CARRIER GROUP

ASSIGNED 9TH AAF/MARCH 1944

303D TrCrSqdn

NO KNOWN INSIGNIA

304TH TrCrSqdn

NO KNOWN INSIGNIA

J7

V4

305TH TrCrSqdn

NO KNOWN INSIGNIA

306TH TrCrSqdn

NO KNOWN INSIGNIA

4J

7H

C-47 'SKYTRAIN' / C-53 'SKYTROOPER'

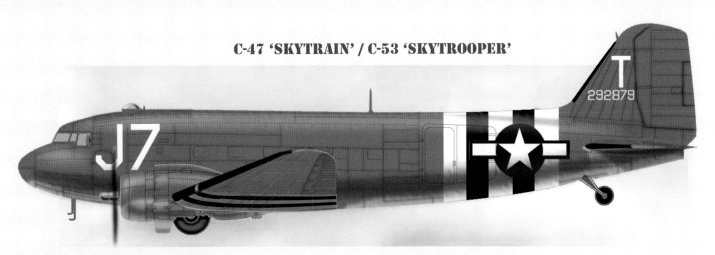

442d Troop Carrier Group:

Motto: unknown

Sobriquet: unknown

Campaign Streamers:

Rome-Arno; Normandy; Northern France; Southern France; Rhineland; Ardennes-Alsace; Central Europe.

Unit Decorations:

Distinguished Unit Citation: France, 6 thru 7 June, 1944

Overseas Combat Commanders

Col. Charles M. Smith, Sep-43

[1.] **Overseas Stations:**

No.488 Fulbeck, Lincolnshire; 29-Mar-44

No.447 Weston Zoyland, Somerset; 27-Apr-44

A-44 Peray / Bonnetable, Basse Normandie; Oct-44

[2.] *B-24* St. Andre-de-l'Eure, Ile-de-France; Nov-44

Combat Operations:

6-Jun-44 thru 8-May-45

[1.] Deployed a detachment to Italy for temporary duty with the Twelfth AF to participate in the pending Allied invasion of Southern France in August 1944.

[2.] RAF airfield utilized by USAAF as temporary staging area.

Insignia / Markings:

Group Insignia: unknown

Squadron Insignia:

303d TCS; unknown

304th TCS; unknown

305th TCS; unknown

306th TCS; unknown

Squadron Codes:

303d TCS - **J 7**

304th TCS - **V 4**

305th TCS - **4 J**

306th TCS - **7 H**

Squadron Colors:

303d TCS; none

304th TCS; none

305th TCS ; none

306th TCS; none

Aircraft Markings:

Standard USAAF two-color camouflage with White or Sky squadron code letters located on forward section of the fuselage, with the a/c call letter positioned on the tail just above the aircraft call number.

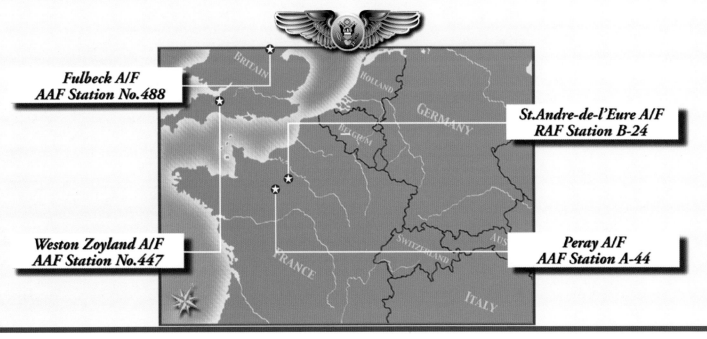

BOMBARDMENT UNITS
OF THE
NINTH U.S.A.A.F.

To anyone new to the study of the air war in World War II, and especially that of the European Theater, the significance and importance of the tactical aircraft markings is often totally overlooked. Unfortunately this is due in no small part to the fact that so much of our contemporary view of this conflict comes to us in the form of black and white photographs. While those of us interested in this page of history are grateful that there exists so much valuable pictorial documentation, it is all to easy to overlook the impact that AAF tactical markings had in the real world of full spectrum color, and just why they were such an important element in the Army Air Forces effort to effectively conduct their part of the war effort.

The two adjacent diagrams have been included herein to illustrate the importance of tactical aircraft markings, especially when it came to the bombing campaign against Hitler's *Festung Europa*. When studying these diagrams it is important to point out that this represents a mission sortie of only one bombardment group.

A single flight was the basic combat element that might be sortied, while a large raid would entail a full combat box formation as depicted herein, only multiplied by the total number of groups participating in that raid.

The rare color photograph at the bottom of this page can be compared to the black and white image on the preceding title page in order to better gain an understanding of the importance color played in aircraft recognition. This same comparison also illustrates how easy it can be to overlook the tactical markings when viewing a black and white period photo. The diagnol yellow (ANA Orange Yellow) stripe of the 97thBG tends to automatically attract the focus of ones eye whereas this very same element blends together with the overall

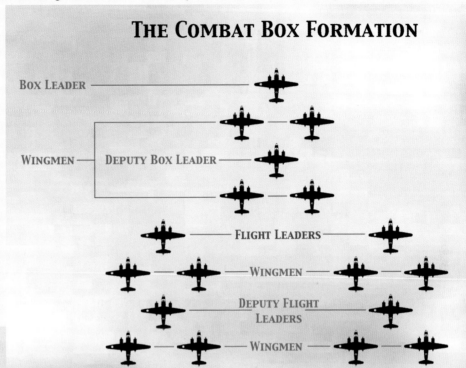

THE COMBAT BOX FORMATION

BOX LEADER

WINGMEN — DEPUTY BOX LEADER

FLIGHT LEADERS

WINGMEN

DEPUTY FLIGHT LEADERS

WINGMEN

gray format of the black and white image. A quick glance over the right shoulder would confirm to a ships co-pilot that their starboard wingman was in his proper position. A good bomber pilot would in fact rely upon every member of his crew to inform him in the event any ship within his respective flight was failing to maintain proper interval.

Maintaining proper formation integrity within ones assigned flight was crucial not only for defensive purposes against enemy aerial attacks, but in order to maximize the effectiveness of the bombing effort. It might be prudent to mention here that maintaining ones proper position within the flight also helped prevent the bombers from knocking each other out of the air via mid-air collision or an accidental hit from a falling bomb.

The means of accomplishing this daunting organizational task began at take-off and did not end until the last ship was safely back down on the ground again at missions end. The pilot of each ship bore the primary responsibility for maintaining his aircrafts proper placement within his respective flight and this task was accomplished only through a means of individual as well as collective aircraft recognition.

NINTH U.S.A.A.F. BOMBARDMENT SQUADRON CODE INDEX

I H } 1stPthfndrSq(P): Pg.98

PN -449ᵀᴴBS • ER -450ᵀᴴBS • SS -451ˢᵀBS • DR -452ᴰBS } 322ᴰBG: Pg.   98

VT -453ᴰBS • RJ -454ᵀᴴBS • YU -455ᵀᴴBS • WT -456ᵀᴴBS } 232ᴰBG: Pg.100

K9 -494ᵀᴴBS • Y5 -495ᵀᴴBS • N3 -496ᵀᴴBS • 7I -497ᵀᴴBS } 344ᵀᴴBG: Pg.102

RG -552ᴰBS • AN -553ᴰBS • RU -554ᵀᴴBS • YA -555ᵀᴴBS } 386ᵀᴴBG: Pg.104

FW -556ᵀᴴBS • KS -557ᵀᴴBS • KX -558ᵀᴴBS • TQ -559ᵀᴴBS } 387ᵀᴴBG: Pg.106

P2 -572ᴰBS • T6 -573ᴰBS • 4L -574ᵀᴴBS • O8 -575ᵀᴴBS } 391ˢᵀBG: Pg.108

K5 -584ᵀᴴBS • 4T -585ᵀᴴBS • H9 -586ᵀᴴBS • 5W -587ᵀᴴBS } 394ᵀᴴBG: Pg.110

X2 -596ᵀᴴBS • 9F -597ᵀᴴBS • U2 -598ᵀᴴBS • 6B -599ᵀᴴBS } 397ᵀᴴBG: Pg.112

W5 -640ᵀᴴBS • 7G -641ˢᵀBS • D6 -642ᴰBS • 5I -643ᴰBS } 409ᵀᴴBG: Pg.114

5D -644ᵀᴴBS • 7X -645ᵀᴴBS • 8U -646ᵀᴴBS • 6Q -647ᵀᴴBS } 410ᵀᴴBG: Pg.116

5H -668ᵀᴴBS • 2A -669ᵀᴴBS • F6 -670ᵀᴴBS • 5C -671ˢᵀBS } 411ᵀᴴBG: Pg.118

IX BOMBER COMMAND
LATER
9TH BOMB DIVISION (M)

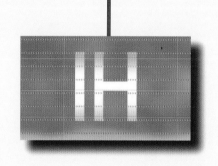

NO KNOWN INSIGNIA

1ST
PATHFINDER SQUADRON
(PROVISIONAL)

ASSIGNED 9TH AAF/JANUARY 1944

IH

1st Pathfinder Squadron (P):

Squadron Insignia: unknown
Motto: unknown
Sobriquet: unknown
Squadron Code: I H
Aircraft Markings:

This unit had its own individual code designation which was generally applied in the prescribed location, along with the respective aircraft call letter, in No. 610 Sky. There were no other known distinguishing marks or colors attributed to this unit.

Overseas Stations:
No.485 / Great Sailing, Essex; 13-Feb-44
Combat Operations:
21-Feb-44 thru 3-May-45

All personnel operating with this special unit were volunteers and serving on a detached duty status from other bomb groups within the IX Bomber Command structure. The speciality of this unit was guiding regular bombers to the target under 10/10 (zero visibility) conditions. The familiarity of the crews of the 1st Pathfinder with state-of-the-art radar and instrumentation flying allowed the Ninth to conduct bombing raids that would have been cancelled prior to this units formation.

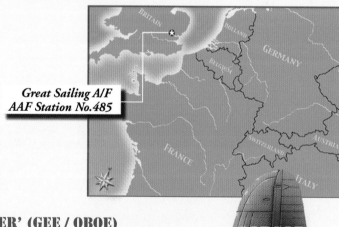

Great Sailing A/F
AAF Station No.485

B-26 'MARAUDER' (GEE / OBOE)

99TH COMBAT
BOMBARDMENT
WING (MEDIUM)
(NOVEMBER 1943)

IX BOMBER COMMAND
LATER
9TH BOMB DIVISION (M)

322D
BOMBARDMENT
GROUP (MEDIUM)
'RECTO FACIENDO NEMINEM TIMEO'
ASSIGNED 9TH AAF/NOVEMBER 1943

RECTO FACIENDO NEMINEM TIMEO

449TH
BOMBSQDN

450TH
BOMBSQDN

PN   ER

SS   DR

451ST
BOMBSQDN

452D
BOMBSQDN

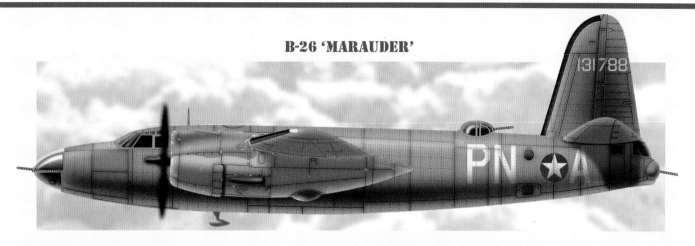

B-26 'MARAUDER'

131788

322d Bomb Group (M):

Motto: '*Recto Faciendo Neminem Timeo*'
('*I Fear None In Doing Right*')

Sobriquet: '*Nye's Annihilators*'

Campaign Streamers:

Air Offensive, Europe; Normandy;
Northern France; Southern France;
Rhineland; Ardennes-Alsace; Central Europe.

Unit Decorations:

Distinguished Unit Citation: ETO, 14-May-43 thru 24-Jul-44

Overseas Combat Commanders:

Lt.Col. Robert M. Stillman, 17-Mar-43
Col. Glenn C. Nye, 19-May-43
Col.-John S. Samuel, Jul-44

Overseas Stations:

No.468 Rougham (Bury St. Edmunds), Suffolk; 1-Dec-42
No.485 Great Sailing / Andrews Field, Essex; Jan-43
A-61 Beauvais-Tille, Picardie; Sep-44
A-89 LeCulot, Province de Namur; Mar-44

Combat Operations:

14-May-43 thru 24-Apr-45
(originally assigned to Eighth AAF).

Insignia / Markings:

Group Insignia: officially approved 9-Jan-43

Squadron Insignia:

449th BS; officially approved 12-Jul-43
450th BS; officially replaced 13-Jun55
451st BS; officially replaced 2-May-55
452d BS; officially replaced 22-Jul-55

Squadron Codes:

449th BS - **P N**
450th BS - **E R**
451st BS - **S S**
452d BS - **D R**

Squadron Colors: none

Aircraft Markings:

Squadron code and call letters were positioned on both sides of fuselage directly fore and aft of the national insignia. Colors used were RAF or ANA 610 Sky on camouflaged surfaces and later black on natural metal finishes. The 322d never developed a distinctive group marking for use on the tail section of their aircraft but carried only the call number in Identification Yellow.

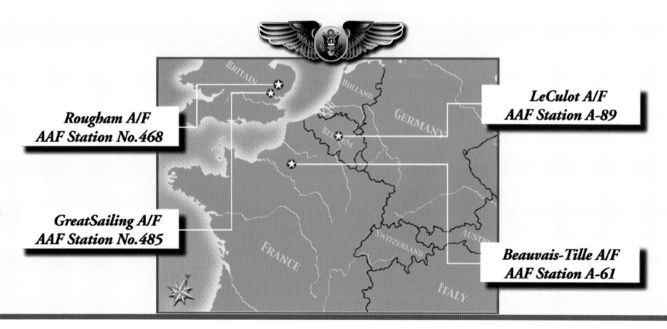

Rougham A/F
AAF Station No.468

GreatSailing A/F
AAF Station No.485

LeCulot A/F
AAF Station A-89

Beauvais-Tille A/F
AAF Station A-61

IX BOMBER COMMAND
LATER
9TH BOMB DIVISION (M)

VINCAMUS SINE TIMORIS

323D
BOMBARDMENT
GROUP (MEDIUM)

'VINCAMUS SINE TIMORIS'

ASSIGNED 9TH AAF/NOVEMBER 1943

453D
BOMB SQDN

VT

RJ

454TH
BOMB SQDN

YU

WT

455TH
BOMB SQDN

456TH
BOMB SQDN

B-26 'MARAUDER'

323d Bomb Group (M):

Motto: *'Vincamus Sine Timoris'*
        ('Without Fear We Conquer')
Sobriquet: *'The White Tails'*
Campaign Streamers:
Air Offensive, Europe; Normandy; Northern France;
Rhineland; Ardennes-Alsace; Central Europe.
Unit Decorations:
Distinguished Unit Citation: Belgium/Germany,
24 thru 27 December, 1944
Overseas Combat Commanders:
Col. Wilson R. Wood, 13-Mar-43
Col. Rollin M. Winingham, 14-Feb-45
Overseas Stations:
No.119 Horham, Suffolk; 12-May-43
No.358 Earls Colne, Essex; 14-Jun-43
No.408 Beaulieu, Hampshire; 21-Jul-44
A-20 Lessay, Basse-Normandie; 26-Aug-44
A-40 Chartres, Centre-Val-de-Loire; 21-Sep-44
A-69 Laon-Athies, Picardie; 13-Oct-44
A-83 Denain-Prouvy, Nord-Pas-De-Calais; 9-Feb-45
Combat Operations:
15-Jul-43 thru April 1945
(originally served in combat with Eighth AAF)

Insignia / Markings:

Group Insignia: officially approved 16-Feb-43
Squadron Insignia:
453d BS; unofficial, replaced 1-Feb-57
454th BS; unofficial, replaced 6-Dec-56
455th BS; unofficial, replaced 7-Jan-57
456th BS; unofficial
Squadron Codes:
453d BS - **V T**
454th BS - **R J**
455th BS - **Y U**
456th BS - **W T**
Squadron Colors: none
Aircraft Markings:

Squadron code and call letters were positioned on both sides
of fuselage directly fore and aft of the national insignia. Colors
used were RAF or ANA 610 Sky on camouflaged surfaces and
later black on natural metal finishes. The 323d adopted the use
of a white horizontal stripe measuring approximately 30 inches
in height, whence was derived the *White Tails* sobriquet.

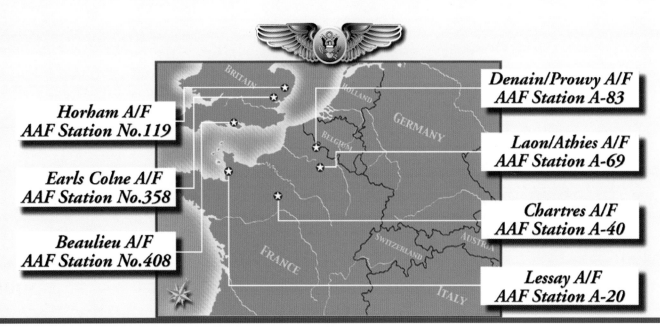

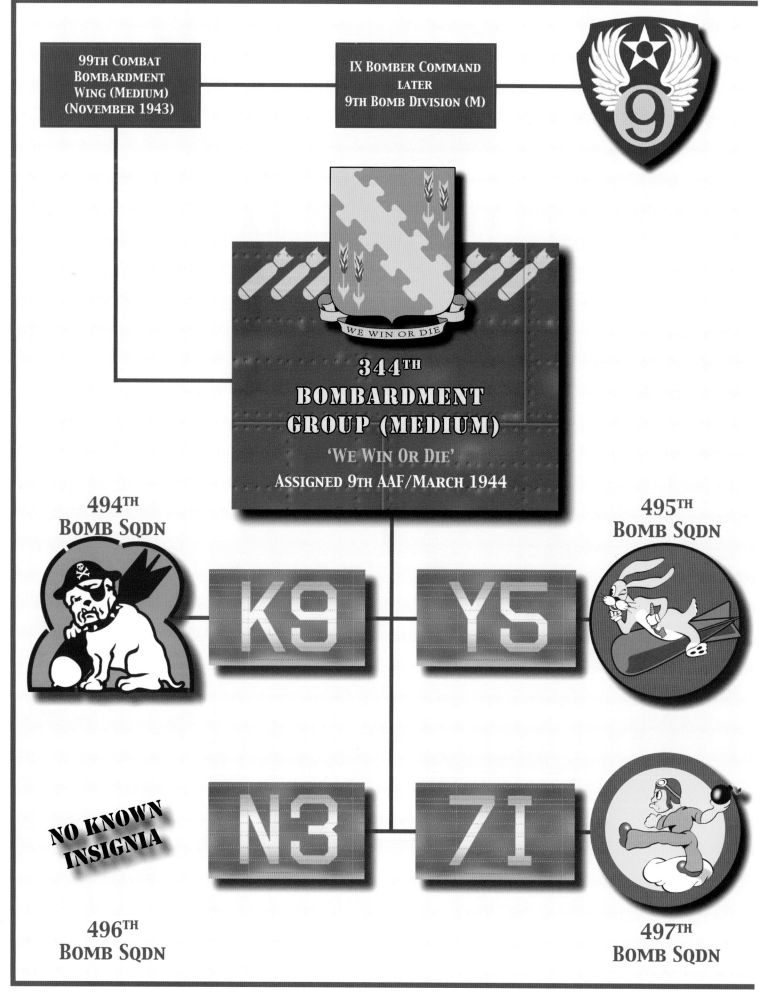

99TH COMBAT BOMBARDMENT WING (MEDIUM) (NOVEMBER 1943)

IX BOMBER COMMAND LATER 9TH BOMB DIVISION (M)

WE WIN OR DIE

344TH BOMBARDMENT GROUP (MEDIUM)
'WE WIN OR DIE'
ASSIGNED 9TH AAF/MARCH 1944

494TH BOMB SQDN

K9

Y5

495TH BOMB SQDN

NO KNOWN INSIGNIA

N3

7I

496TH BOMB SQDN

497TH BOMB SQDN

344th Bomb Group (M):

Motto: '*We Win Or Die*'

Sobriquet: '*The Silver Streaks*'

Campaign Streamers:

American Theatre, Air offensive Europe; Normandy;
Northern France; Rhineland; Ardennes-Alsace; Central Europe.

Unit Decorations:

Distinguished Unit Citation: France, 24 thru 26 July, 1944

Overseas Combat Commanders

Col. Reginald F.C. Vance, 19-Sep-43

Col. Robert W. Witty, 7-Nov-44

Overseas Stations:

No.169 Stansted, Essex; 9-Feb-44

A-59 Cormeilles-en-Vexin, Ile-de-France; 30-Sep-44

A-78 Florennes-Juzaine, Province de Namur; 5-Apr-45

Combat Operations:

6-Mar-44 thru April, 1945

Insignia / Markings:

Group Insignia: officially approved 9-Jan-43

Squadron Insignia:

494th BS; officially approved 7-Jul-44

495th BS; unofficial

496th BS; unknown

497th BS; officially approved 15-May-43

Squadron Codes:

494th BS - **K 9**

495th BS - **Y 5**

496th BS - **N 3**

497th BS - **7 I**

Squadron Colors: none

Aircraft Markings:

The group marking for the 344th was the application of an equilateral triangle to the aircraft's upper tail section immediately above the call number. These triangles were white on both camouflaged and natural metal surfaces, the difference being that in the latter case there was an inner 3-4 inch black border. Squadron codes and aircraft call letters were located fore and aft the fuselage national insignia and were painted No.610 Sky on camouflaged airframes, black on natural metal surfaces.

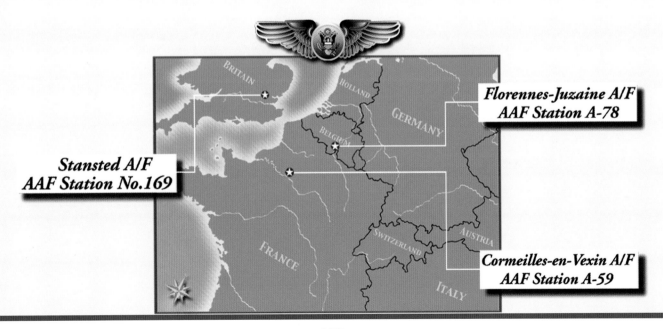

Stansted A/F
AAF Station No.169

Florennes-Juzaine A/F
AAF Station A-78

Cormeilles-en-Vexin A/F
AAF Station A-59

99TH COMBAT
BOMBARDMENT
WING (MEDIUM)
(OCTOBER 1944)

IX BOMBER COMMAND
LATER
9TH BOMB DIVISION (M)

9

386TH BOMBARDMENT GROUP (MEDIUM)

ASSIGNED 9TH AAF/OCTOBER 1944

552D
BOMBSQDN

RG

AN

553D
BOMBSQDN

554TH
BOMBSQDN

RU

YA

555TH
BOMBSQDN

B-26 'MARAUDER' / A-26 'INVADER'

386th Bomb Group (M):

Motto: unknown

Sobriquet: unknown

Campaign Streamers:

Air Offensive, Europe; Normandy; Northern France; Rhineland; Ardennes-Alsace; Central Europe.

Unit Decorations:

Distinguished Unit Citation: ETO, 30-Jul-43 thru 30-Jul-44

Overseas Combat Commanders:

Col. Lester J. Maitland, 1-Dec-42

Col. Richard C. Sanders, 18-Nov-43

Col. Joe W. Kelly, 22-Jan-44

Col. Thomas G. Corbin, 25-Aug-44

Overseas Stations:

No.138 Snetterton Heath, Norfolk; 3-Jun-43

No.150 Boxted, Essex; 10-Jun-43

No.164 Great Dunmow, Essex; 24-Sep-43

A-60 Beaumont-sur-Oise, Picardie; 2-Oct-44

A-92 St. Trond, Province Limburg; 9-Apr-45

Combat Operations:

15-Jul-43 thru 3-May-45

(Previously served in combat with the Eighth AAF).

Insignia / Markings:

Group Insignia: unofficial (signage)

Squadron Insignia:

552d BS; officially approved 16-Apr-43

553d BS; unofficial

554th BS; officially approved 2-Apr-43

555th BS; unofficial

Squadron Codes:

552d BS - **R G**

553d BS - **A N**

554th BS - **R U**

555th BS - **Y A**

Squadron Colors: none

Aircraft Markings:

Squadron code and call letters were positioned on both sides of fuselage directly fore and aft of the national insignia. Colors used were RAF or ANA 610 Sky on camouflaged surfaces and later black on natural metal finishes. The 323d adopted the use of a yellow horizontal stripe measuring approximately 30 inches in height. This marker was accented with 3-4 inch black stripes top and bottom on natural metal finishes and was thus applied on both the B-26 and later (21-Feb-45) the groups A-26 aircraft.

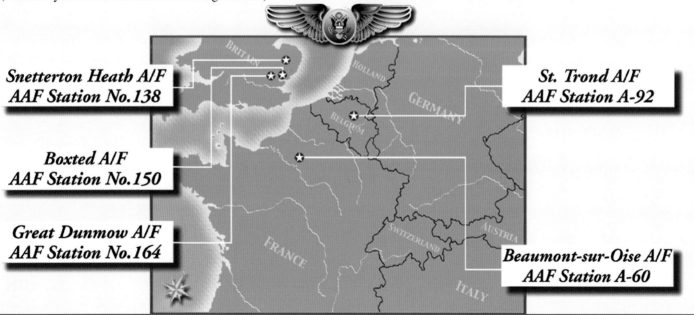

Snetterton Heath A/F
AAF Station No.138

Boxted A/F
AAF Station No.150

Great Dunmow A/F
AAF Station No.164

St. Trond A/F
AAF Station A-92

Beaumont-sur-Oise A/F
AAF Station A-60

98TH COMBAT BOMBARDMENT WING (MEDIUM) (NOVEMBER 1943)	IX BOMBER COMMAND LATER 9TH BOMBARDMENT DIV (M)

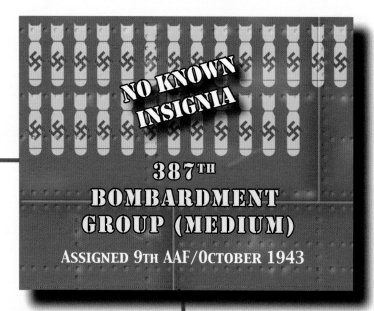

NO KNOWN INSIGNIA

387TH BOMBARDMENT GROUP (MEDIUM)

ASSIGNED 9TH AAF/OCTOBER 1943

556TH BOMBSQDN

FW

KS

557TH BOMBSQDN

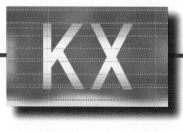

KX

TQ

558TH BOMBSQDN

559TH BOMBSQDN

B-26 'MARAUDER'

387th Bomb Group (M):

Motto: unknown

Sobriquet: *'Tiger Tails'*

Campaign Streamers:

Air offensive Europe; Normandy; Northern France; Rhineland; Ardennes-Alsace; Central Europe.

Unit Decorations:

Distinguished Unit Citation: Germany, 23-Dec-44

Overseas Combat Commanders

Col. Carl R. Storrie, 19-Jan-43

Col.Jack E. Caldwell, 8-Nov-43

Col. Thomas M Seymour, 13-Apr-44

Col. Grover C. Brown, 18-Jul-44

Overseas Stations:

No.162 Chipping Ongar, Essex; 25-Jun-43

No.452 Stony Cross, Hampshire; 18-Jul-44

A-15 Maupertus, Basse-Normandie; 22-Aug-44

A-39 Chateaudun, Centre-Val-de-Loire; 18-Sep-44

A-71 Clastres, Picrdie; 30-Oct-44

Y-44 Maastricht, Provincie Limburg; 29-Apr-45

Combat Operations:

Aug-43 thru April, 1945

Insignia / Markings:

Group Insignia: unknown

Squadron Insignia:

456th BS; officially replaced 25-Apr-62

457th BS; officially approved 19-Apr-43

458th BS; unofficial

459th BS; unofficial

Squadron Codes:

456th BS - **F W**

457th BS - **K S**

458th BS - **K S**

459th BS - **T Q**

Squadron Colors: none

Aircraft Markings:

The tail marking of the 387th was one of the best recognized of all the medium bomb group identification markers. The alternating pattern of yellow and black stripes of equal width created a distinctive and unmistakable image and was incorporated without modification to both camouflaged and natural metal finished airframes. The location of squadron codes and call letters was consistent with other medium bomb groups within the Ninth AAF, i.e. RAF or ANA No.610 Sky on painted surfaces, black on natural metal finishes.

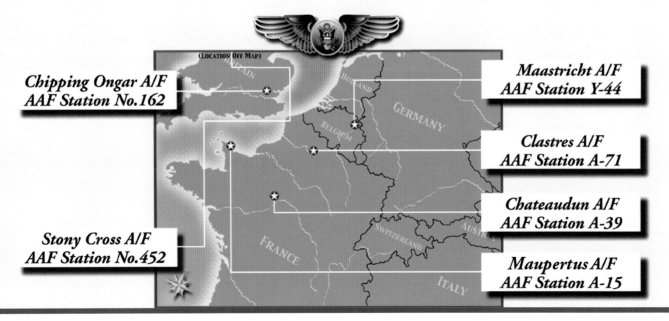

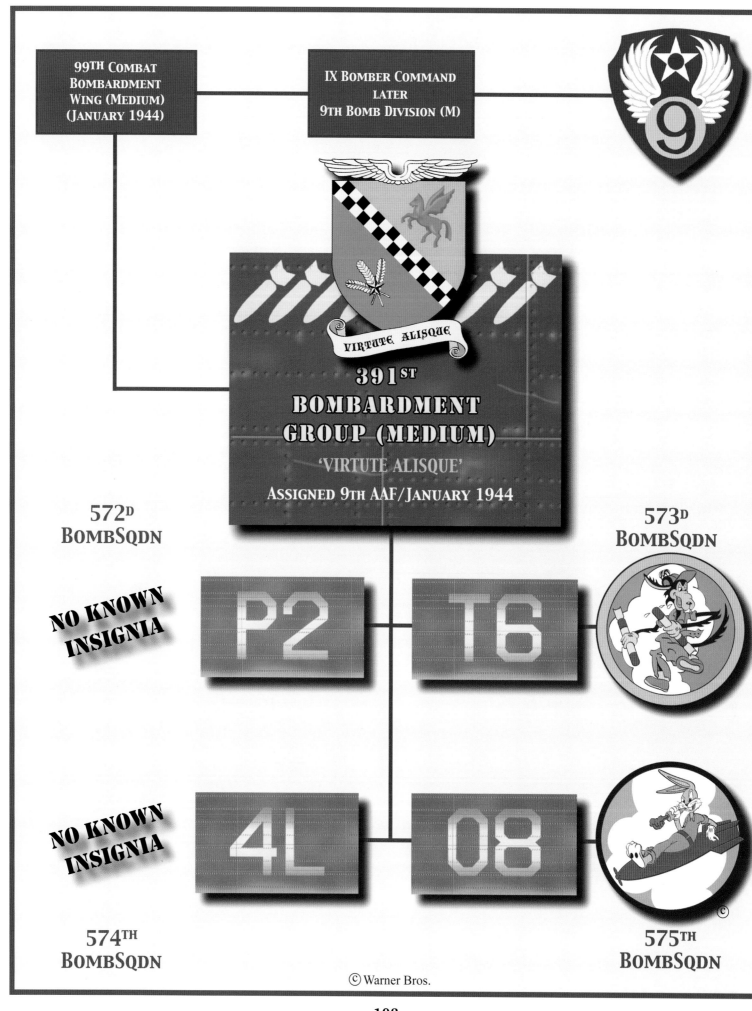

99TH COMBAT BOMBARDMENT WING (MEDIUM) (JANUARY 1944)

IX BOMBER COMMAND LATER 9TH BOMB DIVISION (M)

VIRTUTE ALISQUE

391ST BOMBARDMENT GROUP (MEDIUM)
'VIRTUTE ALISQUE'
ASSIGNED 9TH AAF/JANUARY 1944

572D BOMBSQDN

NO KNOWN INSIGNIA

P2

T6

573D BOMBSQDN

NO KNOWN INSIGNIA

4L

08

574TH BOMBSQDN

575TH BOMBSQDN

© Warner Bros.

391st Bomb Group (M):

Motto: *'Virtute Alisque'*
('With Wings and Courage')

Sobriquet: unknown

Campaign Streamers:

Air offensive Europe; Normandy; Northern France;
Rhineland; Ardennes-Alsace; Central Europe.

Unit Decorations:

Distinguished Unit Citation: Germany,
23 thru 26 December, 1944

Overseas Combat Commanders

Col. Gerald E. Williams, 23-Jan-43

Overseas Stations:

No.166 Matching, Essex; 25-Jan-44

A-73 Roye-Amy, Picardie; 19-Sep-44

Y-29 Assche, Province de Brabant; 16-Apr-45

Combat Operations:

15-Feb-44 thru 3-May-45

1.) Converted to A-26 'Invaders' on 10-Apr-45

Insignia / Markings:

Group Insignia: approved 11-Jan-54 from WWII design

Squadron Insignia:

572d BS; unknown

573d BS; unofficial

574th BS; unknown

575th BS; officially approved 2-Dec-43

Squadron Codes:

572d BS - **P 2**

573d BS - **T 6**

574th BS - **4 L**

575th BS - **O 8**

Squadron Colors: none

Aircraft Markings:

The 391st adopted a yellow equilateral triangle as their Group identification marker. This geometric symbol was positioned on the upper tail section directly above the aircraft call number and included a 3-4 inch black border on natural metal finishes.

Squadron codes and aircraft call letter were applied to the fuselage with Sky on camouflaged finishes, black on metal surfaces, and positioned fore and aft the national insignia.

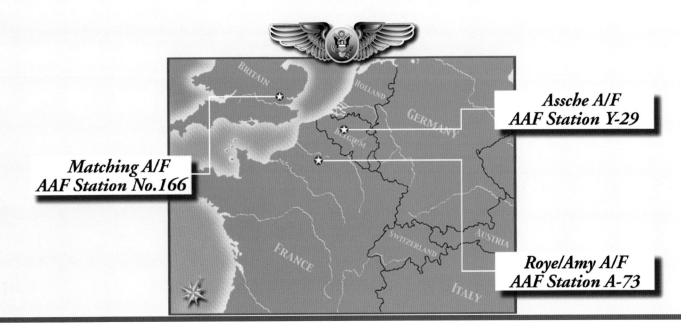

Matching A/F
AAF Station No.166

Assche A/F
AAF Station Y-29

Roye/Amy A/F
AAF Station A-73

98TH COMBAT BOMBARDMENT WING (MEDIUM) (MARCH 1944)

IX BOMBER COMMAND LATER 9TH BOMB DIVISION (M)

394TH BOMBARDMENT GROUP (MEDIUM)

'READINESS STRENGTHENS LIBERTY'

ASSIGNED 9TH AAF/MARCH 1944

584TH BOMBSQDN

585TH BOMBSQDN

K5

4T

H9

5W

586TH BOMBSQDN

587TH BOMBSQDN

394th Bomb Group (M):

Motto: '*Readiness Strengthens Liberty*'

Sobriquet: '*Bridge Busters*'

Campaign Streamers:

American Theater; Air offensive Europe; Normandy; Northern France; Rhineland; Ardennes-Alsace; Central Europe.

Unit Decorations:

Distinguished Unit Citation: France, 7 thru 9 August, 1944; *French Croix de Guerre with Palm*, France, 6-June thru 14-September, 1944

Overseas Combat Commanders

Col. Thomas B. Hall, 6-Apr-43

Col. Gove C. Celio Jr., c. 24-Jan-45

Overseas Stations:

No.161 Boreham, Essex; c. 11-Mar-44

No.455 Holmsley, Hampshire; 24-Jul-44

A-13 Tour-en-Bassin, Basse-Normandie; 25-Aug-44

A-50 Orleans / Bricy, Centre-Val-de-Loire; 18-Sep-44

A-74 Cambrai / Niergnies, Nord-Pas-De-Calais; 8-Oct-44

Y-55 Venlo, Provincie Limburg; 21-May-45

Combat Operations:

23-Mar-44 thru 8-May-45

Insignia / Markings:

Group Insignia: approved 15-Apr-54 from WWII design

Squadron Insignia:

584th BS; officially approved 31-Dec-43

585th BS; officially approved 9-Dec-43

586th BS; officially approved 29-Jun-43

587th BS; officially approved 26-Oct-43

Squadron Codes:

584th BS - **K 5**

585th BS - **4 T**

586th BS - **H 9**

587th BS - **5 W**

Squadron Colors: none

Aircraft Markings:

The location and colors of squadron codes and call letters were consistent with other medium bomb groups within the Ninth AAF. The group marker was a diagonal white stripe, approximately 24 inches in width, ascending from the lower front base of the vertical stabilizer at an angle of 45⁰, and terminating at the stabilizers upper trailing edge. This device was accompanied by 3 to 4 inch diagonal border stripes running the length, top and bottom, of the white marker band on natural metal surfaces.

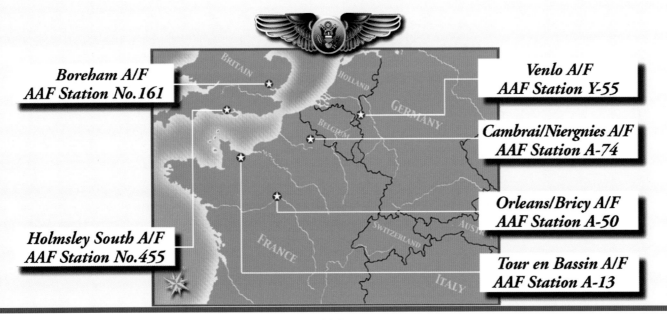

Boreham A/F
AAF Station No.161

Venlo A/F
AAF Station Y-55

Cambrai/Niergnies A/F
AAF Station A-74

Orleans/Bricy A/F
AAF Station A-50

Holmsley South A/F
AAF Station No.455

Tour en Bassin A/F
AAF Station A-13

98TH COMBAT
BOMBARDMENT
WING (MEDIUM)
(APRIL 1944)

IX BOMBER COMMAND
LATER
9TH BOMBARDMENT DIV (M)

NO KNOWN
INSIGNIA

397TH
BOMBARDMENT
GROUP (MEDIUM)

ASSIGNED 9TH AAF/APRIL 1944

596TH
BOMBSQDN

597TH
BOMBSQDN

X2

9F

U2

6B

598TH
BOMBSQDN

599TH
BOMBSQDN

B-26 'MARAUDER'

397th Bomb Group (M):

Motto: unknown

Sobriquet: unknown

Campaign Streamers:

Air offensive Europe; Normandy; Northern France; Rhineland; Ardennes-Alsace; Central Europe.

Unit Decorations:

Distinguished Unit Citation: Germany, 23-December, 1944;

Overseas Combat Commanders

Col. Richard T. Coiner Jr., 5-October, 1943

Overseas Stations:

No.154 Gosfield, Essex; 5-Apr-44

No.168 Rivenhall, Essex; 15-Apr-44

No.492 Hurn, Hampshire; 4-Aug-44

A-26 Gorges, Basse-Normandie; Aug-44

A-41 Dreux, Centre-Val-de-Loire; c.11-Sep-44

A-72 Peronne, Picardie; 6-Oct-44

Y-55 Venlo, Provincie Limburg; 25-Apr-45

Combat Operations:

May-44 thru 25-Apr-45

Insignia / Markings:

Group Insignia: unknown

Squadron Insignia:

596th BS; officially approved 20-Mar-45

597th BS; officially approved 20-Dec-43

598th BS; officially approved 5-Feb-44

599th BS; officially approved 10-Jun-44

Squadron Codes:

596th BS - **X 2**

597th BS - **9 F**

598th BS - **U 2**

599th BS - **6 B**

Squadron Colors: none

Aircraft Markings:

The identification marker specifications for the 397thBG were identical as those for the 394thBG except for the base color which was yellow in the case of the 397th. The common practice with both of these two groups when applying their respective diagonal markers, was to block-mask out the aircraft call numbers prior to the actual marker application.

Squadron codes and aircraft call letters were located fore and aft the fuselage national insignia, black on metal finishes, ANA No. 610 Sky on camouflaged surfaces.

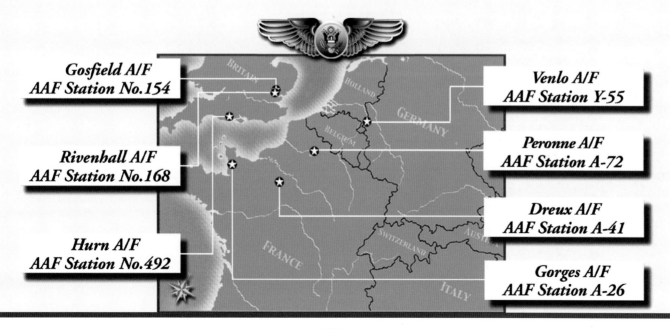

Gosfield A/F
AAF Station No.154

Rivenhall A/F
AAF Station No.168

Hurn A/F
AAF Station No.492

Venlo A/F
AAF Station Y-55

Peronne A/F
AAF Station A-72

Dreux A/F
AAF Station A-41

Gorges A/F
AAF Station A-26

97TH COMBAT BOMBARDMENT WING (MEDIUM) LATER (LIGHT) (NOVEMBER 1943)

IX BOMBER COMMAND LATER 9TH BOMBARDMENT DIV (M)

NO KNOWN INSIGNIA

409TH BOMBARDMENT GROUP (LIGHT)

ASSIGNED 9TH AAF/MARCH 1944

640TH BOMBSQDN

641ST BOMBSQDN

WS

7G

D6

5I

642D BOMBSQDN

643D BOMBSQDN

409th Bomb Group (L):

Motto: unknown

Sobriquet: unknown

Campaign Streamers:

Air offensive Europe; Normandy; Northern France; Rhineland; Ardennes-Alsace; Central Europe.

Unit Decorations: none

Overseas Combat Commanders

Col. Preston P. Pender, Jun-43

Col. Thomas R. Ford, 4-Jul-44

Overseas Stations:

No.165 Little Walden, Essex; 7-Mar-44

A-48 Bretigny, Ile-de-France; Sep-44

A-70 Laon / Couvron, Picardie; 15-Feb-44

Combat Operations:

14-Apr-44 thru 3-May-45

Insignia / Markings:

Group Insignia: unknown

Squadron Insignia:

640th BS; officially approved 14-Mar-44

641st BS; officially approved 21-Dec-43

642d BS; unofficial

643d BS; officially approved 18-Jan-44

Squadron Codes:

640th BS - **5 W**

641st BS - **7 G**

642d BS - **D 6**

643d BS - **5 I**

Squadron Colors: none

Aircraft Markings:

The tail marking of the 409th was the simple application of a yellow color band along the trailing edge of the tail rudder, approximately 30-36 inches in width. The location of squadron codes and call letters was consistent with other medium bomb groups within the Ninth AAF, and applied to both the A-20 'Havoc' and A-26 'Invader' to which the 409thBG converted in December 1944.

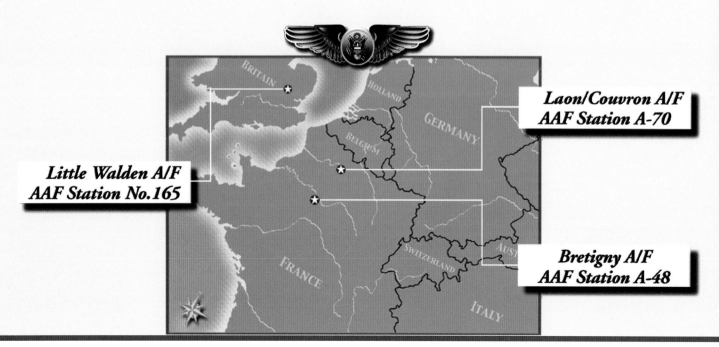

97TH COMBAT BOMBARDMENT WING (MEDIUM) LATER (LIGHT) (NOVEMBER 1943)

IX BOMBER COMMAND LATER 9TH BOMBARDMENT DIV (M)

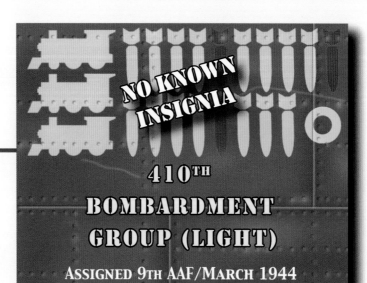

NO KNOWN INSIGNIA

410TH BOMBARDMENT GROUP (LIGHT)

ASSIGNED 9TH AAF/MARCH 1944

644TH BOMB SQDN

645TH BOMBSQDN

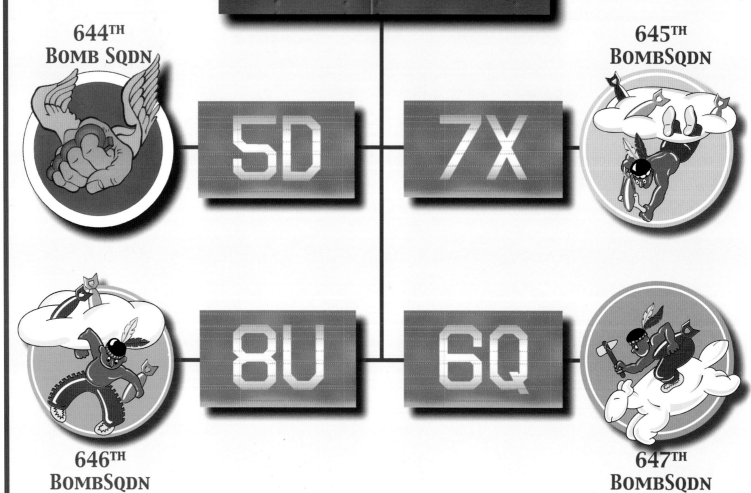

5D

7X

8U

6Q

646TH BOMBSQDN

647TH BOMBSQDN

410th Bomb Group (L):

Motto: unknown

Sobriquet: unknown

Campaign Streamers:

Air offensive Europe; Normandy; Northern France; Rhineland; Ardennes-Alsace; Central Europe.

Unit Decorations:

Distinguished Unit Citation: Germany, 23 thru 25 December, 1944

Overseas Combat Commanders:

Col. Ralph Rhudy, 17-Sep-43

Col. Sherman R. Beaty, 3-Jul-44

Col. Robert J. Hughey, Dec-44

Overseas Stations:

No.149 Birch, Essex; c. 4-Apr-44

No.154 Gosfield, Essex; c.16-Apr-44

A-58 Coulommiers, Ile-de-France; Sep-44

A-68 Juvincourt, Champagne-Ardenne; Feb-45

Combat Operations:

1-May-44 thru April, 1945

1.) The 410th was in the process of converting to the A-26 'Invader' when the war ended.

Insignia / Markings:

Group Insignia: unknown

Squadron Insignia:

644th BS; officially approved 21-Dec-43

645th BS; officially approved 29-Dec-43

646th BS; officially approved 29-Dec-43

647th BS; officially approved 15-Nov-43

Squadron Codes:

644th BS - **5 D**

645th BS - **7 X**

646th BS - **8 U**

647th BS - **6 Q**

Squadron Colors: Some use of colors was utilized within the four squadrons on spinners and engine cowlings but this appears to have been sporadic and somewhat random. As best can be determined these colors were as follows: 644thBS-red; 647thBS-yellow; 646thBS-medium blue; 645thBS-white.

Aircraft Markings:

The 410th group marking consisted of painting the trailing edge of the tail rudder white with the subsequent addition of three black stripes. The overall effect was very much in keeping with the fuselage Invasion Stripes. Squadron codes and call letters were applied to the fuselage with white paint.

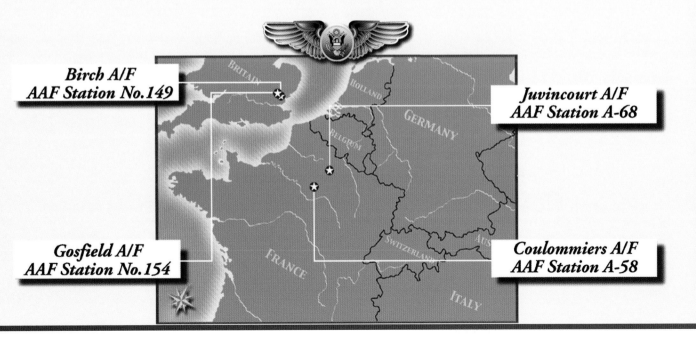

Birch A/F
AAF Station No.149

Juvincourt A/F
AAF Station A-68

Gosfield A/F
AAF Station No.154

Coulommiers A/F
AAF Station A-58

97TH COMBAT BOMBARDMENT WING (MEDIUM) LATER (LIGHT) (NOVEMBER 1943)

IX BOMBER COMMAND LATER 9TH BOMBARDMENT DIV (M)

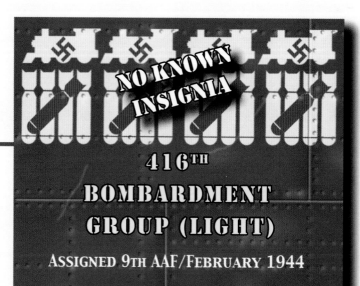

NO KNOWN INSIGNIA

416TH BOMBARDMENT GROUP (LIGHT)

ASSIGNED 9TH AAF/FEBRUARY 1944

668TH BOMBSQDN

5H

2A

669TH BOMBSQDN

'SURE SHOT SULLY'

670TH BOMBSQDN
'BEAKY THE BOMBER'

F6

5C

671ST BOMBSQDN

A-20 'HAVOC' / A-26 'INVADER'

416th Bomb Group (L):

Motto: unknown

Sobriquet: unknown

Campaign Streamers:

Air offensive Europe; Normandy; Northern France; Rhineland; Ardennes-Alsace; Central Europe.

Unit Decorations:

Distinguished Unit Citation: France, 6 thru 9 August, 1944

Overseas Combat Commanders

Col. Harold L. Mace, Oct-43

Col. Theodore R. Aylesworth, 3-Aug-44

Overseas Stations:

No.170 Wethersfield, Essex; Feb-44

A-55 Melun, Ile-de-France; Sep-44

A-69 Laon / Athies, Picardie; Feb-45

Combat Operations:

3-Mar-44 thru 3-Mar-45

Insignia / Markings:

Group Insignia: unknown

Squadron Insignia:

668th BS; officially approved 3-Jun-43

669th BS; officially approved 28-Jul-43

670th BS; officially approved 29-Jun-43

671st BS; officially approved 13-May-43

Squadron Codes:

668th BS - **5 H**

669th BS - **2 A**

670th BS - **F 6**

671st BS - **5 C**

Squadron Colors: none

Aircraft Markings:

The tail marking of the 387th was the application of a white diagonal stripe emanating inwards from the trailing edge of the tail rudder. This device was carried over to the A-26 'Invader' when the group converted to that aircraft in November 1944. Fuselage tactical markings were consistent with Ninth AAF specifications and were applied with white paint on camouflaged surfaces, black on natural metal finishes

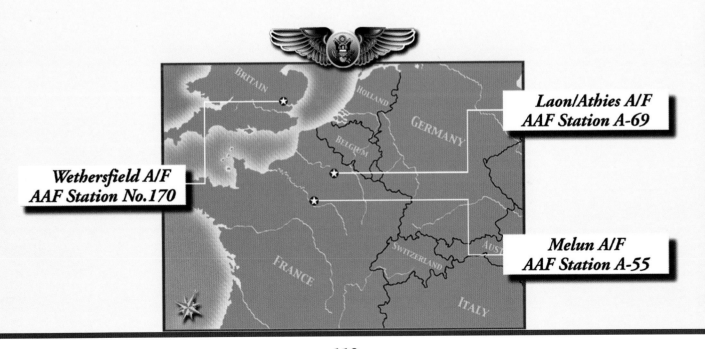

Laon/Athies A/F
AAF Station A-69

Wethersfield A/F
AAF Station No.170

Melun A/F
AAF Station A-55

LIAISON UNITS
OF THE
NINTH U.S.A.A.F.

Although greatly appreciated within the army in which they served, little attention is today given these diminutive single engine aircraft, yet the pilots of these slow unarmed ships made an invaluable contribution to the war effort throughout the entire conflict and in every theater of operation throughout the world.

The first rule of thumb if one found oneself assigned to an overseas liaison unit was 'don't unpack'. The length of stay at any given duty station might be a matter of weeks or mere hours, it all depended upon any number of variables. There were of course, as in all matters, exceptions to the rule, but for the most part duty with a liaison outfit in a combat area was one of constant movement.

The duties involved with being a liaison pilot varied greatly and often depended largely upon the immediate needs of the unit being currently served. One of the more important duties from a tactical perspective was that of Forward Artillery Observer.

Upon returning to your assigned field (presuming of course you did return) you may have a few post-mission drinks at the local officers or enlisted men's club (provided there was one) and listen to some fighter jock regale you with his tales and tell you what 'real flying' was all about.

There were many other types of missions carried out by liaison pilots throughout the war. These operations involved the medical evacuation of the critically wounded, relaying communications, battle plans and personnel between the front lines and rear command centers. The rescue of downed airmen, sometimes behind enemy lines, was another fun filled mission. Then of course the Liaison pilot could invariably be called upon at any given time to act as an airborne taxi driver to whomever had enough clout to move   from Point-A to Point-B by means other than routine ground transportation.

L-4 PIPER 'CUB'

L-4 STINSON 'SENTINEL'

The job of an artillery observer, or Spotter, entailed flying close enough to enemy lines to have everything up to and including the kitchen sink thrown at them while maintaining radio contact with the artillery commander in order to direct fire upon enemy positions. The enemy of course was all to aware of the presence and purpose of this harmless looking aircraft and this is where the kitchen sink part comes in. Everything that could shoot would focus its undivided attention upon this slow moving, tubular famed, fabric covered, unarmed and unarmored target in an earnest attempt to terminate its mission, permanently if possible.

Aerial reconnaissance was another fun job. Here again one was likely to find ones self over enemy held territory, unarmed except for perhaps a pistol, a pair of binoculars and maybe an aerial camera. The key point to these operations was that in order to locate the enemy you had to fly low and slow enough to see them, which meant that they could see you, which meant that they would once again begin shooting at you. Here's where that proverbial kitchen sink comes into play once more, and while the enemy is throwing it at you, you're watching him do it through your binoculars, or perhaps in your cameras view finder. The term 'Sitting Duck' might well have been coined with these types of missions in mind.

The question often arises as to the difference between reconnaissance conducted by a liaison outfit as opposed to that of a photo recon unit. In simplest terms, and this is admittedly an over simplification, formal photo reconnaissance generally took place immediately before and immediately following a raid or battle. Reconnaissance by a liaison unit generally took place while that battle was in progress.

Many types of aircraft were utilized by liaison pilots but by far the most common, and recognizable, were the two types depicted above, the Piper L-4 'Cub' and Stinson L-5 'Sentinel'. Within the 'L' Series, the L-2, L-3, L-4 and L-6 type shared a common but unpopular Army nickname, the 'Grasshopper'. Most pilots and ground crew generally referred to these aircraft by their civilian sobriquets or more simply with their respective designator, i.e. L-4, L-6, etc. Prior to the AAF redesignation from Observation to Liaison in April 1942, these aircraft were labeled with an 'O' designator. Thus O-57, O-58, O-59, O-54, and O-63 became the L-2, L-3, L-4, L-5 and L-6 respectively.

The inherit low landing speed of these single engine liaison aircraft (approximately 35 miles per hour with an L-4), made them the ideal means of accessing places unusable by other aircraft. The down side, as mentioned earlier, was the lack of armor or armament. These aircraft were all powered by efficient, but low horsepower engines, as such they were handicapped when it came to payload capacity, ceiling and range.

All things considered, the exploits of many a liaison pilot would have, under different circumstances, been widely acclaimed and accompanied with all honors bestowed upon their fellow pilots in the fighters or bombers. Unfortunately, the harmless, almost friendly appearance of the average liaison aircraft just didn't quite strike a chord with those writing about the war. Even with the occasional addition of sharks teeth nose art, an L-4 was none-the-less the same type of airplane one well might have seen traversing the pre-war skies. In all fairness to the journalists, liaison aircraft may have faithfully performed many invaluable duties, but no matter how hard they worked, how dangerous their missions or how well they did their job, they just weren't a P-51.

14ᵀᴴ LIAISON SQUADRON

Squadron Insignia: officially approved 5-Sep-42
Motto: unknown
Sobriquet: unknown
Aircraft: L-1 'Vigilant'; L-4 'Cub'; L-5 'Sentinel'
Campaign Streamers:
Antisubmarine, American Theater; Normandy;
Northern France; Rhineland; Ardennes-Alsace; Central Europe.
Unit Decorations: none

Overseas Stations:
(no AAF/AF listing) Alderley Edge, Cheshire England; 9-Apr-44
(no AAF/AF listing) Knutsford, Cheshire England; 11-May-44
No.347 / Ibsley, Hampshire England; 29-Jun-44
(no ALG code) Nehou, Basse-Normandie France; 6-Jul-44
(no ALG code) Le Repas, Basse-Normandie France; 2-Aug-44
(no ALG code) Beauchamps, Basse-Normandie France; 4-Aug-44
(no ALG code) Poilley, Basse-Normandie France; 7-Aug-44
(no ALG code) St. Germain, Basse-Normandie France; 12-Aug-44
(no ALG code) Dampierre, Basse-Normandie France; 20-Aug-44
(no ALG code) Courcy, Centre-Val-de-Loire France; 25-Aug-44
(no ALG code) St. Maurice-aux-Riches-Hommes, France; 30-Aug-44
(no ALG code) Marson, Alsace France; 4-Sep-44
(no ALG code) Gussainville, Alsace France; 14-Sep-44
Y-42 / Nancy-Essey, Alsace France; 12-Oct-44
A-97 / Sandweiler, District de Luxembourg, Luxembourg; 31-Dec-44
(no ALG code) Idar-Oberstein, Rheinland-Pfalz Germany; 27-Mar-45
(no ALG code) Berkersheim, Land Hessen Germany; 3-Apr-45
(no ALG code) Hersfeld, Land Hessen Germany; 11-Apr-45
R-96 / Erlangen, Land Bayern Germany; 22-Apr-45
R-66 / Regensburg/Prufening, Land Bayen Germany; 2-May-45
Overseas Operations:
Combat, ETO; Jul-44 thru May-45

47ᵀᴴ LIAISON SQUADRON

Overseas Stations:
(no AAF/AF listing) Cheltenham, Gloucestershire England; 9-Apr-44
[1.] *No.510 /* Heston, Middlesex England; 25-Apr-44
(no ALG code) St. Sauveur-le-Vicomte, Auvergne France; 10-Aug-44
A-57 / Laval, Champagne-Ardenne France; 21-Aug-44
Y-4 / Buc, Il-de-France (Paris), France; 2-Sep-44
A-82 / Verdun, Lorraine France; 17-Sep-44
Y-80 / Wiesbaden, Land Hessen Germany; 2-May-45
Overseas Operations:
ETO; May-44 thru May-45
[1.] Detachment assigned to Colombieres, Basse Normandie
    France; c.24-Jul thru c.10-Aug 1944

Squadron Insignia: officially approved 19-Sep-44
Motto: unknown
Sobriquet: unknown
Aircraft: L-1 'Vigilant'; L-2 'Tee-Cart";
L-3 'Defender'; L-4 'Cub'; L-5 'Sentinel';
Campaign Streamers:
Northern France; Rhineland; Ardennes-Alsace; Central Europe.
Unit Decorations: none

72ᴰ LIAISON SQUADRON

Squadron Insignia: officially approved 6-Nov-43
Motto: unknown
Sobriquet: unknown
Aircraft: L-1 'Vigilant' ; L-4 'Cub'; L-5 'Sentinel';
L-6 'Cadet'; A-24 'Banshee'
Campaign Streamers: Rome-Arno; Northern France; Southern France; Rhineland; Ardennes-Alsace; Central Europe.
Unit Decorations: Army Meritorious Unit Commendation,
15-Aug thru 31-December, 1944

1.) Overseas Stations:
Epinal, Alsace France; 30-Sep-44 / 2-Jan-45
2.) Buhl, Alsace France; 1-Dec-44 / 11-Mar-45
Sarreguemines, Alsace France; 22-Mar-45
Kaiserlautern, Rhineland-Pfalz Germany; 26-Mar-45
Darmstadt, Hessen Germany; 1-Apr-45
Kitzingen, Bavaria Bayern Germany; 15-Apr-45
Gmund, Bavaria Bayern Germany; 27-Apr-45
Augsburg, Bavaria Bayern Germany; 2-Jul-45
Overseas Operations:
ETO/MTO; Apr-44 thru May-45
1.) The duty stations listed reflect only those to which the 72d
Liaison was assigned during its tenure with the Ninth AAF
2.) Detachment at Steinbourg, France; c.8-Dec-44 thru 1-Jan-45

112ᵀᴴ LIAISON SQUADRON

Squadron Insignia: officially replaced 9-Mar-54
Motto: unknown
Sobriquet: unknown
Aircraft: L-2 'Tee-Cart'; L-4 'Cub'; L-5 'Sentinel';
L-6 'Cadet'; A-24 'Banshee'; UC-78 'Bobcat'
Campaign Streamers: Antisubmarine, American Theater
Northern France; Rhineland; Central Europe.
Unit Decorations: none

Overseas Stations:
(no AAF/AF listing) Kingston Deverill, England; 9-Jun-44
No.508 / Hurst Park, Surry England; 20-Jun-44
1.) *No.517 /* Heston, Middlesex England; 30-Jun-44
(no ALG code) Jullouville, France; 27-Aug-44
2.) Y-4 / Buc, Ile-de-France (Paris) France; 24-Sep-44
Overseas Operations:
ETO; Jun-44 thru May-45
1.) Detachment assigned to Valognes, France;
c.6-Aug thru c.9-Sep 1944
2.) Detachment operating from Namur, Belgium;
26-Oct-44 thru c.11-Feb-45

121ˢᵀ LIAISON SQUADRON

Overseas Stations:
(no ALG listing) St. Tropez, France; 1-Sep-44
Y-6 / Lyon-Bron, Lorraine France; 15-Sep-44
(no ALG listing) Vittel, Alsace France; 3-Oct-44
Overseas Operations:
Combat in ETO and MTO; Sep-44 thru 3-May-45
1.) Detachments were assigned for various periods of time to both the Ninth AAF and the First Tactical Air Force (Prov). The 121st Liaison Squadron spent most of the war operating in the Mediterranean Theater with bases ranging from North Africa to Italy.

Squadron Insignia: officially replaced 4-Sep-51
Motto: unknown
Sobriquet: unknown
Aircraft: L-4 'Cub'; L-5 'Sentinel'; L-6 'Cadet';
RA-24; A-20 'Havoc'; UC-78 'Bobcat'
Campaign Streamers: Antisubmarine, American Theater;
Rome-Arno; Rhineland; North Apennines; Po Valley.
Unit Decorations: none

125ᵀᴴ LIAISON SQUADRON

Overseas Stations:
(no AAF/AF listing) Cheltenham, Glouchestershire England; c.8-Jun-44
(no AAF/AF listing) Chedworth, Glouchestershire England; 19-Jun-44
1.) *No.435* / Erle Stoke Village, Wiltshire England; 9-Jul-44
(no ALG listing) St. Sauveur Lendelin, France; 1-Sep-44
A-27 / Rennes, Bretagne France; 3-Sep-44
(no ALG listing) Arlon, Provincie de Luxembourg Belgium; c.1-Oct-44
Y-44 / Maastricht, Provincie Limburg Holland; 21-Oct-44
Y-56 / Munchen-Gladbach, Nordrhein-Westphalia Germany; 9-Mar-45
(no ALG listing) Haltern, Nordrhein-Westphalia Germany; 4-Apr-45
Y-99 / Gutersloh, Nordrhein-Westphalia Germany; 12-Apr-45
R-38 / Brunswick-Broitzem, Niedersachsen Germany; 24-Apr-45
Overseas Operations:
Combat, ETO; Aug-44 thru May-45
1.) Detachments began operating from France in late August '44.

Squadron Insignia: officially approved 15-Sep-43
Motto: unknown
Sobriquet: unknown
Aircraft: L-5 'Sentinel'
Campaign Streamers:
Northern France; Rhineland; Ardennes-Alsace; Central Europe.
Unit Decorations: *Order of the Day,* Belgian Army; 20-Oct thru 17-Dec 1944 and 18-Dec-44 thru 15-Jan-45:
Belgian Fourragere.

158ᵀᴴ LIAISON SQUADRON

Overseas Stations:
(no AAF/AF listing) Nantwich, Cheshire England; 13-Dec-44
(no ALG listing) Somme-Suippe, Alsace France; 4-Feb-45
(no ALG listing) Celles, Province de Namur Belgium; 16-Feb-45
(no ALG listing) Ahrweiler, Rheinland-Pfaltz Germany; 17-Apr-45
Overseas Operations:
Combat, ETO; March thru May 1945

Squadron Insignia: officially approved 16-Dec-44
Motto: unknown
Sobriquet: unknown
Aircraft: A-24 'Banshee'; BT-13 'Valiant'; L-5 'Sentinel'
RA-24; UC-78 'Bobcat';
Campaign Streamers:
Rhineland; Central Europe.
Unit Decorations: none

167ᵀᴴ LIAISON SQUADRON

NO KNOWN INSIGNIA

Overseas Stations:
(no ALG listing) Vittel, Alsace France; 19-Feb-45
(no ALG listing) Kaiserslautern, Rheinland-Pfalz Germany; 5-Apr-45
(no ALG listing) Pfaffengrun, Sachsen Germany; 14-Apr-45
Overseas Operations:
ETO; 10-March thru May 1945
Squadron Insignia: unknown
Motto: unknown
Sobriquet: unknown
Aircraft: L-4 'Cub'; L-5 'Sentinel'
Campaign Streamers: Rhineland; Central Europe.
Unit Decorations: none

173ᴰ LIAISON SQUADRON

Overseas Stations:
A-47 / Orly, Il-de-France (Paris) France; 24-Oct-44
Overseas Operations:
ETO; Nov-44 thru May-45
Squadron Insignia: none
Motto: unknown
Sobriquet: unknown
Aircraft: L-4 'Cub'; L-5 'Sentinel'; UC-78 'Bobcat'
Campaign Streamers:
Rhineland; Central Europe.
Unit Decorations: none

NO KNOWN INSIGNIA

RECONNAISSANCE
UNITS OF THE
NINTH U.S.A.A.F.

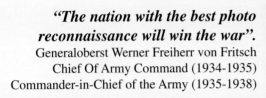

"Our photo reconnaissance pilots were instructed to fly on the theory that fighter planes win battles while camera planes win wars".
General of the Air Force Henry Harley 'Hap' Arnold,
Chief of the U.S. Army Air Forces (1941-1946)
Member / Joint Chiefs of Staff (1942-1946)
Combined British-American Chiefs of Staff (1942-1946)

"The nation with the best photo reconnaissance will win the war".
Generaloberst Werner Freiherr von Fritsch
Chief Of Army Command (1934-1935)
Commander-in-Chief of the Army (1935-1938)

The above quotes are included to illustrate a long standing paradox within the study of military history. Both of the men quoted were exceptional military officers with a full understanding of their profession and each understood the critical importance of timely photographic intelligence as it equated to success on the battlefield. With this thought in mind the question arises as to just why so little attention has been given to a subject these two influential leaders, and many other visionary military thinkers like them, thought so important to the outcome of a modern armed conflict..

The importance of accurate and timely military intelligence is certainly nothing new and in fact has been a sought after commodity of any field commander worth his salt since time immemorial. The means of obtaining this intelligence has evolved dramatically however, and this is especially true with the advent of men taking to the air. Until this time field reconnaissance was done either on foot, horseback or boat, depending upon various factors prevalent at the time. Later still the advent and advances in the field of photography would come into play and reconnaissance became an entirely new but equally dangerous ball game.

The French were among the first to use visual aerial reconnaissance in the form of hot air balloons as far back as the Napoleonic Wars. Less than half a century later both sides involved in the American Civil War, and especially the Union, employed gas operated balloons in much the same way the French had earlier. Just how effective these early attempts at aerial reconnaissance were is a subject of study unto itself, suffice to say that these first crude efforts were indeed successful enough for some of the better

military minds of all nations with foresight to see the potential of tactical aerial reconnaissance. Thus the stage was set for revolutionary advances in the field of intelligence gathering.

The dawning of the Twentieth Century soon found the world embroiled in The War To End All Wars, which with the benefit of hindsight we now know it wasn't. It would be difficult, if not impossible, to find a conflict in all of human history that saw so many radical changes from its beginning to its end.

The balloons, though bigger and better than their predecessors, were soon to be replaced by fixed wing, tactical aerial reconnaissance utilizing carrier pigeons as a means of communicating enemy positions to local artillery commanders. Photography soon came into its own as a strategic reconnaissance tool, assisting battle planners on both sides of the conflict as to their opponents precise location and strength.

Both camera and film technologies experienced giant strides between WWI and WWII, and with the outbreak of hostilities both the Germans and Allies put forth extreme efforts to perfect the practice of combat aerial photo reconnaissance. Special training programs were established in order to maximize the end result of any given recon mission. Gone forever were the days when someone would inform a fighter pilot that he would be going out today to take a couple of pictures of a battle field, the age of the specialists had arrived and this applied not only to the taking of the aerial surveillance photos, but in analyzing the content of these photos as well. Men and women on both sides of the conflict became skilled at interpreting aerial combat photographs to a point where each side was forced to elevate the art of camouflage to a new level. The failure of those on the ground to adequately make provisions for the adequate concealment of

ones position was to invite your adversary to pay you a visit with a load of bombs. Governments went to great lengths to educate both their soldiers and civilians as well in the principles of aerial reconnaissance and the necessary countermeasures. This was done in an effort to garner civilian support in areas subject to aerial bombardment to do what they could to help in an ongoing effort to thwart the effectiveness of photo reconnaissance by the enemy.

Part of the main Allied effort in this education process was to deploy operatives behind enemy line for the specific purpose of educating local resistance networks on just what to look for when engaged in their own ground surveillance efforts. These measures proved highly effective to the Allies, especially when it came to the planning for the invasion of the European continent. The intelligence received from these on-the-ground sources quickly evolved into an aerial reconnaissance mission with the end result being that by the time the Normandy Invasion took place, the overall German defences on and around the Atlantic Wall had,

at one time or another, most certainly been photographed and documented, paving the way for a successful landing.

This type of activity was taking place at varying levels in virtually every theatre of operation during the course of World War II and aerial surveillance did not cease with the surrender of the Axis powers. The barrel that fired the last shot of World War II had not yet cooled before we found ourselves immersed in the Cold War, during the course of which aerial reconnaissance took quantum leaps forward, leaving the achievements and technological advances of the previous conflict far behind. These latter advances however should in no way detract from the achievements and accomplishments of the war years, which brings us back to the original question as to why the subject of aerial reconnaissance during World War II has received but scant attention in the post war years.

These pilots were certainly deserving of as much praise and public adulation as their contemporaries in the other air branches. With the exception of the F-6 Mustang, most all other reconnaissance aircraft flew deep into enemy territory unarmed, depending upon speed and stealth alone. In some cases photo recon aircraft would be escorted by a fighter to supply top cover but these served more as an extra pair of eyes than any real tangible protection. If jumped by a flight of enemy fighters the only hope the reconnaissance pilot had was swift evasion.

Whether flying a low level 'oblique' or high level vertical photo mission, a reconnaissance pilot had to function in much the same manner as the pilot of a bomber, only alone. There was a set course to follow with a pre-assigned mission target, and like a bombing mission, failure one time meant going back to the same target until that mission was successfully completed.

Aerial reconnaissance might well be compared to a pair of winter socks; unseen, glamorless but absolutely vital when needed.

NINTH U.S.A.A.F. RECONNAISSANCE SQUADRON CODE INDEX

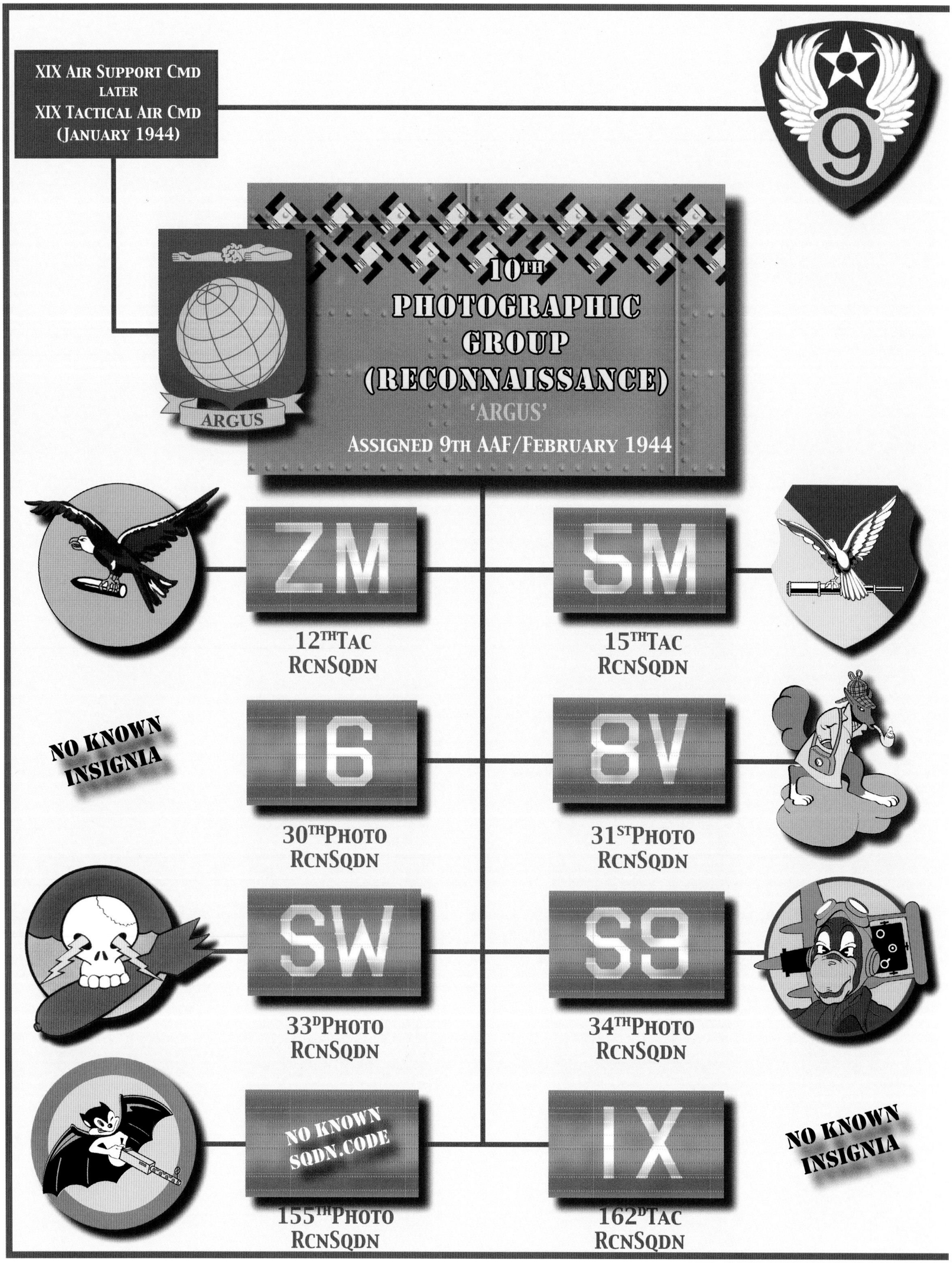

XIX Air Support Cmd
LATER
XIX Tactical Air Cmd
(JANUARY 1944)

ARGUS

10TH PHOTOGRAPHIC GROUP (RECONNAISSANCE)

'ARGUS'

ASSIGNED 9TH AAF/FEBRUARY 1944

ZM

12TH TAC
RcnSqdn

5M

15TH TAC
RcnSqdn

NO KNOWN INSIGNIA

16

30TH PHOTO
RcnSqdn

8V

31ST PHOTO
RcnSqdn

SW

33D PHOTO
RcnSqdn

S9

34TH PHOTO
RcnSqdn

NO KNOWN SQDN.CODE

155TH PHOTO
RcnSqdn

IX

162D TAC
RcnSqdn

NO KNOWN INSIGNIA

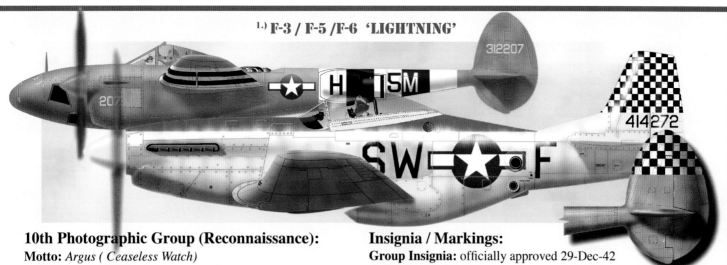

1.) F-3 / F-5 /F-6 'LIGHTNING'

312207

H 5M

414272

SW ✦ F

10th Photographic Group (Reconnaissance):

Motto: *Argus (Ceaseless Watch)*

Sobriquet: unknown

Campaign Streamers:

American Theater; Air Offensive,

Europe; Normandy; Northern France;

Rhineland; Ardennes-Alsace; Central Europe.

Unit Decorations:

Distinguished Unit Citation - France, 6 thru 20 May 1944

Overseas Combat Commanders:

Col. William B. Reed, 9-Sep-43

Col. Russell A. Berg, 20-Jun-44

2.) Overseas Stations:

No. 456 Chalgrove, Oxforfshire; Feb-44

A-27 Rennes / St. Jacques, Bretagne; c.11-Aug-44

A-39 Chateaudun, Centre-Val-de-Loire; Aug-44

A-64 St. Dizier / Robinson, Champagne-Ardenne; Sep-44

A-94 Conflans / Doncourt, Lorraine; Nov-44

Y-57 Trier / Eren, Rineland-Palatinate; Mar-45

Y-64 Ober Olm, Hessen; c.5Apr-44

R-28 Furth, Bavaria Bayern; c.28-Apr-45

Combat Operations:

Feb-44 thru 8-May-45

1.) Additional operational aircraft: L-1 / L-5 / L-5

2.) Numerous detachments were assigned for duty with other
   units at varying locations throughout the course of the war.

Insignia / Markings:

Group Insignia: officially approved 29-Dec-42

Squadron Insignia:

12th TRS; WWI insignia, officially approved 2-Feb-24

15th TRS; officially approved 2-Apr-24

30th PRS; unknown

31st PRS; officially approved 30-May-44

33d PRS; officially approved 10-Oct-42

34th PRS; officially replaced 23-Oct-54

155th TRS; originally 423d NFS. Redesignated 155th 22-Jun-44

162d TRS; unknown

Squadron Codes:

12th TRS - **Z M** • *15th TRS -* **5 M** • *30th PRS -* **I 6**

31st TRS - **8 V** • *33d PRS -* **S W**

34th PRS - **S 9** (Mar - Oct 1944) **X X** - (Oct-44 thru May-45)

155thTRS - unkwn • *162d TRS -* **I X**

Squadron Colors: unknown. Photographic material of the period
suggests that some use of color existed on a number of aircraft
within the group. To date however, no documentation has surfaced
that would indicate any uniform applications.

Aircraft Markings:

In the final months of the war the 10th Photographic Group
adopted a tactical identification marker which involved the application of a checkerboard pattern to the upper third of both inner
and outer tail fin surfaces. This pattern consisted of six to ten rows
of black and white rectangles on camouflaged (PRB) surfaces or
sometimes black only when applied to a metal finished surface.

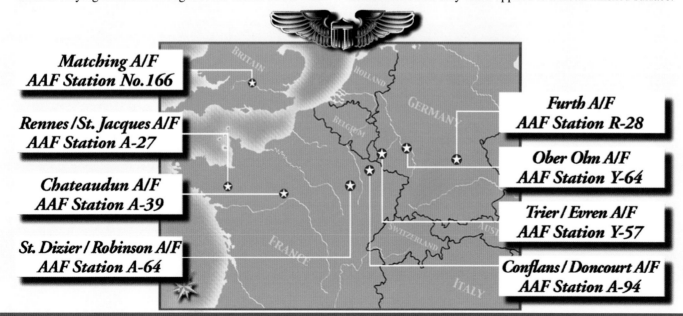

Matching A/F
AAF Station No.166

Rennes /St. Jacques A/F
AAF Station A-27

Chateaudun A/F
AAF Station A-39

St. Dizier / Robinson A/F
AAF Station A-64

Furth A/F
AAF Station R-28

Ober Olm A/F
AAF Station Y-64

Trier / Evren A/F
AAF Station Y-57

Conflans / Doncourt A/F
AAF Station A-94

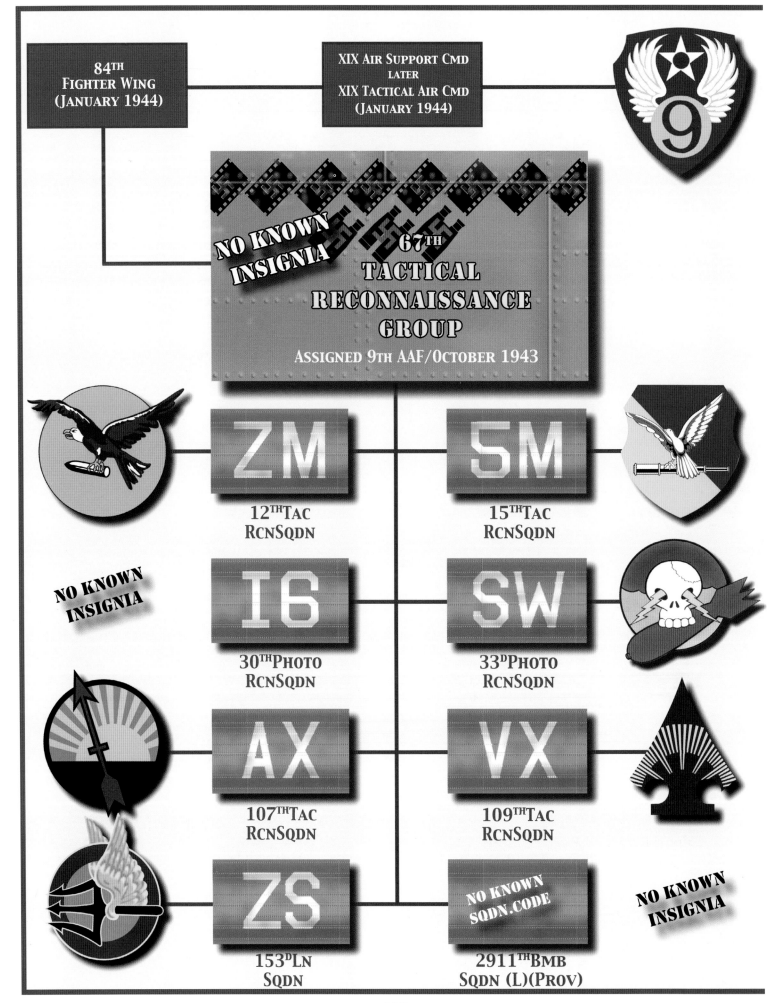

84TH
FIGHTER WING
(JANUARY 1944)

XIX AIR SUPPORT CMD
LATER
XIX TACTICAL AIR CMD
(JANUARY 1944)

NO KNOWN INSIGNIA

67TH
TACTICAL
RECONNAISSANCE
GROUP

ASSIGNED 9TH AAF/OCTOBER 1943

ZM

12THTAC
RCNSQDN

5M

15THTAC
RCNSQDN

NO KNOWN INSIGNIA

I6

30THPHOTO
RCNSQDN

SW

33DPHOTO
RCNSQDN

AX

107THTAC
RCNSQDN

VX

109THTAC
RCNSQDN

ZS

153DLN
SQDN

NO KNOWN SQDN.CODE

2911THBMB
SQDN (L)(PROV)

NO KNOWN INSIGNIA

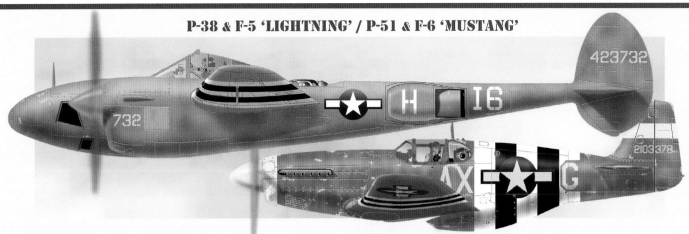

P-38 & F-5 'LIGHTNING' / P-51 & F-6 'MUSTANG'

67th Tactical Reconnaissance Group:

Motto: unknown

Sobriquet: unknown

Campaign Streamers:
Antisubmarine, American Theater; Air Offensive, Europe;
Normandy; Northern France; Rhineland;
Ardennes-Alsace; Central Europe.

Unit Decorations:
Distinguished Unit Citations - Le Havre and
Straits of Dover, 15-February thru 20-March, 1944

Overseas Combat Commanders:
Col. Fredrick R. Anderson, c.4-May-42
Col. George W. Peck, 6-Dec-43

Overseas Stations:
[1.] *No. 466* Membury; Berkshire; Sep-42
No.449 Middle Wallop, Hampshire; Dec-43
A-9 Le Molay, Basse-Normandie; Jul-44
A-46 Toussus le Noble, Ile-de-France; Aug-44
A-87 Charleroi, Province de Hainaut; Sep-44
Y-51 Vogelsang, Nordrhein-Westphalia; Mar-45
Y-83 Limburg, Hessen; c.2-Apr-44
R-11 Eschwege, Hessen; c.10-Apr-45

Combat Operations:
Dec-43 thru 8-May-45

[1.] Duty station when originally assigned to 8thAAF.

Insignia / Markings:

Group Insignia: unknown

Squadron Insignia:
12th TRS; WWI insignia, officially approved 2-Feb-24
15th TRS; officially approved 2-Apr-24
30th PRS; unknown
33d PRS; officially approved 10-Oct-42
107th TRS; officially replaced 16-Sep-54
109th TRS; officially approved 7-Mar-39
153d LS; officially replaced 15-Dec-53
2911th BS (L)(P); unknown. Organized from former 153d LnSq.

Squadron Codes:
12th TRS - **Z M** • *15th TRS* - **5 M** • *30th PRS* - **I 6**
33d PRS - **S W** • *107th TRS* - **A X** • *109th TRS* - **V X**
153d LS - **Z S** • *2911th BS* - unknown. This Provisional Bomb
Squadron (L) was organized from the former 153d Liaison
Squadron after that unit was inactivated on 15-Dec-45.

Squadron Colors: unknown.

Aircraft Markings:

There is currently no evidence relating to tactical markings for
the 67th Tactical Reconnaissance Group. Most reconnaissance
units did in fact adopt such a device in the final months of the war,
however, to date no conclusive documentation or photographic
material pertaining to this subject has been located.

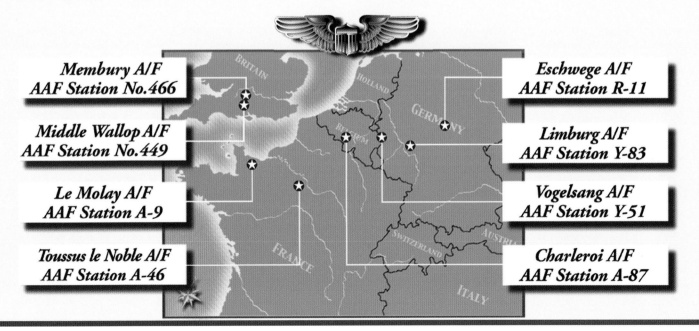

Membury A/F
AAF Station No.466

Middle Wallop A/F
AAF Station No.449

Le Molay A/F
AAF Station A-9

Toussus le Noble A/F
AAF Station A-46

Eschwege A/F
AAF Station R-11

Limburg A/F
AAF Station Y-83

Vogelsang A/F
AAF Station Y-51

Charleroi A/F
AAF Station A-87

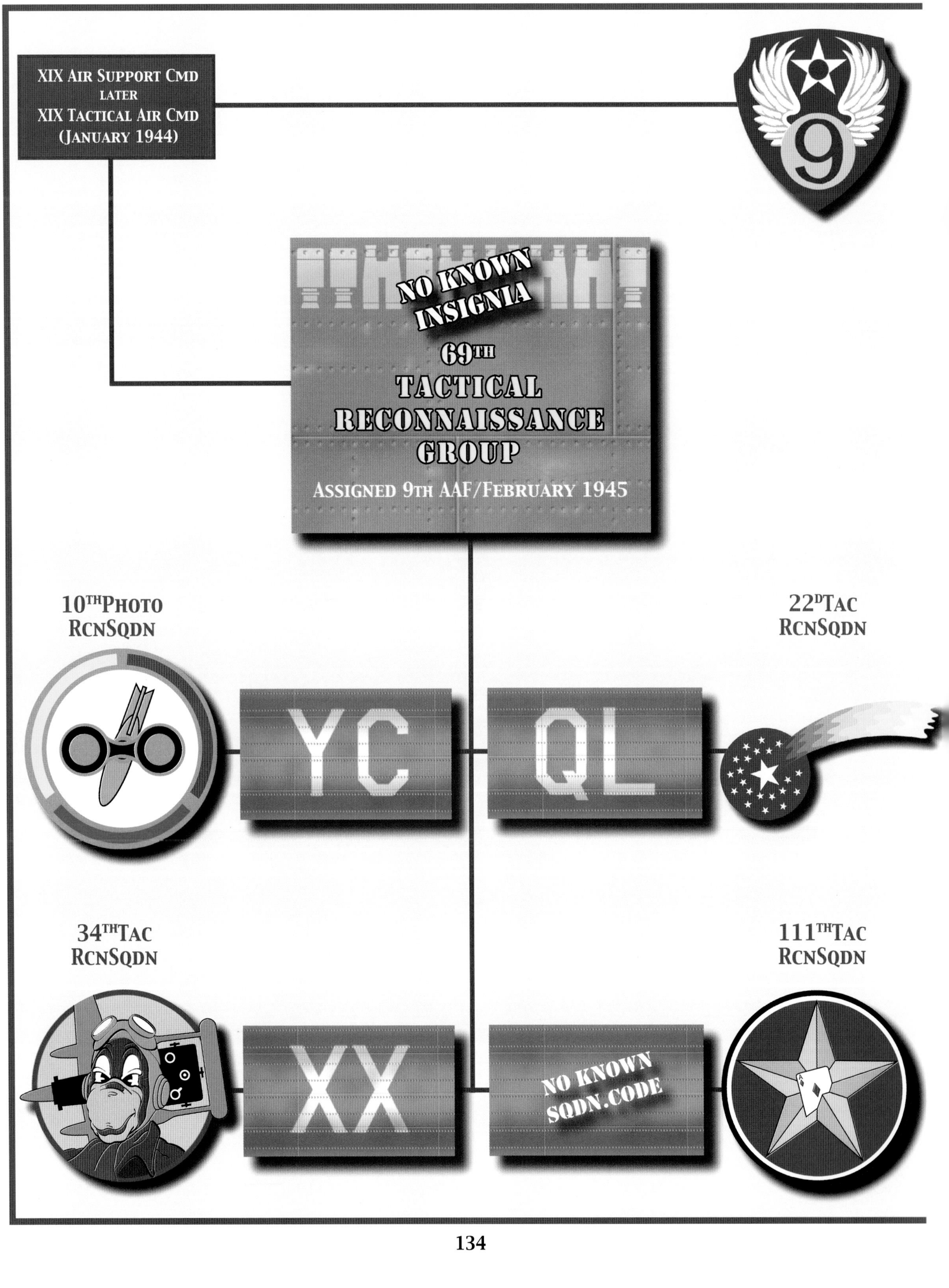

9

NO KNOWN
INSIGNIA

**69TH
TACTICAL
RECONNAISSANCE
GROUP**

ASSIGNED 9TH AAF/FEBRUARY 1945

**10TH PHOTO
RCNSQDN**

**22D TAC
RCNSQDN**

YC

QL

**34TH TAC
RCNSQDN**

**111TH TAC
RCNSQDN**

XX

NO KNOWN
SQDN. CODE

69th Tactical Reconnaissance Group:

Motto: unknown

Sobriquet: unknown

Campaign Streamers:

Antisubmarine, American Theater; Central Europe.

Unit Decorations:

Overseas Combat Commanders:

Col. John T. Shields, 21-Jan-45

Overseas Stations:

A-95 Nancy-Azelot, Lorraine; c.22-Mar-45

Y-39 Hagunau, Alsace; c.2-Apr-45

Combat Operations:

March thru May 1945

Insignia / Markings:

Group Insignia: unknown

Squadron Insignia:

10th PRS; pre-war design of 10thRcnSq, details unknown

22d TRS; WWI design officially approved 1-Mar-24

34th TRS; unofficial

111th TRS; officially approved 6-Jun-33

Squadron Codes:

10th PRS - **Y C** (from Mar-44) • *22d TRS* - **Q L** (from Mar-45)

34th TRS - **X X** (from Mar-45) • *111th TRS* - unknown

Squadron Colors: unknown.

Aircraft Markings:

There is currently no evidence relating to tactical markings for the 69th Tactical Reconnaissance Group.

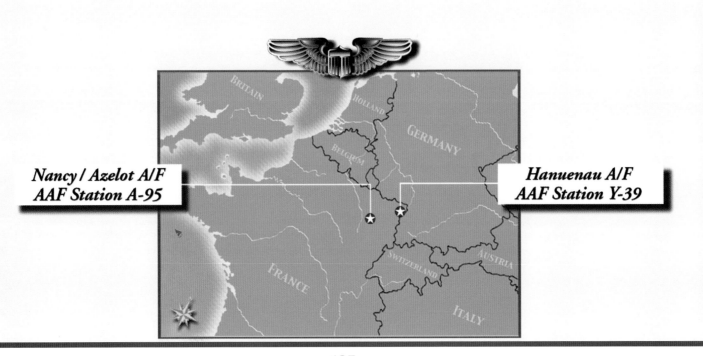

Nancy / Azelot A/F
AAF Station A-95

Hanuenau A/F
AAF Station Y-39

XIX Tactical Air Command (September 1944)

NO KNOWN INSIGNIA

363ᴅ TACTICAL RECONNAISSANCE GROUP

1.)Assigned 9th AAF/December 1943

33ᴅPhoto RcnSqdn

2W

160ᵀᴴPhoto RcnSqdn

A9

NO KNOWN INSIGNIA

161ˢᵀPhoto RcnSqdn

NO KNOWN INSIGNIA

B3

C3

162ᴅPhoto RcnSqdn

NO KNOWN INSIGNIA

363d Tactical Reconnaissance Group:

Motto: unknown

Sobriquet: unknown

Campaign Streamers:

Air Offensive, Europe; Normandy; Northern France; Rhineland; Ardennes-Alsace; Central Europe.

Unit Decorations:

Order of the Day, Belgian Army, 1-Oct-44, 18-Dec-44 thru 15-Jan-45, *Belgian Fourragere.*

Overseas Combat Commanders:

Col. John R Ulricson, 5-Jun-43 (363d FG)

Col. James B. Tipton, 7-May-44 (363d FG)

Col. James M. Smelley, c.1-Sep-44

Overseas Stations:

A-97 Sandweiler,District de Luxembourg; c.1-Oct-44

Y-10 Le Culot, East; Provience de Brabant Wallon; c.29-Oct-44

Y-55 Venlo, Provincie Limburg; Mar-45

Y-99 Gutersloh, Nordhein-Westphalia; c.15-Apr-45

R-37 Brunswick / Waggum, Sachsen-Anhalt; c.22-Apr-45

[1.] Refer to pages 32-33 for earlier duty stations when operating as the 363d Fighter Group)

Combat Operations:

[1.] 23-Feb-44 thru 3-Sep-44 (363d FG)
  12-Sep-44 thru 8-May-45 (363d TRG)

Insignia / Markings:

Group Insignia: unknown

Squadron Insignia:

33d PRS; officially approved 10-Oct-42

160th PRS; unknown

161st PRS; unknown

162d PRS; unknown

Squadron Codes:

33d PRS - **2 W** (Oct-44 thru May-45)

160th PRS - **A 9** (retained original 363d FS code)

161st PRS - **B 3** (retained original 363d FS code)

162d PRS - **C 3** (retained original 363d FS code)

Squadron Colors:

The 363d utilized individual squadron tactical colors when operating as a fighter unit (see pages 32-33) and there is some indication that this practice was carried over, perhaps semi-officially, subsequent to the units reorganization as a tactical reconnaissance group. These colors would have been consistent with those displayed on the aforementioned pages within the fighter section, however the additional color that may have been adopted for use by the 33d PRS is unknown at this time.

Aircraft Markings:

Squadron codes and call numbers were applied to camouflaged airframes with either white or yellow, black paint was utilized on natural metal surfaces.

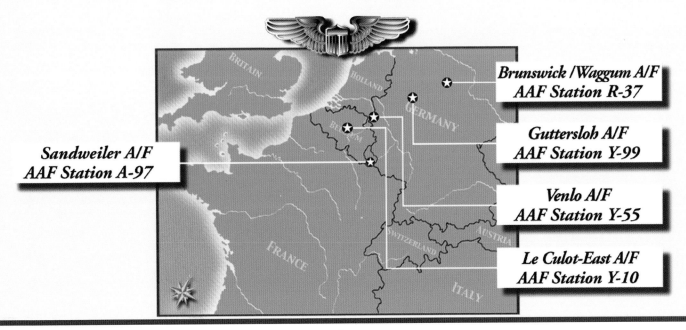

Brunswick /Waggum A/F
AAF Station R-37

Guttersloh A/F
AAF Station Y-99

Venlo A/F
AAF Station Y-55

Le Culot-East A/F
AAF Station Y-10

Sandweiler A/F
AAF Station A-97

9TH TACTICAL RECONNAISSANCE GROUP (PROV)

NO KNOWN INSIGNIA

31ˢᵀTᴀᴄRᴄɴSQᴅɴ

NO KNOWN SQDN.CODE

34ᵀᴴPʜᴏᴛᴏRᴄɴSQᴅɴ

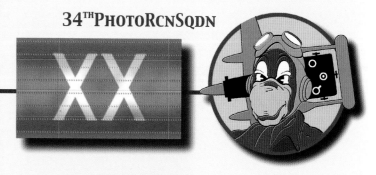

1.)111ᵀᴴTᴀᴄRᴄɴSQᴅɴ

NO KNOWN SQDN.CODE

162ᴰTᴀᴄRᴄɴSQᴅɴ

NO KNOWN INSIGNIA

9th Reconnaissance Group (P)

Motto: unknown
Sobriquet: unknown
Overseas Stations:
Attached squadrons were posted for brief periods at various ALG's located in France, Holland and Germany from October 1944 through V-E Day.
1.) The 111thTRS was on detached duty from the Eighth USAAF. Both the 34thPRS and 111thTRS were re-assigned to the 69thTRG in February 1945.
Combat Operations: October 1944 thru 8-May-45

Insignia / Markings

Group Insignia: unknown
Squadron Insignia:
31stTRS: unofficial, originally developed by Walter Lantz Productions for the original 31stObservation Squadron.
34thPRS: officially replaced 23-Apr-54
111thTRS: officially approved 6-Jun-33
162dTRS: unknown
Aircraft & Markings: This unit operated with a wide assortment within their inventory. Markings were consistent with reconnaissance units operating within the Ninth AAF.

F-4 / F-5 / F-6 / P-40 / UC-64 /A-20

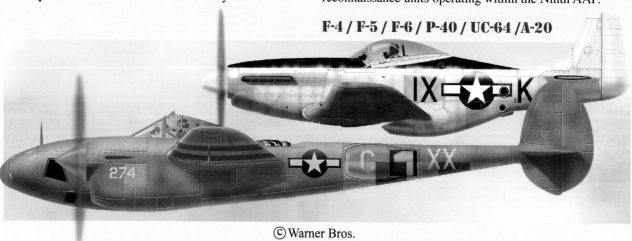

AIRCRAFT MARKINGS OF THE NINTH U.S.A.A.F.

USAAF CAMOUFLAGE & MARKINGS

Since the advent of aerial warfare early in the Twentieth Century it has been observed that one can determine how close any given country is to going to war simply by observing their military aircraft. While this might be an oversimplification, there is nevertheless considerable merit in such a statement.

As war clouds would begin to gather, once shiny military aircraft soon display an assortment of camouflage paint schemes. Although this adage may not necessarily apply today as much as it did in past conflicts, the fact is that in times of peace there simply were few logical reasons for the application of paint to the exterior of a metal finished aircraft. In addition to the obvious investment of materials and man-hours necessary for applying the paint, there is a decrease in fuel efficiency due to the additional weight and increased coefficient of friction or 'drag'. Slower and less maneuverable are characteristics one would not normally assign to any combat aircraft. It is thus easy to see why painting an aircrafts fuselage and wing surface area was something to be avoided unless so mandated by extreme necessity. That necessity arose, and still does arise in time of war, when opposing forces possess similar offensive capabilities i.e. the ability of both belligerents to attack each other's airfields. It was under these very conditions that air forces around the world learned very early on that it was not advisable to present an attacking force with shinny stationary aircraft as targets. Unfortunately the most expedient, versatile method of diminishing the profile of an airframe is with paint. Even the most elaborate of camouflage paint jobs however was no sure guarantee against detection by an attacking aircraft. The photo above depicts how an airframes contour outline can provide convienant aiming points for enemy pilots.

The position of the sun, cloud cover, angle of attack, all are factors that can assist or detract from the effectiveness of almost any attempt to obliterate the profile of a stationary aircraft. Many alternate methods of concealment from attacking forces were utilized to one extent or another during the course of World War II including camouflage netting, foliage canopies and dugout revetments. Effective concealment involved man-hours, materials and a significant reduction to a fighters combat readiness response time. Given the highly mobile nature of WWII, surface paint proved to be the only consistently viable solution to the problem of profile disruption for most belligerents during the majority of this conflict.

The ever increasing presence of USAAF combat aircraft over the skies of Great Britain and Western Europe brought about the need for an improved means of unit identification for both fighter and bombers alike. Eighth AAF aircraft soon displayed a typical two-color overall paint scheme, brightly colored (and highly visible) nose and tail patterns. These obviously offset any concealment advantages obtained with camouflage paint. By the time these high profile unit identification patterns began appearing however, Allied air power had seriously hampered the Luftwaffes ability to mount significant offensive sorties against Allied air bases in England. This was a transitional period in the European air war and the Luftwaffe would soon find itself incapable of virtually any offensive efforts whatsoever. Even so, the Allied air forces were not about to become complacent where the Luftwaffe was concerned. There was considerable discussion regarding the advisability of issuing of SHAEF Operation Memorandum Number 23 of 18Apr44/Distinctive Markings-Aircraft, better known to the world as D-Day or Invasion Stripes. Admittedly there was a definite need for an improved system of 'friendly Allied aircraft' identification marks during and immediately following the Normandy Invasion but a series of large alternating black & white stripes on fuselage, wings and empennage was hardly conducive to conceal-ment from an enemy aerial attack. There was considerable speculation at the time that the Luftwaffe might mount a massive retaliatory raid against Allied air bases in East Anglia and these tactical recognition markings would provide German pilots, gunners and bombardiers with a prime aiming point. Fortunately for the Allied cause the once mighty Luftwaffe found itself incapable of such a reprisal raid and the concern proved to be a moot point, at least until British and American fighter units were later redeployed to the European Continent. Once on European soil the new Allied air bases came within range of the Luftwaffe home defence fighters. The controversial D-Day Invasion Stripes quickly disappeared from upper surfaces of the redeployed Allied units for the reason previously stated.

As the war continued to progress in the Allies favor, the combat aircraft of the Ninth began to take on a new look. With the threat of potential Luftwaffe attacks on Allied airfields based in England virtually eliminated, Ninth USAAF fighters and bombers alike began to rapidly shed their existing camouflage paint schemes and were soon reaping the benefits inherent with a natural metal finished fuselage and wing surface areas. Some ground crews would soon go as far as polishing and waxing the entire fuselage and wings of the fighters in their charge. This was in an effort to maximize airflow over and around the airframe surface areas. The intent was to provide the men flying these aircraft with a little extra advantage, an advantage that in combat will often prove to be the deciding factor separating victory from defeat.

The following diagrams show the official WW II / USAAF specifications for placement of the national insignia and tail numbers as they applied to the fighter aircraft depicted. It is important to note that a combat aircraft might undergo any number of surface modifications, some of which would alter the original size and placement of the factory applications depicted on these diagrams. To those interested in a specific aircraft at a specific time in World War II, it is strongly suggested that a thorough study and comparative analysis of actual wartime photographs pertaining to that subject be conducted. Such research will often reveal variations in positioning, color and configuration of markings and paint schemes differing from those detailed in official USAAF or ANA directives.

The three photographs in the adjacent column are included to address a marking scheme developed and used by the U.S. Army Air Corps prior to the outbreak of hostilities in 1941. These were colored cowling bands and fuselage command stripes. These devises were used to denote group, squadron and flight leaders but were not much used overseas. A few combat units did utilize some form of command stripe during their wartime deployment, but this was not the norm within the Ninth AAF during this organizations wartime deployment.

LOCKHEED P-38 'LIGHTNING'

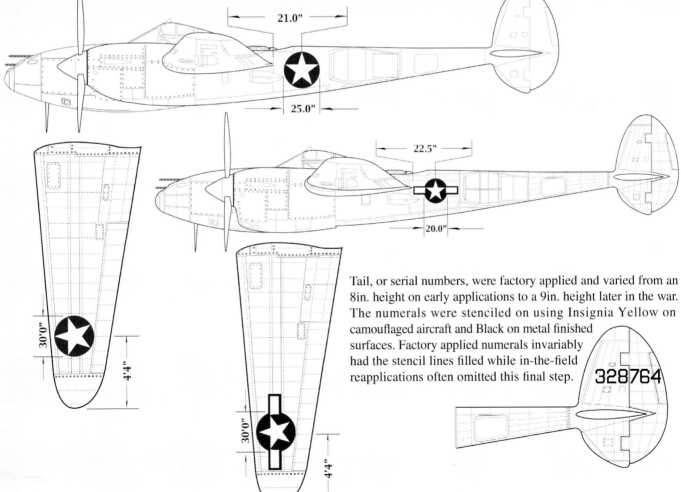

21.0"

25.0"

22.5"

20.0"

30'0"

4'4"

30'0"

4'4"

Tail, or serial numbers, were factory applied and varied from an 8in. height on early applications to a 9in. height later in the war. The numerals were stenciled on using Insignia Yellow on camouflaged aircraft and Black on metal finished surfaces. Factory applied numerals invariably had the stencil lines filled while in-the-field reapplications often omitted this final step.

328764

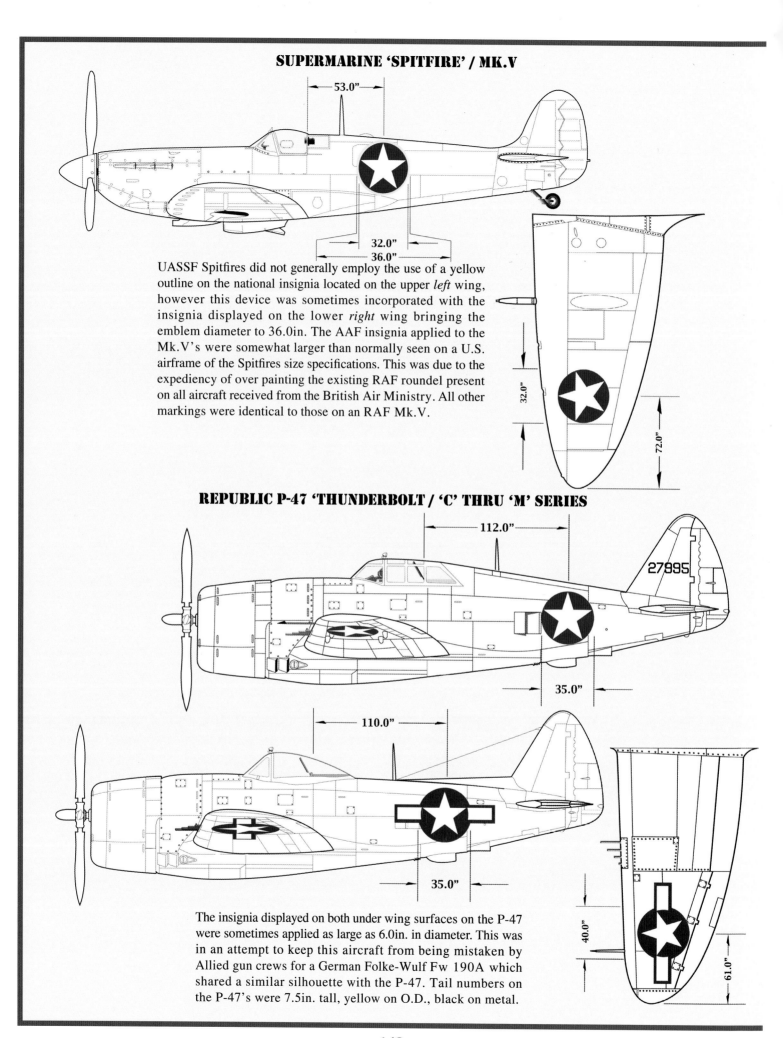

SUPERMARINE 'SPITFIRE' / MK.V

53.0"

32.0"
36.0"

UASSF Spitfires did not generally employ the use of a yellow outline on the national insignia located on the upper *left* wing, however this device was sometimes incorporated with the insignia displayed on the lower *right* wing bringing the emblem diameter to 36.0in. The AAF insignia applied to the Mk.V's were somewhat larger than normally seen on a U.S. airframe of the Spitfires size specifications. This was due to the expediency of over painting the existing RAF roundel present on all aircraft received from the British Air Ministry. All other markings were identical to those on an RAF Mk.V.

32.0"

72.0"

REPUBLIC P-47 'THUNDERBOLT / 'C' THRU 'M' SERIES

112.0"

27995

35.0"

110.0"

35.0"

40.0"

61.0"

The insignia displayed on both under wing surfaces on the P-47 were sometimes applied as large as 6.0in. in diameter. This was in an attempt to keep this aircraft from being mistaken by Allied gun crews for a German Folke-Wulf Fw 190A which shared a similar silhouette with the P-47. Tail numbers on the P-47's were 7.5in. tall, yellow on O.D., black on metal.

P-47 TAIL NUMBERS

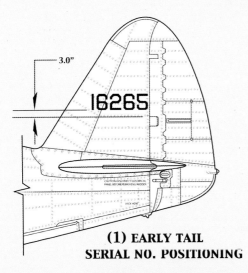

(1) EARLY TAIL SERIAL NO. POSITIONING

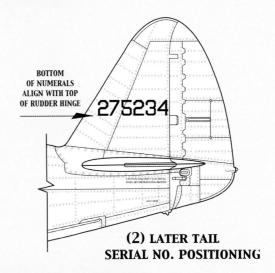

(2) LATER TAIL SERIAL NO. POSITIONING

Increased wartime production resulted in higher aircraft serial numbers, and the addition of another digit to these numbers required a wider space than that of the original positioning (example 1). This minor space-fitting problem was solved by simply dropping the base line down three inches to align with the bottom of the central rudder hinge (example 2). The original location would have required a smaller stencil; this move negated a reduction in numeral size. Tail numbers (also referred to as call-numbers) were factory applied with yellow on standard camouflaged surfaces and black on metal finishes.

P-47 ALLIED EXPEDITIONARY AIR FORCE MARKINGS (QIM'S)

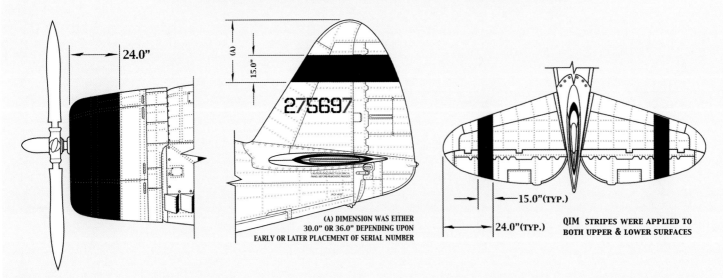

These markings, also known as U.K. Special Recognition, Friendly Fighter and Quick Identification Markings, were adopted early in the original deployment of the U.S. Eighth Army Air Force to Great Britain. Due to a number of friendly fire incidents it was determined that an additional form of recognition was needed to assist Allied gun crews in differentiating between German and American fighter aircraft. The Thunderbolt, as previously stated, was often mistaken for a German Focke-Wulf Fw-190A while the P-51's were just as likely to be erroneously identified as a Mersserschmitt Bf 109.

It was the hope of both the British Air Ministry and AAF / VIII Fighter Command that these markings would alleviate many, if not most, of these 'mistaken identity' problems. There is no way of determining exactly how effective these QIM markings proved to be in reducing friendly fire mishaps. However, even though gradually phased out as the war progressed, a substantial number of 8th and 9th AAF fighter units continued to display these markings until the cession of hostilities. The standard application for the QIM's on these fighters was white on camouflaged surfaces and black on natural metal finishes.

NORTH AMERICAN P-51 'MUSTANG'

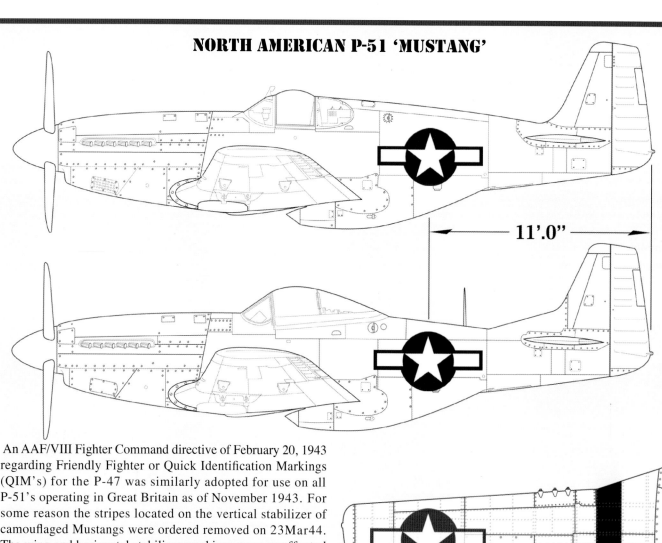

11'.0"

An AAF/VIII Fighter Command directive of February 20, 1943 regarding Friendly Fighter or Quick Identification Markings (QIM's) for the P-47 was similarly adopted for use on all P-51's operating in Great Britain as of November 1943. For some reason the stripes located on the vertical stabilizer of camouflaged Mustangs were ordered removed on 23Mar44. The wing and horizontal stabilizer markings were unaffected by this directive for both painted and unpainted P-51 surfaces.

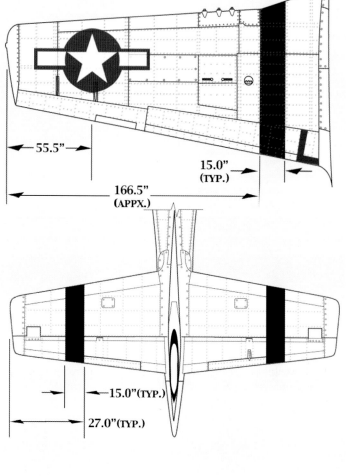

55.5"

15.0"
(TYP.)

166.5"
(APPX.)

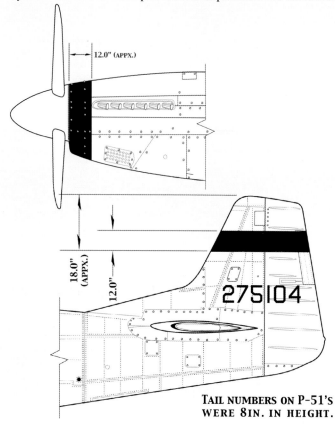

12.0" (APPX.)

18.0"
(APPX.)

12.0"

275104

15.0"(TYP.)

27.0"(TYP.)

TAIL NUMBERS ON P-51'S WERE 8IN. IN HEIGHT.

ALLIED INVASION (D-DAY) STRIPES

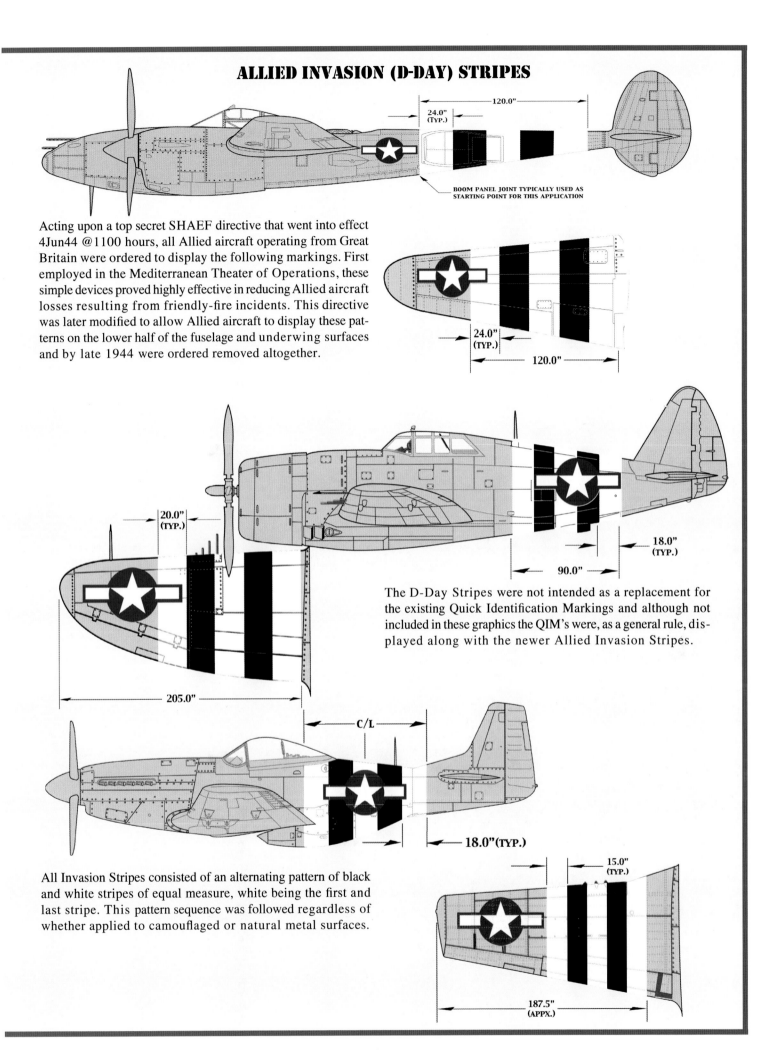

120.0"

24.0"
(TYP.)

**BOOM PANEL JOINT TYPICALLY USED AS
STARTING POINT FOR THIS APPLICATION**

Acting upon a top secret SHAEF directive that went into effect 4Jun44 @1100 hours, all Allied aircraft operating from Great Britain were ordered to display the following markings. First employed in the Mediterranean Theater of Operations, these simple devices proved highly effective in reducing Allied aircraft losses resulting from friendly-fire incidents. This directive was later modified to allow Allied aircraft to display these patterns on the lower half of the fuselage and underwing surfaces and by late 1944 were ordered removed altogether.

24.0"
(TYP.)

120.0"

20.0"
(TYP.)

18.0"
(TYP.)

90.0"

The D-Day Stripes were not intended as a replacement for the existing Quick Identification Markings and although not included in these graphics the QIM's were, as a general rule, displayed along with the newer Allied Invasion Stripes.

205.0"

C/L

18.0"(TYP.)

15.0"
(TYP.)

All Invasion Stripes consisted of an alternating pattern of black and white stripes of equal measure, white being the first and last stripe. This pattern sequence was followed regardless of whether applied to camouflaged or natural metal surfaces.

187.5"
(APPX.)

145

A Wolf In Wolfs Clothing

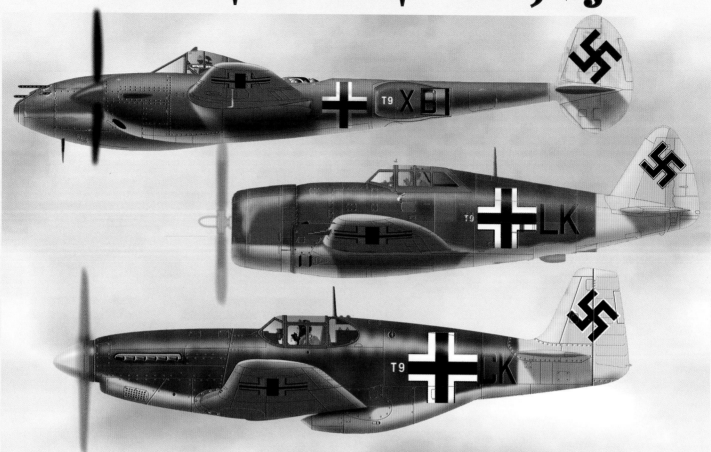

The overriding importance of tactical aircraft markings is that of serving as an organizational tool for any given airforce at virtually all levels. From the initial form-up at a missions beginning to its conclusion, tactical markings serve as a visual aid to pilots, air and ground crew alike. The precision daylight bombing campaign carried out against Germany during World War II would not have been possible without the bombers ability to maintain tight 'combat box' flight formations. Tactical markings made this possible.

The Invasion and Allied Recognition Stripes (QIM's) utilized by both the Eighth and Ninth U.S. Army Air Forces operating from Great Britain were developed for the purpose of reducing the incidence of 'friendly fire' mishaps, and in this they were highly effective. The importance of national insignia on military aircraft however has been the subject of debate for many years.

Some form of national identity is of course necessary if for no other reason then compliance with numerous international treaties. The effectiveness of these symbols from a ground observers perspective was, and is today, a questionable issue.

A major contributing factor to this ongoing debate are represented on this page. These illustrations represent captured American combat aircraft that were pressed into service by the Luftwaffe. These are but a small sampling however of the total number of such aircraft, from many different nations, that were 'drafted' to service against their former owners. These aircraft came in many shapes and sizes, from single engine liaison types to four engine bombers. Some of these were employed by the Luftwaffe solely for pilot training purposes while others, like those depicted above, were utilized for covert reconnaissance purposes.

There are documented instances where captured Allied aircraft were used as decoys by Axis forces. The purpose of these decoys was to lead an unsuspecting Allied pilot into an ambush where he would run the risk of being downed by either by waiting enemy fighters or anti-aircraft batteries.

In order to keep their airmen from being treated as spies in the event they went down behind Allied lines, standard military markings were applied to these aircraft by the Luftwaffe. What is truly interesting is the fact that in spite of these markings these aircraft were known to have not only entered Allied airspace on numerous occasions, but completed their assigned missions with impunity. Despite the presence of both the Balkenkreuz and Swastika on their airframes, these aircraft conducted their missions virtually undetected by Allied ground observers.

These examples and others like them added support to the argument against the necessity for the conspicuous national insignia, and is perhaps one of the underlying reasons many of today's combat aircraft serving the United States and other nations carry national markings of a subdued nature.

U.S.A.A.F. COLORS

Due the inconsistencies inherent with offset printing it would be an exercise in abject futility to attempt to accurately represent the actual colors developed for, and used by the AAF in World War II. The following information may be useful however as a reference for further examination into this complex subject.

This chart represents a bulletin issued by the ANA on 24-Mar-44 (No. 157a) and was intended as a tool to assist those units deployed overseas, especially the European Theater, with a possible means of complying with current AAF color regs when ready access to proper inventory might not be possible.

ARMY/NAVY AERONAUTICAL	[1]AAF EQUIVALENT	BUREAU OF AERONAUTICS	[2]RAF EQUIVALENT
601 Insignia White	Insignia White 46	Insignia White	White
602 Light Gray		Light Gray	
603 Sea Gray	Neutral Gray 43		Extra Dark Sea Gray
			Dark Sea Gray & Ocean Gray
604 Black	Black 44	Black	Black
605 Insignia Blue	Insignia Blue 47	Insignia Blue	Dull Blue
606 Semi-Gloss Sea Blue		Semi-Gloss Sea Blue	
607 Non-Specular Blue		Non-Specular Sea Blue, Dark Blue & Blue Gray	
608 Intermediate Blue		Intermediate Blue	
609 Azure Blue		Light Blue	Azure Blue & Deep Sky
610 Sky			Sky
611 Interior Green	[3]	[3]	[3]
612 Medium Green	Medium Green 42	Light Green	
613 Olive Drab	Dark Olive Drab 41		Dark Slate Gray & Dark Green
614 Orange Yellow	Identification Yellow 48	Orange Yellow	Yellow
615 Middlestone			Middlestone
616 Sand	Sand 49		
617 Dark Earth			Dark Earth
618 Dull Red	Insignia Red 45	Insignia Red	Red
619 Bright Red[4]		Insignia Red[4]	

[1] AAF Bulletin No. 41

[2] Ministry of Aircraft Production Color Standards

[3] 611 Interior Green is intended for standardization of the product obtained by tinting zinc chromate primer (Spec.AN-TT-P-656) for shop coat or interior finish purposes.

[4] 619 Bright Red, formerly called Insignia Red is intended for use as specified by the Bereau of Aeronautics.

ALLIED 'FRIENDLY FORCES' RECOGNITION FLASH

This device was first adopted by Allied forces serving early in the war in the Mediterranean Theatre of Operations. This symbol was applied to both sides of an aircrafts vertical stabilizer in order to reduce the incidence of 'friendly fire'. Many aircraft belonging to the Ninth AAF continued to display this device after this organizations transfer to the United Kingdom. Although not authorized in the UK it was considered something of a status symbol by the air crews of the Ninth, and thus its continued use was, for the most part, overlooked by many AAF officials until these images either wore-off, were re-painted or the aircraft was lost.

THE 'GOLDFISH' AWARD

Although neither a tactical marking nor a unit insignia, this image is included here to help preserve its existence, use and historical significance. This 'award' originated with the RAF and was 'conferred' upon any pilot or air crew member who had the dubious distinction, and equally dubious experience, of spending time floating in the ocean after being forced to ditch over open water. This device was quickly adopted by U.S. air crews upon their deployment to the ETO and were the source of pride among those select few who had earned the right to wear one. The original 'awards' were hand embroidered cloth patches which, in order to comply with uniform regulations, were generally sewn onto the underside of a lapel. Multiple 'dunking's as they were known, were denoted by the addition of 'hash marks'. These duplicate waves were sewn on below the original 'award'.

UNITED STATES ARMY AIR FORCE
AIRFIELDS & ADVANCE LANDING GROUNDS/ETO

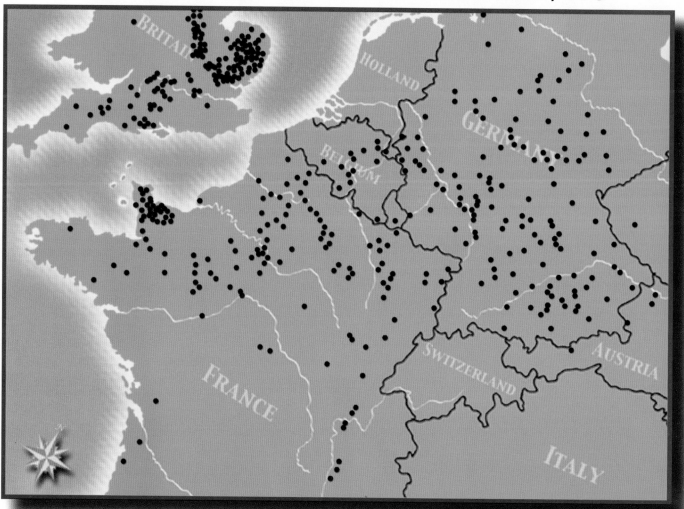

Often overlooked in the study of the air war in Europe during World War II is the logistical side of this story. During this conflict, it has been estimated that an average of ten to twelve noncombatant personnel were required to support each man sent directly into harms way. This ratio may in fact have been even slightly higher where the USAAF is concerned due to the nature of the technology involved at that time.

The accompanying map on this page will help in presenting a portion of the overall logistics involved in waging an effective offensive air campaign in the mid-Twentieth Century.

A typical USAAF medium bomb group at full strength during WWII was made up of four squadrons totalling 1,442 men and 64 aircraft. A twin engine fighter group consisted of three squadrons comprised of 1,037 personnel with 75 aircraft, while a single engine fighter group had the same number of aircraft with a compliment of 950. The amount of tools, equipment, materials, spare parts and other supplies necessary for any one of these groups to keep their aircraft operational would in itself fill volumes.

Each dot shown on the map above represents the location, at one time or another, of an Eighth or Ninth AAF combat group between mid 1942 to 8-May-45. It is important here to point out that this does in no way represent the full picture of the

total deployment of AAF units in this theatre during the war. Numerous bases in the north of England, Scotland and Ireland do not show up on this particular map. Also not indicated are the Royal Air Forces bases which were shared at various times with several AAF units, these being primarily troop transport groups or Liaison Squadrons.

The logistics involved in relocating any one of these units is staggering, and yet they all had their beginnings in the United States, relocated to Great Britain, and many still went on to the European Continent proper. And of course these units were expected to maintain their normal combat operations while in transit. Ground crews worked feverishly after every move in order to keep the aircraft in their charge flying, while the Engineers kept expanding and improving the landing strips. If a group was assigned to an ALG with no existing structures, ground and air echelon alike slept in tents. This leap-frog scenario would continue as the Allied air elements followed the continuing advances of the ground forces into Germany itself.

It should be reemphasized here that these dots represent *only* airfields of the Eighth and Ninth Air Forces. When one factors in the deployment of the RAF and other Allied air units, and than considers all of the Allied ground elements, the overall complexity of this conflict is staggering.

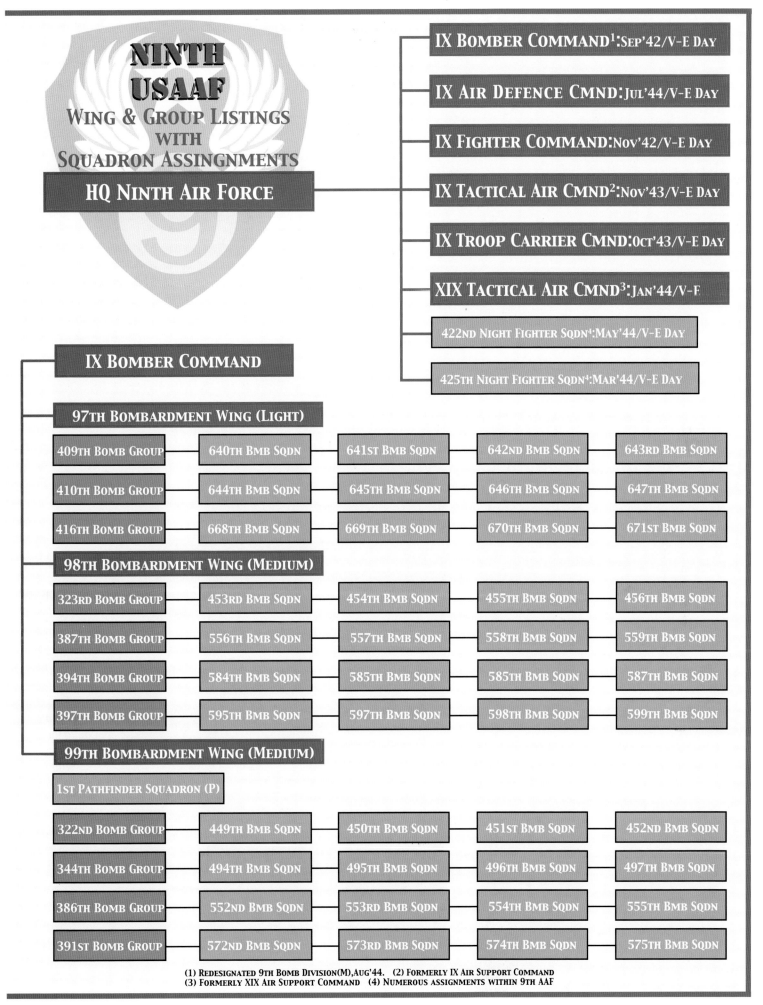

NINTH USAAF
WING & GROUP LISTINGS WITH SQUADRON ASSINGNMENTS

HQ NINTH AIR FORCE

- IX BOMBER COMMAND[1]: SEP'42/V-E DAY
- IX AIR DEFENCE CMND: JUL'44/V-E DAY
- IX FIGHTER COMMAND: NOV'42/V-E DAY
- IX TACTICAL AIR CMND[2]: NOV'43/V-E DAY
- IX TROOP CARRIER CMND: OCT'43/V-E DAY
- XIX TACTICAL AIR CMND[3]: JAN'44/V-E
- 422ND NIGHT FIGHTER SQDN[4]: MAY'44/V-E DAY
- 425TH NIGHT FIGHTER SQDN[4]: MAR'44/V-E DAY

IX BOMBER COMMAND

97TH BOMBARDMENT WING (LIGHT)

409TH BOMB GROUP	640TH BMB SQDN	641ST BMB SQDN	642ND BMB SQDN	643RD BMB SQDN
410TH BOMB GROUP	644TH BMB SQDN	645TH BMB SQDN	646TH BMB SQDN	647TH BMB SQDN
416TH BOMB GROUP	668TH BMB SQDN	669TH BMB SQDN	670TH BMB SQDN	671ST BMB SQDN

98TH BOMBARDMENT WING (MEDIUM)

323RD BOMB GROUP	453RD BMB SQDN	454TH BMB SQDN	455TH BMB SQDN	456TH BMB SQDN
387TH BOMB GROUP	556TH BMB SQDN	557TH BMB SQDN	558TH BMB SQDN	559TH BMB SQDN
394TH BOMB GROUP	584TH BMB SQDN	585TH BMB SQDN	585TH BMB SQDN	587TH BMB SQDN
397TH BOMB GROUP	595TH BMB SQDN	597TH BMB SQDN	598TH BMB SQDN	599TH BMB SQDN

99TH BOMBARDMENT WING (MEDIUM)

1ST PATHFINDER SQUADRON (P)

322ND BOMB GROUP	449TH BMB SQDN	450TH BMB SQDN	451ST BMB SQDN	452ND BMB SQDN
344TH BOMB GROUP	494TH BMB SQDN	495TH BMB SQDN	496TH BMB SQDN	497TH BMB SQDN
386TH BOMB GROUP	552ND BMB SQDN	553RD BMB SQDN	554TH BMB SQDN	555TH BMB SQDN
391ST BOMB GROUP	572ND BMB SQDN	573RD BMB SQDN	574TH BMB SQDN	575TH BMB SQDN

(1) REDESIGNATED 9TH BOMB DIVISION(M),AUG'44. (2) FORMERLY IX AIR SUPPORT COMMAND
(3) FORMERLY XIX AIR SUPPORT COMMAND (4) NUMEROUS ASSIGNMENTS WITHIN 9TH AAF

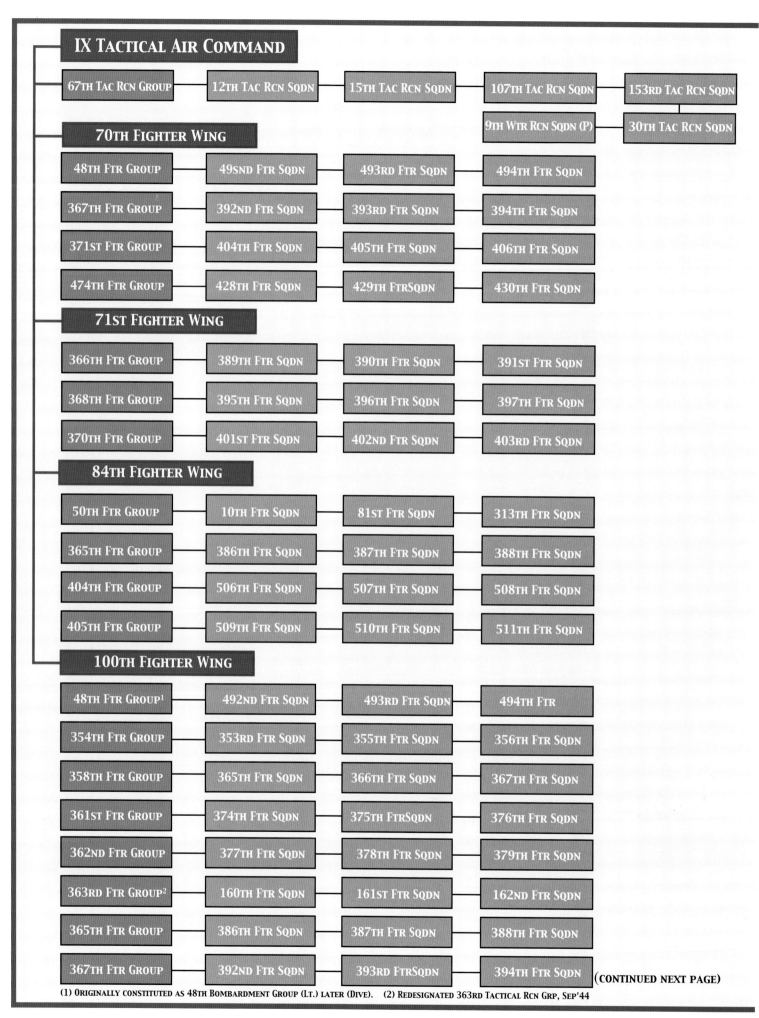

IX Tactical Air Command

67th Tac Rcn Group	12th Tac Rcn Sqdn	15th Tac Rcn Sqdn	107th Tac Rcn Sqdn	153rd Tac Rcn Sqdn
			9th Wtr Rcn Sqdn (P)	30th Tac Rcn Sqdn

70th Fighter Wing

48th Ftr Group	49snd Ftr Sqdn	493rd Ftr Sqdn	494th Ftr Sqdn
367th Ftr Group	392nd Ftr Sqdn	393rd Ftr Sqdn	394th Ftr Sqdn
371st Ftr Group	404th Ftr Sqdn	405th Ftr Sqdn	406th Ftr Sqdn
474th Ftr Group	428th Ftr Sqdn	429th FtrSqdn	430th Ftr Sqdn

71st Fighter Wing

366th Ftr Group	389th Ftr Sqdn	390th Ftr Sqdn	391st Ftr Sqdn
368th Ftr Group	395th Ftr Sqdn	396th Ftr Sqdn	397th Ftr Sqdn
370th Ftr Group	401st Ftr Sqdn	402nd Ftr Sqdn	403rd Ftr Sqdn

84th Fighter Wing

50th Ftr Group	10th Ftr Sqdn	81st Ftr Sqdn	313th Ftr Sqdn
365th Ftr Group	386th Ftr Sqdn	387th Ftr Sqdn	388th Ftr Sqdn
404th Ftr Group	506th Ftr Sqdn	507th Ftr Sqdn	508th Ftr Sqdn
405th Ftr Group	509th Ftr Sqdn	510th Ftr Sqdn	511th Ftr Sqdn

100th Fighter Wing

48th Ftr Group[1]	492nd Ftr Sqdn	493rd Ftr Sqdn	494th Ftr
354th Ftr Group	353rd Ftr Sqdn	355th Ftr Sqdn	356th Ftr Sqdn
358th Ftr Group	365th Ftr Sqdn	366th Ftr Sqdn	367th Ftr Sqdn
361st Ftr Group	374th Ftr Sqdn	375th FtrSqdn	376th Ftr Sqdn
362nd Ftr Group	377th Ftr Sqdn	378th Ftr Sqdn	379th Ftr Sqdn
363rd Ftr Group[2]	160th Ftr Sqdn	161st Ftr Sqdn	162nd Ftr Sqdn
365th Ftr Group	386th Ftr Sqdn	387th Ftr Sqdn	388th Ftr Sqdn
367th Ftr Group	392nd Ftr Sqdn	393rd FtrSqdn	394th Ftr Sqdn

(CONTINUED NEXT PAGE)

(1) Originally constituted as 48th Bombardment Group (Lt.) later (Dive). (2) Redesignated 363rd Tactical Rcn Grp, Sep'44

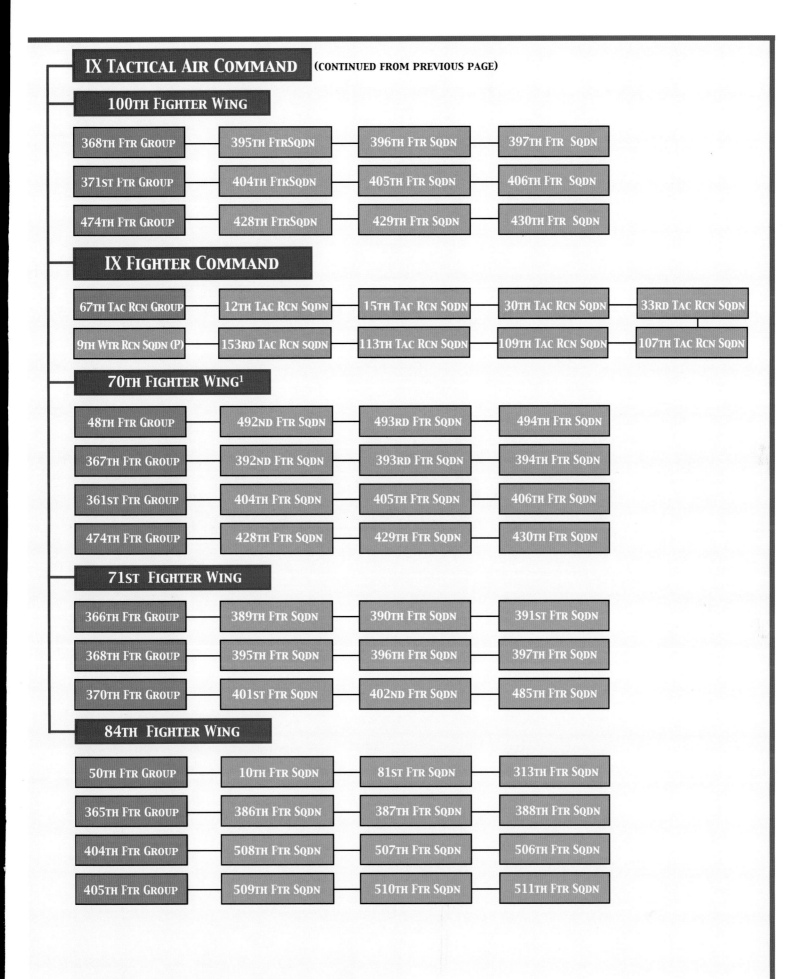

IX TACTICAL AIR COMMAND (CONTINUED FROM PREVIOUS PAGE)

100TH FIGHTER WING

368TH FTR GROUP	395TH FTRSQDN	396TH FTR SQDN	397TH FTR SQDN
371ST FTR GROUP	404TH FTRSQDN	405TH FTR SQDN	406TH FTR SQDN
474TH FTR GROUP	428TH FTRSQDN	429TH FTR SQDN	430TH FTR SQDN

IX FIGHTER COMMAND

| 67TH TAC RCN GROUP | 12TH TAC RCN SQDN | 15TH TAC RCN SQDN | 30TH TAC RCN SQDN | 33RD TAC RCN SQDN |
| 9TH WTR RCN SQDN (P) | 153RD TAC RCN SQDN | 113TH TAC RCN SQDN | 109TH TAC RCN SQDN | 107TH TAC RCN SQDN |

70TH FIGHTER WING[1]

48TH FTR GROUP	492ND FTR SQDN	493RD FTR SQDN	494TH FTR SQDN
367TH FTR GROUP	392ND FTR SQDN	393RD FTR SQDN	394TH FTR SQDN
361ST FTR GROUP	404TH FTR SQDN	405TH FTR SQDN	406TH FTR SQDN
474TH FTR GROUP	428TH FTR SQDN	429TH FTR SQDN	430TH FTR SQDN

71ST FIGHTER WING

366TH FTR GROUP	389TH FTR SQDN	390TH FTR SQDN	391ST FTR SQDN
368TH FTR GROUP	395TH FTR SQDN	396TH FTR SQDN	397TH FTR SQDN
370TH FTR GROUP	401ST FTR SQDN	402ND FTR SQDN	485TH FTR SQDN

84TH FIGHTER WING

50TH FTR GROUP	10TH FTR SQDN	81ST FTR SQDN	313TH FTR SQDN
365TH FTR GROUP	386TH FTR SQDN	387TH FTR SQDN	388TH FTR SQDN
404TH FTR GROUP	508TH FTR SQDN	507TH FTR SQDN	506TH FTR SQDN
405TH FTR GROUP	509TH FTR SQDN	510TH FTR SQDN	511TH FTR SQDN

(1) NUMEROUS FTRGRPS WERE ATTACHED OR ASSIGNED TO THE 70TH FTRWNG DURING THE WAR. THE GROUPS LISTED HEREIN WERE ASSIGNED TO THE 70THFW AS OF D-DAY, JUNE 6TH 1944.

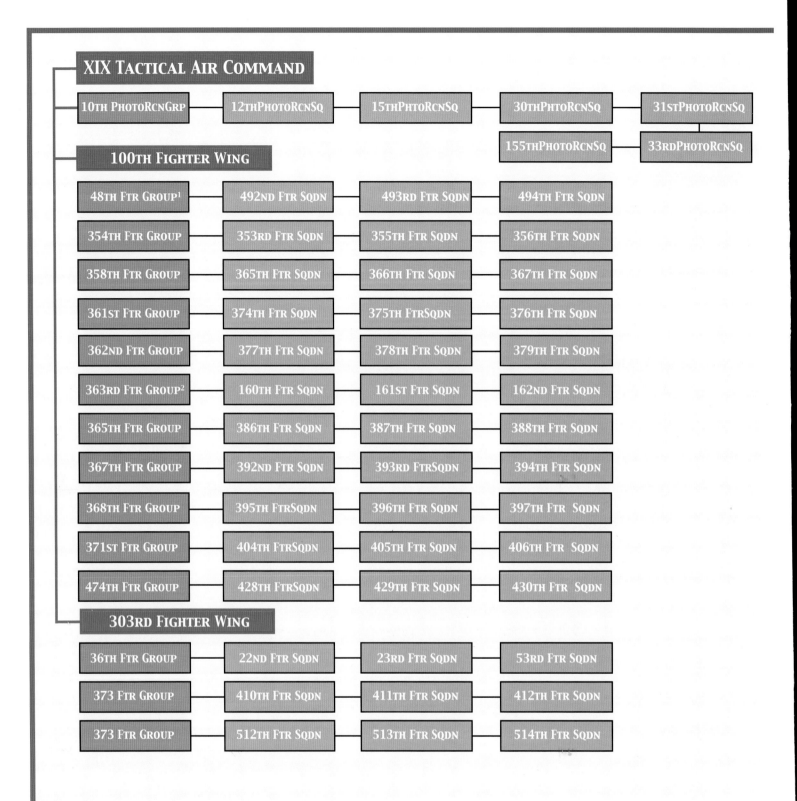

XIX TACTICAL AIR COMMAND

10TH PHOTORCNGRP	12THPHOTORCNSQ	15THPHTORCNSQ	30THPHTORCNSQ	31STPHOTORCNSQ
			155THPHOTORCNSQ	33RDPHOTORCNSQ

100TH FIGHTER WING

48TH FTR GROUP[1]	492ND FTR SQDN	493RD FTR SQDN	494TH FTR SQDN
354TH FTR GROUP	353RD FTR SQDN	355TH FTR SQDN	356TH FTR SQDN
358TH FTR GROUP	365TH FTR SQDN	366TH FTR SQDN	367TH FTR SQDN
361ST FTR GROUP	374TH FTR SQDN	375TH FTRSQDN	376TH FTR SQDN
362ND FTR GROUP	377TH FTR SQDN	378TH FTR SQDN	379TH FTR SQDN
363RD FTR GROUP[2]	160TH FTR SQDN	161ST FTR SQDN	162ND FTR SQDN
365TH FTR GROUP	386TH FTR SQDN	387TH FTR SQDN	388TH FTR SQDN
367TH FTR GROUP	392ND FTR SQDN	393RD FTRSQDN	394TH FTR SQDN
368TH FTR GROUP	395TH FTRSQDN	396TH FTR SQDN	397TH FTR SQDN
371ST FTR GROUP	404TH FTRSQDN	405TH FTR SQDN	406TH FTR SQDN
474TH FTR GROUP	428TH FTRSQDN	429TH FTR SQDN	430TH FTR SQDN

303RD FIGHTER WING

36TH FTR GROUP	22ND FTR SQDN	23RD FTR SQDN	53RD FTR SQDN
373 FTR GROUP	410TH FTR SQDN	411TH FTR SQDN	412TH FTR SQDN
373 FTR GROUP	512TH FTR SQDN	513TH FTR SQDN	514TH FTR SQDN

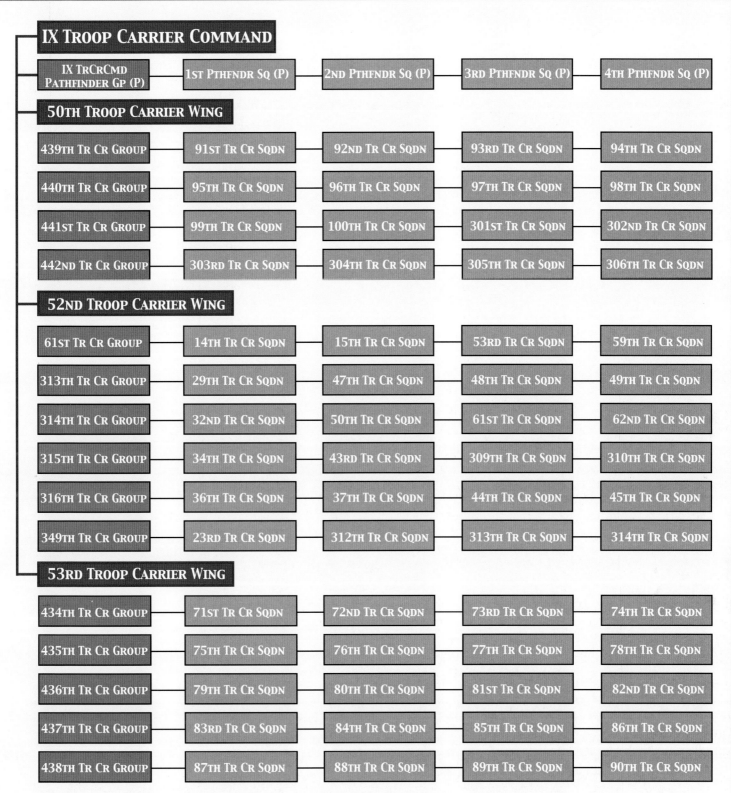

IX Troop Carrier Command

IX TrCrCmd Pathfinder Gp (P)	1st Pthfndr Sq (P)	2nd Pthfndr Sq (P)	3rd Pthfndr Sq (P)	4th Pthfndr Sq (P)

50th Troop Carrier Wing

439th Tr Cr Group	91st Tr Cr Sqdn	92nd Tr Cr Sqdn	93rd Tr Cr Sqdn	94th Tr Cr Sqdn
440th Tr Cr Group	95th Tr Cr Sqdn	96th Tr Cr Sqdn	97th Tr Cr Sqdn	98th Tr Cr Sqdn
441st Tr Cr Group	99th Tr Cr Sqdn	100th Tr Cr Sqdn	301st Tr Cr Sqdn	302nd Tr Cr Sqdn
442nd Tr Cr Group	303rd Tr Cr Sqdn	304th Tr Cr Sqdn	305th Tr Cr Sqdn	306th Tr Cr Sqdn

52nd Troop Carrier Wing

61st Tr Cr Group	14th Tr Cr Sqdn	15th Tr Cr Sqdn	53rd Tr Cr Sqdn	59th Tr Cr Sqdn
313th Tr Cr Group	29th Tr Cr Sqdn	47th Tr Cr Sqdn	48th Tr Cr Sqdn	49th Tr Cr Sqdn
314th Tr Cr Group	32nd Tr Cr Sqdn	50th Tr Cr Sqdn	61st Tr Cr Sqdn	62nd Tr Cr Sqdn
315th Tr Cr Group	34th Tr Cr Sqdn	43rd Tr Cr Sqdn	309th Tr Cr Sqdn	310th Tr Cr Sqdn
316th Tr Cr Group	36th Tr Cr Sqdn	37th Tr Cr Sqdn	44th Tr Cr Sqdn	45th Tr Cr Sqdn
349th Tr Cr Group	23rd Tr Cr Sqdn	312th Tr Cr Sqdn	313th Tr Cr Sqdn	314th Tr Cr Sqdn

53rd Troop Carrier Wing

434th Tr Cr Group	71st Tr Cr Sqdn	72nd Tr Cr Sqdn	73rd Tr Cr Sqdn	74th Tr Cr Sqdn
435th Tr Cr Group	75th Tr Cr Sqdn	76th Tr Cr Sqdn	77th Tr Cr Sqdn	78th Tr Cr Sqdn
436th Tr Cr Group	79th Tr Cr Sqdn	80th Tr Cr Sqdn	81st Tr Cr Sqdn	82nd Tr Cr Sqdn
437th Tr Cr Group	83rd Tr Cr Sqdn	84th Tr Cr Sqdn	85th Tr Cr Sqdn	86th Tr Cr Sqdn
438th Tr Cr Group	87th Tr Cr Sqdn	88th Tr Cr Sqdn	89th Tr Cr Sqdn	90th Tr Cr Sqdn

Note on assignment lists: duplicate or multiple listings reflect reorganizing and/or reassignment of numerous units within the Ninth Air Force structure while this organization was deployed in the ETO during the war.

IX Fighter Command was reorganized under the Tactical Air Command designation.

CLOSING ARGUMENT

From time to time the question invariably arises as to why one would dedicate so much time and effort to a subject so obscure as unit insignia and tactical markings. The source of this type of query are generally from the 'Big Picture' advocates, those individuals who prefer to view history from the perspective of cause and affect, and while there is nothing wrong with this approach to the study of history, it is often the smaller elements comprising the whole that afford us insight into the human aspect of any given point in historical study.

The organizational, or practical side of tactical markings has already been addressed earlier in this text, what remains is the subject of wartime unit insignia. Like the study of USAAF aircraft nose art during World War II, much of the individual character of the men actually tasked with carrying out the day to day operations of the war can be gleaned through those images they created. Several things become obvious when these images are viewed as a whole, the first of which was, even lacking supportive information, that the men of the USAAF at this moment in history were little more than boys at the time, perhaps a more apt description would be young men.

As such they were preoccupied with the opposite sex, a fact reflected primarily through their nose art, but what we learn through the study of their unit insignia tells even more about these young men. It tells us that taken as a whole, in addition to their youth, they were somewhat unsophisticated by European standards but possessed of a keen sense of humor which, given the dire circumstances to which they were subjected, equated directly with confidence, and confidence in war is often a major determining factor between ultimate victory or defeat.

It must be pointed out however that interest in the subject of unit insignia was not confined to the respective units themselves, in fact the full reality concerning these images was quite the opposite during the war years. Those on the Home Front expressed a great deal of interest in these symbols as will be demonstrated within the following pages.

Virtually anyone could design and submit a concept for a squadron and even group insignia. In order to become officially authorized for display by a unit a design concept had to be submitted to the U.S. Army's Heraldric Department where it would subsequently be scrutinized by a review board. The regulations governing Army Air Force insignia at the time stated that a submission, "may be of caricature design, not necessarily classic or heraldic, but must be in good taste and of composition to enable painting on airplanes by simple stencil." If a design met these basic guidelines it was

forwarded up the line for the next phase. There were several additional prerequisites that a proposed insignia had to meet. Each design had to be sufficiently concise as to be distinguishable at a maximum distance of 150 yards. The gereral submission criteria further prohibited the following specific data from

inclusion within a design format: numerals of any kind; the flag or coat of arms of the United States; the letters 'U.S.'; geographical maps; military decorations; motto's or coat of arms of any state, country or United States service branch.

Many units elected to request the services of professionals within the civilian sector to assist in the development of their respective insignia designs. Those within this art profession who gladly contributed their services included such notable names as Al Capp, Walter Lantz, Milt Canniff and V.T. Hamlin. By far the largest contributor to this design pool however was

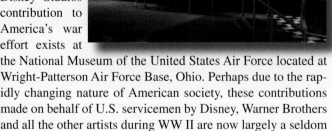

Disney Studios. Walt Disney designed his first unit insignia for the U.S. Naval Reserve Squadron in 1933 and by the end of World War II Disney had created over 1,200 pro-bono designs for virtually every branch of government service. Requests for these designs reached such a large scale that a special five man department was created to meet this overwelming demand.

By far however the majority of this effort seems to have gone into designing insignia for the U.S. Army Air Force and this effort was not to be totally forgotten. A special exhibit commemorating Disney Studios contribution to America's war effort exists at the National Museum of the United States Air Force located at Wright-Patterson Air Force Base, Ohio. Perhaps due to the rapidly changing nature of American society, these contributions made on behalf of U.S. servicemen by Disney, Warner Brothers and all the other artists during WW II are now largely a seldom acknowledged footnote in the history of this conflict.

Interest in the subject of unit, or combat insignia as it was popularly known, was by no means confined to active duty personnel. Pearl Harbor had galvanized the country and the Home Front stood unified in the war effort and expressed great interest in a wide variety of subjects connected with their servicemen overseas, unit insignia among them. The interest in combat insignia was so keen in fact that entire marketing /advertising campaigns and promotional programs were developed utilizing these insignia as the central theme.

Not Just For Kids! Lest those unfamiliar with this period in American history go away with the wrong idea, it wasn't only youngsters who were attracted to the 'cartoon' images of combat insignia. The popularity of these designs among adults is perhaps best illustrated by a lengthy ad campaign launched in 1943 by the Oldsmobile Division of General Motors. This series of full page, full color ads featured a different unit insignia each month for almost two years, and while the series depicted insignia of all service branches, for some reason those of the Army Air Force dominated the campaign. Although General Motors was neither manufacturing civilian transportation during the war years, like all other automobile manufactures in the United States, this campaign was designed both to foster patriotism while simultaneously keeping the product name before the buying public against that time when the company was again in the business of manufacturing cars.

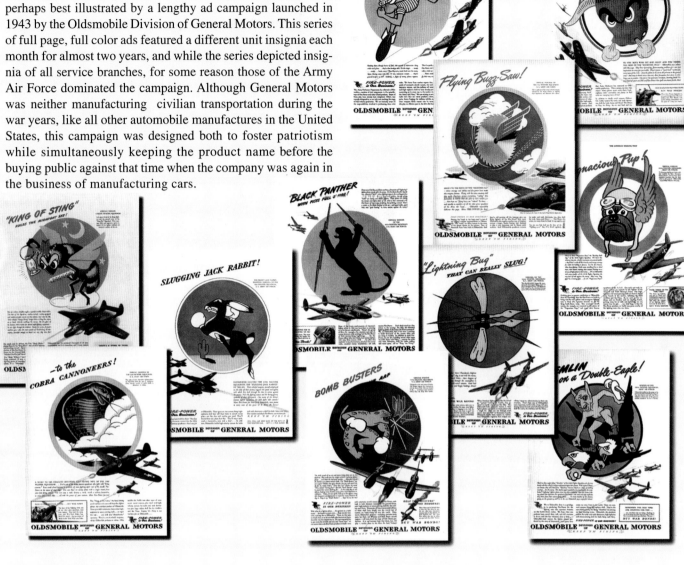

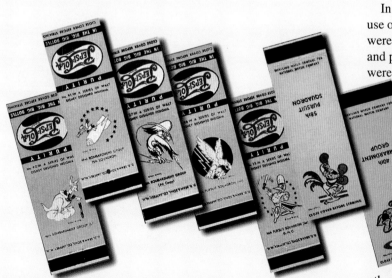

In the 1940's a large portion of Americans indulged in the use of tobacco in much greater quantities than today. Cigarettes were included in C-rations issued to troops until as late as 1975, and pipe and cigar smoking, while not as popular as cigarettes, were never the less common in virtually every sector of American life. Throughout the war Disney allowed many of the unit insignia his studio had designed to be utilized as the central theme for a series of matchbook covers. One series of these covers depicted only a single insignia design and very little text copy. Later Pepsi-Cola Co. sponsored a similar series licensed incorporating additional Disney designs.

Today these give-away items of the 1940's are a sought after collectors item but at the time they were simply an everyday utility, used as a subtle reminder of a nations young fighting men. These and other reminders were intended to curb, among other things, civilian grumbling about shortages of many items due to war time rationing.

Further proof that the American publics interest in unit insignia went well beyond an adolescence audience can be perhaps best illustrated in the selected examples depicted at left.

Cover art and feature articles on the subject of combat insignia appeared in virtually every major publication during the war years. Periodicals such as Colliers, Life, Popular Mechanics and many others published everything from full length articles to one page write-ups on the images representing U.S. fighting forces both at home and abroad.

Perhaps one of the most compelling examples of just how popular this subject was is evidenced by The National Geographic Magazine. In their June 1943 issue this publication ran a feature story entitled *Insignia of the United States Armed Forces*. This article covered many aspects of regulation U.S. military uniform insignia but included a full color section entitled *Army Aircraft Insignia*. These images depicted some, but by no means all, of the current inventory of USAAF squadron and group insignia. Reader response to this article was so great that National Geographic published a special edition issue dedicated to this same subject in December of the following year. The section of this special issue devoted to combat insignia was expanded to include not only those images of the AAF but unit insignia of the U.S. Navy and Marine Corps as well. Both of these editions were a huge success in their day and are now a highly sought after collectors item.

And speaking of collectors items, the composite grouping below is an assemblage of a series of four booklets produced by Hearst Publishing during World War II These particular items were indeed produced with an adolescent audience in mind. Each booklet was designed to contain fifty collectors stamps especially printed for this series. Both the booklets as well as the stamps themselves were distributed free for the asking and were intended to help foster patriotism and involve Americas youth by allowing them feel a part of their nations war effort. It was hoped that the images would help promote something of a spiritual bond between the youthful collector and Americas fighting forces, and to this end they appear to have been effective.

All of this brings us back to the original question: Why expend so much time and effort on a subject as esoteric as World War II combat insignia? The answer should by now be self explanatory. These images were not only a patriotic aspect of many civilians on the Home Front but first and foremost they were a part of the daily lives of the men belonging to each respective unit. In virtually every theatre of operation around the globe U.S. airmen displayed these same designs on their clothing, equipment and aircraft. Just as these men are deserving of our remembrance, so to are the images that represented them deserving of at least a little of our remembrance as well.

In the relatively short span of time since the end of World War II, many of these designs are already at risk of being lost to history forever. It doesn't matter that these combat insignia were not essential to the war effort, what is important is how much they are able to tell us years later of the personalities of an entire generation of young Americans who left home to fight in far away skies for something they believed was greater than themselves.

USAAF ABBREVIATIONS

AAA	Anti-Aircraft Artillery
AAF	Army Air Force
AB	Air Base
AAB	Army Air Base
A/C	Aircraft
AD	Air Division
Air.Div	Air Division
A/D	Air Depot
AEF	American Expeditionary Force
AF	Air Force
A/F	Airfield
ANA	Army-Navy Aeronautical
AS / Antisub	Anti-Submarine
A/S	Airstrip
ATO	American Theater of Operations
Avn.	Aviation
BD	Bombardment (later Air) Division
BG	Bombardment (Bomb) Group
BG(H)	Bomb Group (Heavy)
BG(M)	Bomb Group (Medium)
BG(L)	Bomb Group (Light)
Bmr.	Bomber
Bomb	Bombardment
BS	Bombardment (Bomb) Squadron
BW	Bombardment (Bomb) Wing
c.	circa (approximate time period)
Carr.	Carrier
CBI	China-Burma-India (Theater of Operations)
Cmbt.	Combat
Cmd.	Command
Cmdo.	Commando
CO	Commanding Officer
Cmpst.	Composite
Crgo.	Cargo
CW	Combat Wing
DB	Dive Bomber
Det.	Detachment
EAME	European-African-Middle Eastern (Theater of Operations)
ERS	Emergency Rescue Squadron
ETO	European Theater of Operations
F/B	Fighter-Bomber
FG / FtrGrp	Fighter Group
FLAK	Anti-Aircraft Fire
Fld.	Field
Flt.	Flight
Ftr.	Fighter
FS / FtrSqdn	Fighter Squadron
FW / FtrWng	Fighter Wing
GB	Great Britain
GHQ	General Headquarters
GP / Grp.	Group
HQ	Headquarters
Incpt.	Interceptor
LN	Liaison
MTO	Mediterranean Theater of Operations
Mpng.	Mapping
NLS	Night Leaflet Squadron
PS	Photographic Squadron
OBS	Observation
OPS	Operations
QIM	Quick Identification Markings (Allied)
OSS	Office Of Strategic Services (US)
(P) / Prov.	Provisional
PG	Photographic Group
Photo	Photographic
POM	Preparation for Overseas Movement
POW	Prisoner Of War
PR	Photographic Reconnaissance
PRG	Photographic Reconnaissance Group
PS	Photographic Squadron
PTO	Pacific Theater of Operations
Pur.	Pursuit
RAF	Royal Air Force (British)
RCM	Radio Counter Measures
Rcn.	Reconnaissance
RG	Reconnaissance Group
RS	Reconnaissance Squadron
SF	Scouting Force
SHAEF	Supreme Headquarters Allied Expeditionary Force
SOE	Special Operations Executive (British)
Spt.	Support
Sq. / Sqdn.	Squadron
Srch.	Search
Stn.	Station
Tac.	Tactical
Trng.	Training
Tr.	Troop
Trnsp.	Transport
T/O	Theater Of Operations
TRG	Tactical Reconnaissance Group
TRS	Tactical Reconnaissance Squadron
Triple-A	Anti-Aircraft Artillery
USA	United States Army
UK	United Kingdom
USN	United States Navy
US	United States
USAAF	United States Army Air Force
USSAFE	United States Strategic Air Forces, Europe
WR	Weather Reconnaissance
Wthr.	Weather
Wng.	Wing

SPECIAL OPERATIONS CODES

Argument: Concentrated AAF attacks on luftwaffe fighter factories from 11-Jun thru 1-Mar 1944.

Aphrodite: USAAF's initial experiments with radio and video controlled aircraft and guided bombs. Joseph P. Kennedy Jr. was killed 12-Aug-44 after volunteering for this operation.

Azon: Acronym for AZimuth ONly. Worlds first radio controlled 'smart bomb' was officially designated the VB-1.

Batty: Experimentation with TV controlled bombs dropped from B-17's resulted in three unsuccessful attacks against German U-boat pens

Blue Stocking: Standard code for all weather reconnaissance flights.

Carpetbagger: name for night missions on behalf of OSS / underground operations behind enemy lines

Castor: Partially radio controlled bombers. Integrated with the Aphrodite Operation.

Chattanooga: Fighter staffing attacks on enemy railroad network.

Chowhound: Airborne drop to civilians of badly need food supplies over Holland in May 1945.

Circus: Ambush tactics employed by the AAF to draw out and destroy the Luftwaffe in the air.

Crossbow: Allied air offensive on German rocket sites beginning 17-Aug-43.

Disney: Some of the first bunker busters. These were rocket assisted bombs designed to penetrate concrete before denotation

Duck: A decoy mission in the area of the North Sea.

Frantic: AAF Shuttle missions between Great Britain, Russia and Italy.

Jackpot: Concentrated AAF aerial attacks on Luftwaffe airfields inside Germany proper.

Joker: Nighttime photo reconnaissance mission utilizing 'flash bombs' to illuminate surveillance area.

Moling: Bad weather probing missions designed to test effectiveness of enemy early warning systems.

Moonshine: Specialized equipment designed to produce a false radar signature.

Nickeling: Dropping propaganda leaflets over enemy occupied territory.

Noball: AAF missions directed specifically towards German V-1 / V-2 rocket facilities and launch sites.

Ramrod: A round trip fighter escort of heavy bombers, both to and from a target.

Revival: Reunification of former Allied POW's following Germany's formal surrender on 8-May-45.

Rhubarb: Characteristically a smaller fighter sortie against enemy ground targets in bad weather.

Roadstead: Fighter escort for bombing mission against open water targets.

Rodeo: A coordinated fighter sweep of enemy air facilities. The intent was to destroy enemy aircraft on the ground if they couldn't be lured into the skies .

Skywave: Purely navigational flights for the express purpose of calibrating airborne LORAN equipment.

Spoof: A 'Rubber Duck', or decoy mission where a relatively small number of aircraft would attempt to divert enemy defensive efforts away from the real mission target.

Title Wave: Ninth AAF attacks on the Rumanian oil fields located at Ploesti

Trolley: Sometimes called Taxi Rides. Transports and even bombers were used to fly ground personnel over Germany following V-E Day.

Trucking: Using heavy bombers as opposed to transports to relay supplies to distribution points on continental Europe.

Varsity: Airborne invasion over the Rhine River by elements of the 17th Airborne Division deployed primarily by units of the Ninth AAF.

INDEX

INDEX

INDEX

INDEX

INDEX

BIBLIOGRAPHY / ACKNOWLEDGEMENTS

Aircraft Insignia-Spirit Of Youth:
   National Geographic, June 1943 / Gerard Hubbard

Air Force Units Of World War II:
   Dr. M. Maurer

Army Air Force Stations in the
United Kingdom During World War II
   USAF Historical Research Center

Battles With The Luftwaffe:
   Theo Boiten & Martin Bowman

C-47 / R4d Units Of The ETO & MTO:
   David Isby

B-26 Marauder Units of The Eighth And Ninth Air Forces:
   Jerry Scutts

Combat Insignia Stamps Of The United States Army & Navy:
   Hearst Publications

Combat Squadrons Of The Air Force, World War II:
   Dr. M. Maurer

Command And Employment Of Air Power:
   War Department Field Manual / FM 100-20

From The Zenith To The Deck:
   Eighth Fighter Command / Gen. Francis Griswold

Insignia & Decorations Of The US Armed Forces:
   National Geographic, 1944

Jagdwaffe / Holding The West, 1941-1943:
   David Wadman / Martin Pegg

Jagdwaffe / Defending The Reich, 1943-1944:
   Robert Forsyth / Eddie J. Creek

Jagdwaffe / Defending The Reich, 1944-1945:
   Robert Forsyth

L-Birds / American Combat Liaison Aircraft Of World War II:
   Terry M. Love

Martin B-26 Marauder:
   Fredrick A. Johnsen

P-38 Lightning:
   Bert Kinzey

Strangers In A Strange Land:
   Hans-Heiri Stapfer

The Army Air Forces In World War II;
Combat Chronology / 1941-1945
   Kit C. Carter / Robert Mueller

The Luftwaffe / Strategy For Defeat:
   Williamson Murray

The Ninth Air Force in World War II:
   Ken C. Rust

The Official Guide To The Army Forces:
   Army Air Forces Aid Society

The Organization And Lineage Of The United States Air Force:
   Charles A. Ravenstein

The United States Strategic Bombing Surveys / European War:
   United States Air Force

USAAF Markings & Camouflage:
   Robert Archer

U.S. Army Air Forces Continental
Airfields [ETO] D-Day To V-E Day:
   USAF Historical Research Center

War Insignia Stamp Album / Vol's.2,3 & 4:
   Robert Lash Robbins

Grateful appreciation is extended to the following institutions for providing much of the invaluable historical data and photo images used in the creation of this work:

American Battle Monuments Commission
National Air and Space Museum
P-38 National Association
Planes of Fame / Air Museum
United States Air Force Museum / Wright-Patterson AFB
United States National Archives and Records
9th Air Force Association

A special thanks is tendered to the following individuals;

Cpt. Robert 'Punchy' Powell
Pilot, 352ndFG, Eighth USAAF

Sgt. Chester Gavryck,
Ordinance Specialist
Eighth USAAF

Lt. H.C. 'Pete' Henry
Pilot, 44th BG
Eighth USAAF

Norman Malaney, 25th Bomb Group Association
Michael Faley, 100th Bomb Group Historian
Johnny 'Siggy' Signor, IRS (Insignia Reproduction Specialist)
Readers looking for quality reproductions of unit insignia are encouraged to contact Siggy.

J.'Siggy' Signor
714 Atlantis Road S.E.
Palm Beach FL 32909-4811

Think where man's glory most begins and ends,

And say my glory was, I had such friends

William Butler Yeats

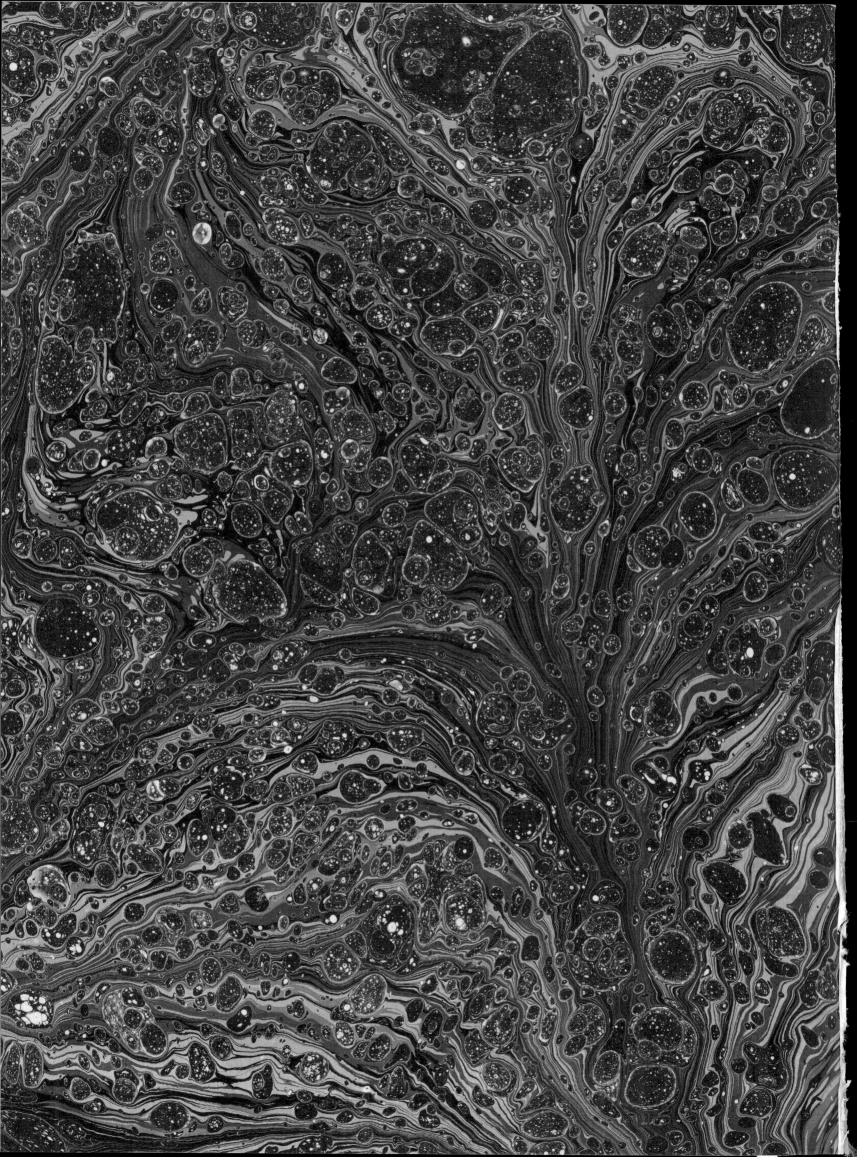